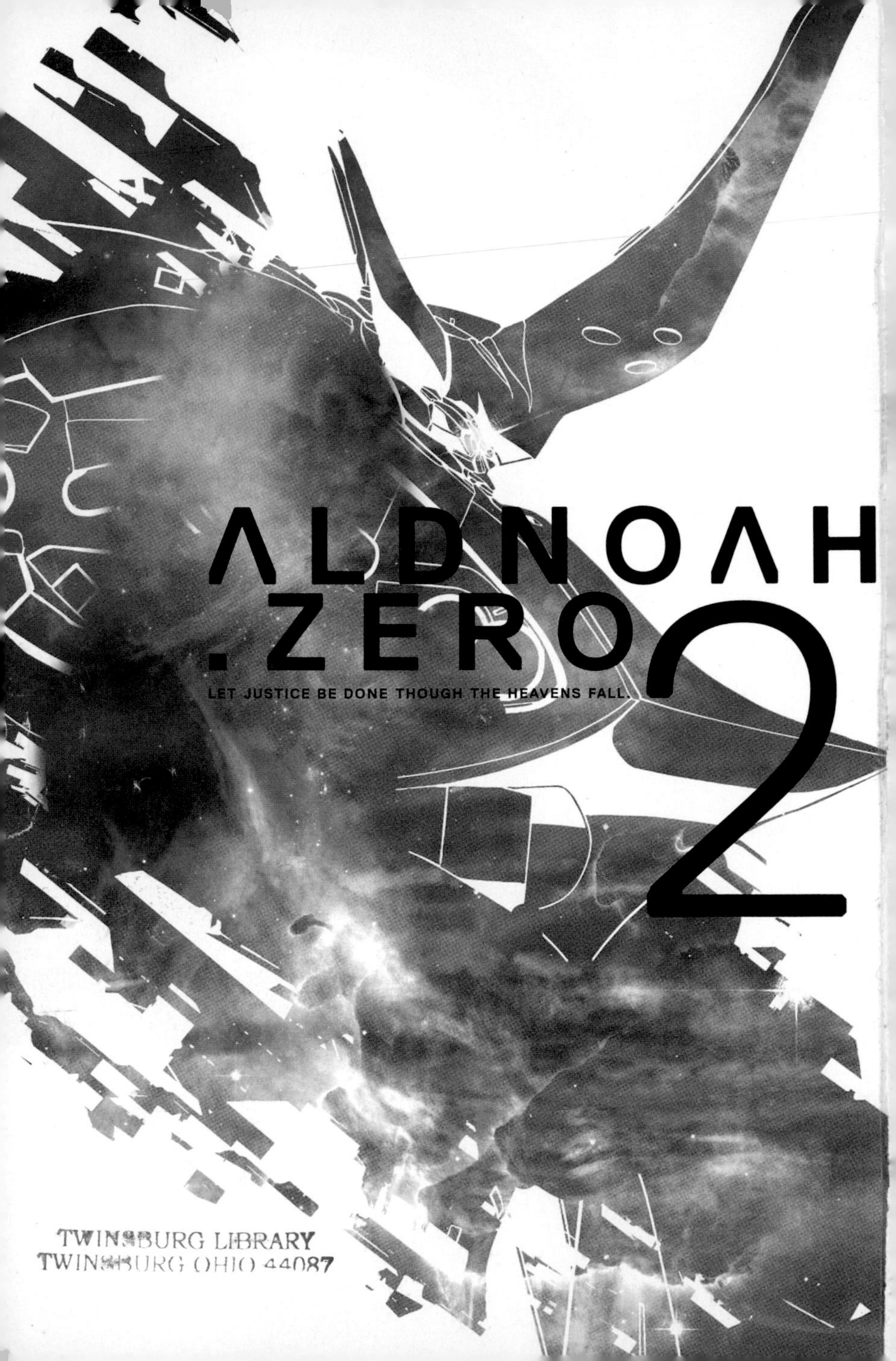
ALDNOAH.ZERO
LET JUSTICE BE DONE THOUGH THE HEAVENS FALL.
2

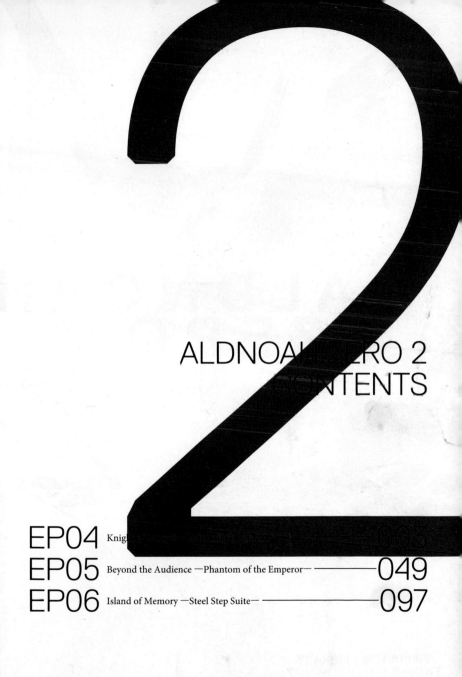

ALDNOAH.ZERO 2
CONTENTS

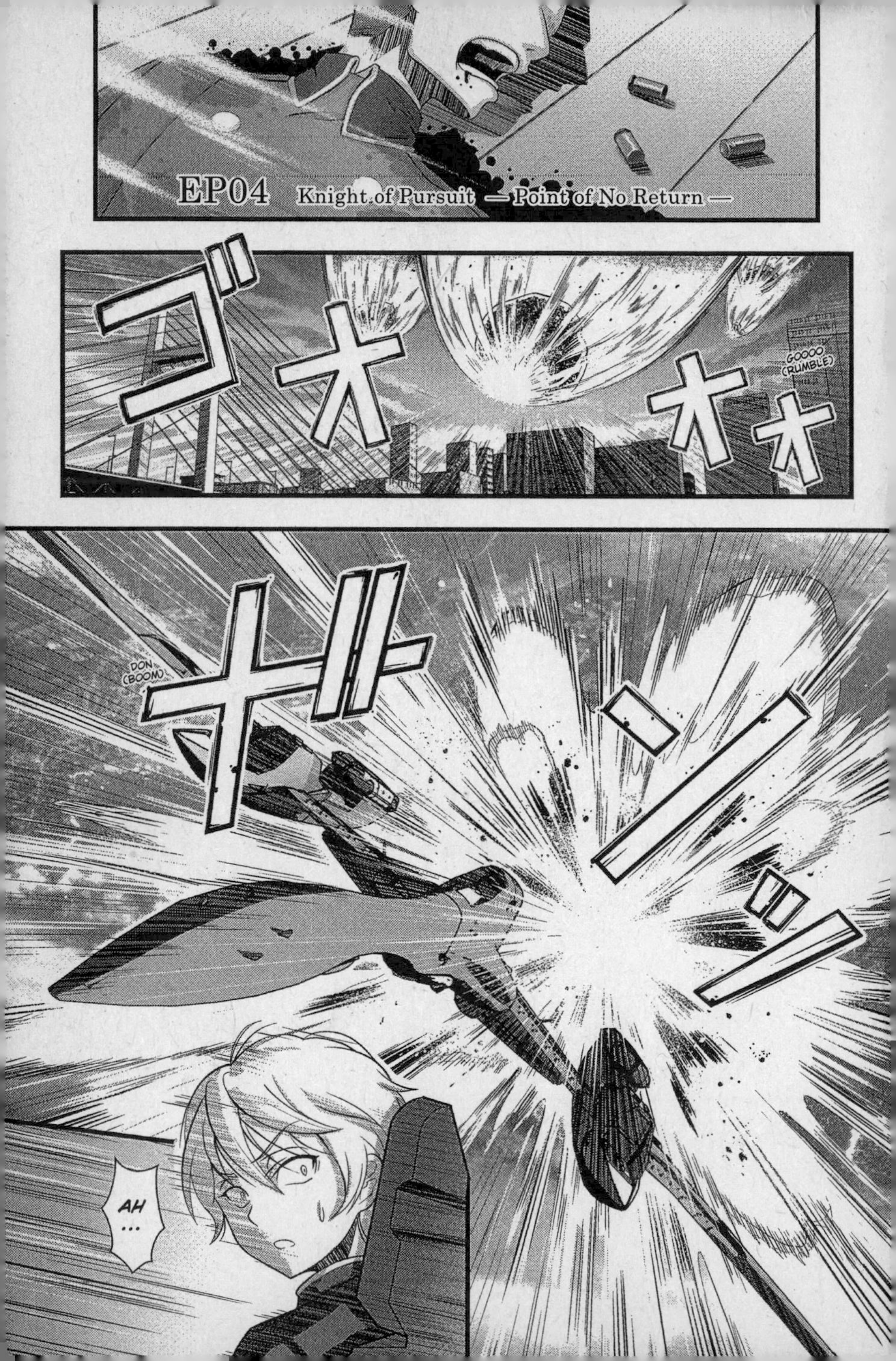
EP04 Knight of Pursuit — Point of No Return —
ゴオオォ
GOOOO (RUMBLE)
ドンッ
DON (BOOM)
AH ...

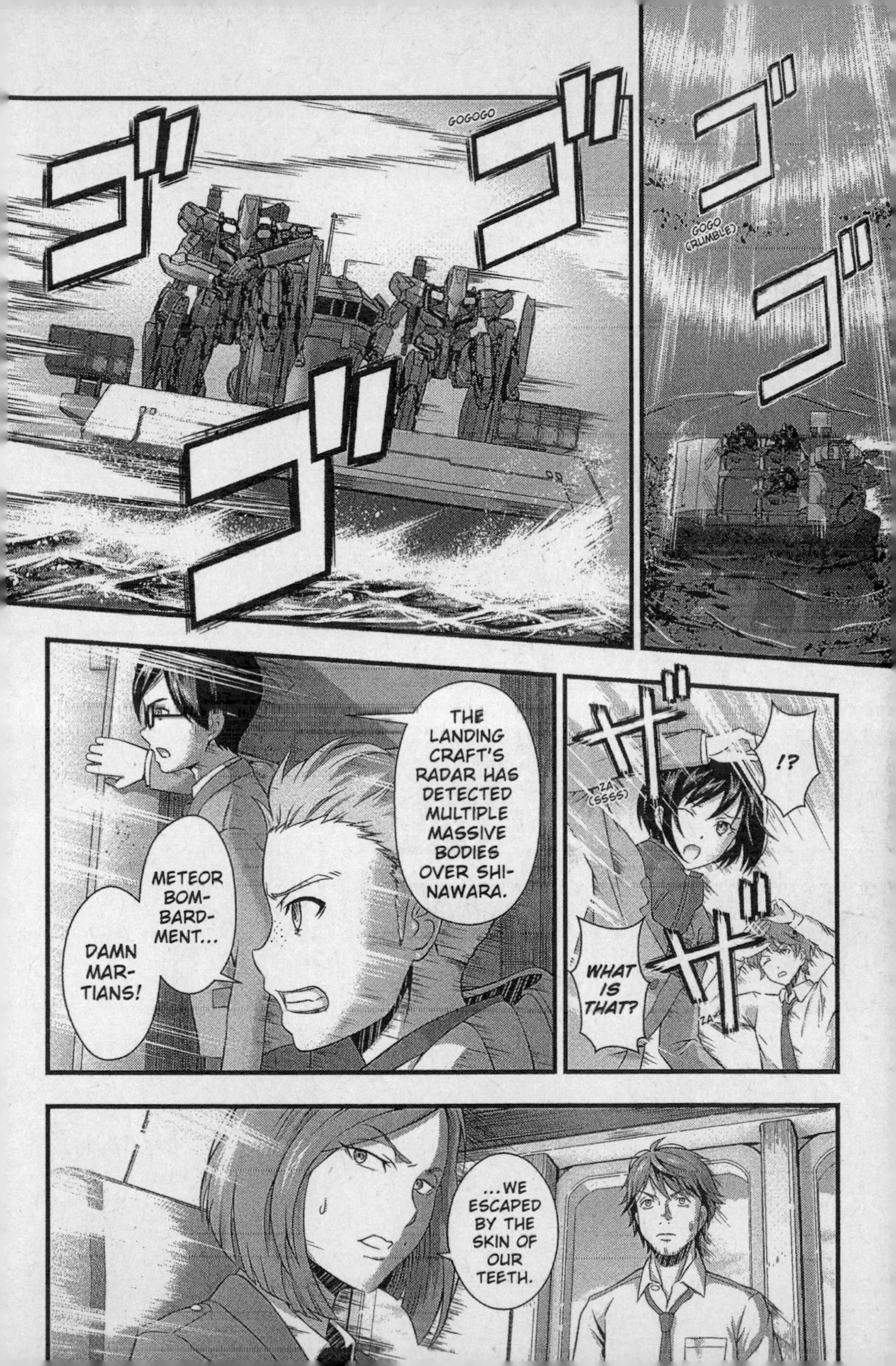
GOGO (RUMBLE)
GOGOGO
!?
ZA (SSSS)
WHAT IS THAT?
ZA
THE LANDING CRAFT'S RADAR HAS DETECTED MULTIPLE MASSIVE BODIES OVER SHINAWARA.
METEOR BOMBARDMENT...
DAMN MARTIANS!
...WE ESCAPED BY THE SKIN OF OUR TEETH.

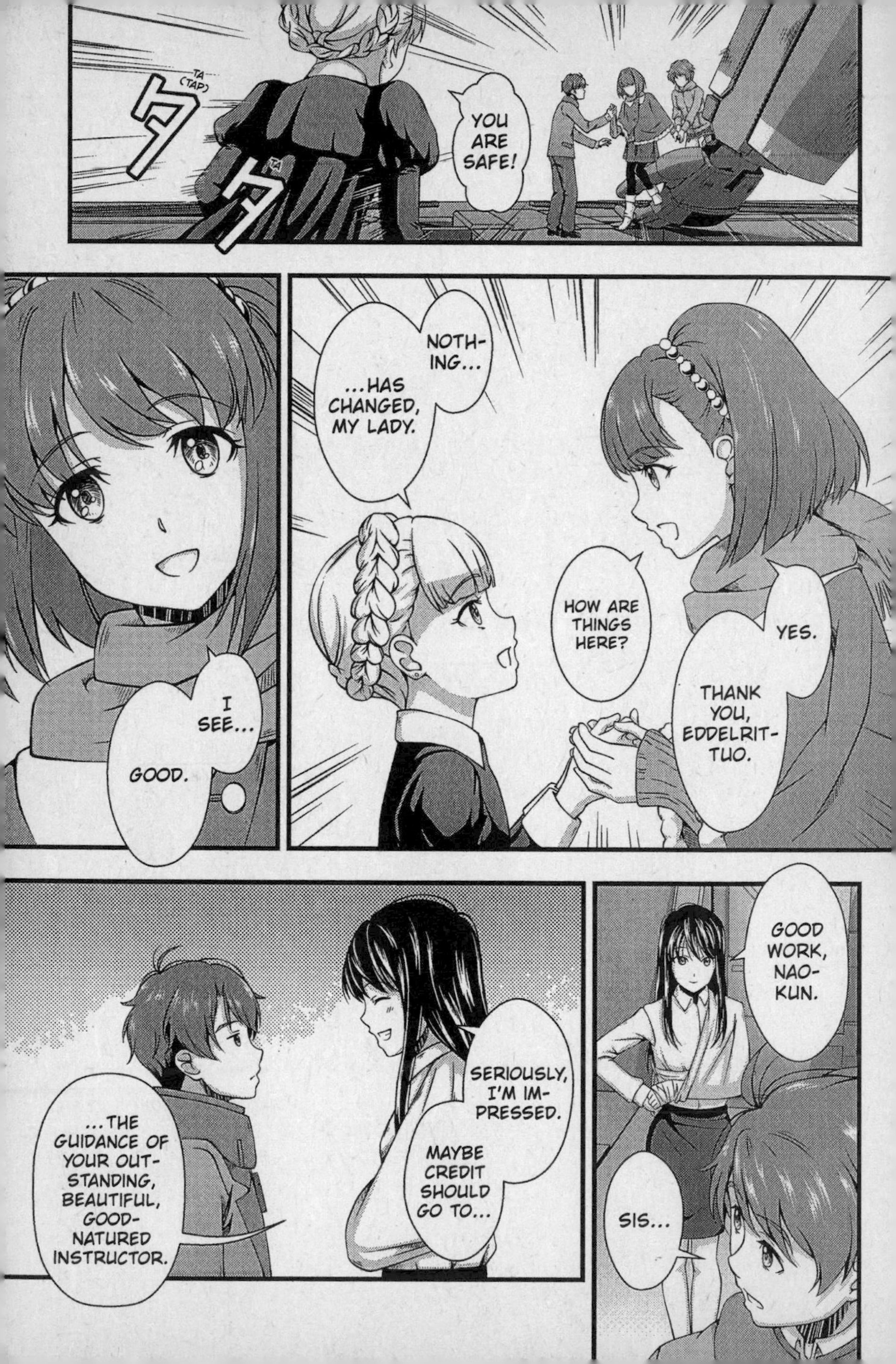
TA (TAP)
TA
YOU ARE SAFE!
YES. THANK YOU, EDDELRITTUO.
HOW ARE THINGS HERE?
NOTHING... ...HAS CHANGED, MY LADY.
I SEE... GOOD.
GOOD WORK, NAO-KUN.
SIS...
SERIOUSLY, I'M IMPRESSED.
MAYBE CREDIT SHOULD GO TO...
...THE GUIDANCE OF YOUR OUTSTANDING, BEAUTIFUL, GOOD-NATURED INSTRUCTOR.

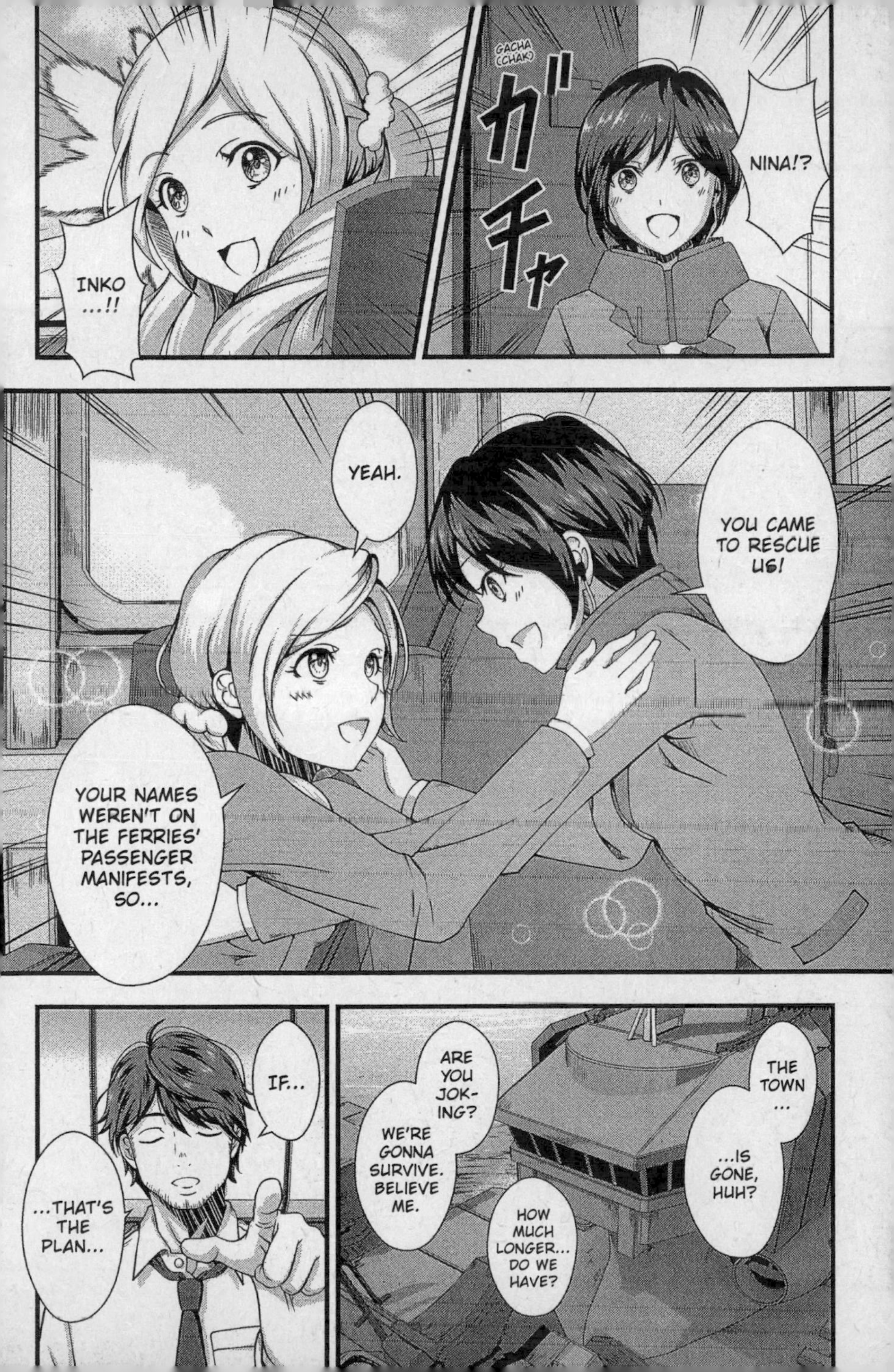
NINA!?
GACHA (CHAK)
ガチャ
INKO ...!!
YOU CAME TO RESCUE US!
YEAH.
YOUR NAMES WEREN'T ON THE FERRIES' PASSENGER MANIFESTS, SO...
THE TOWN ...
...IS GONE, HUH?
ARE YOU JOK-ING?
WE'RE GONNA SURVIVE. BELIEVE ME.
HOW MUCH LONGER... DO WE HAVE?
IF...
...THAT'S THE PLAN...

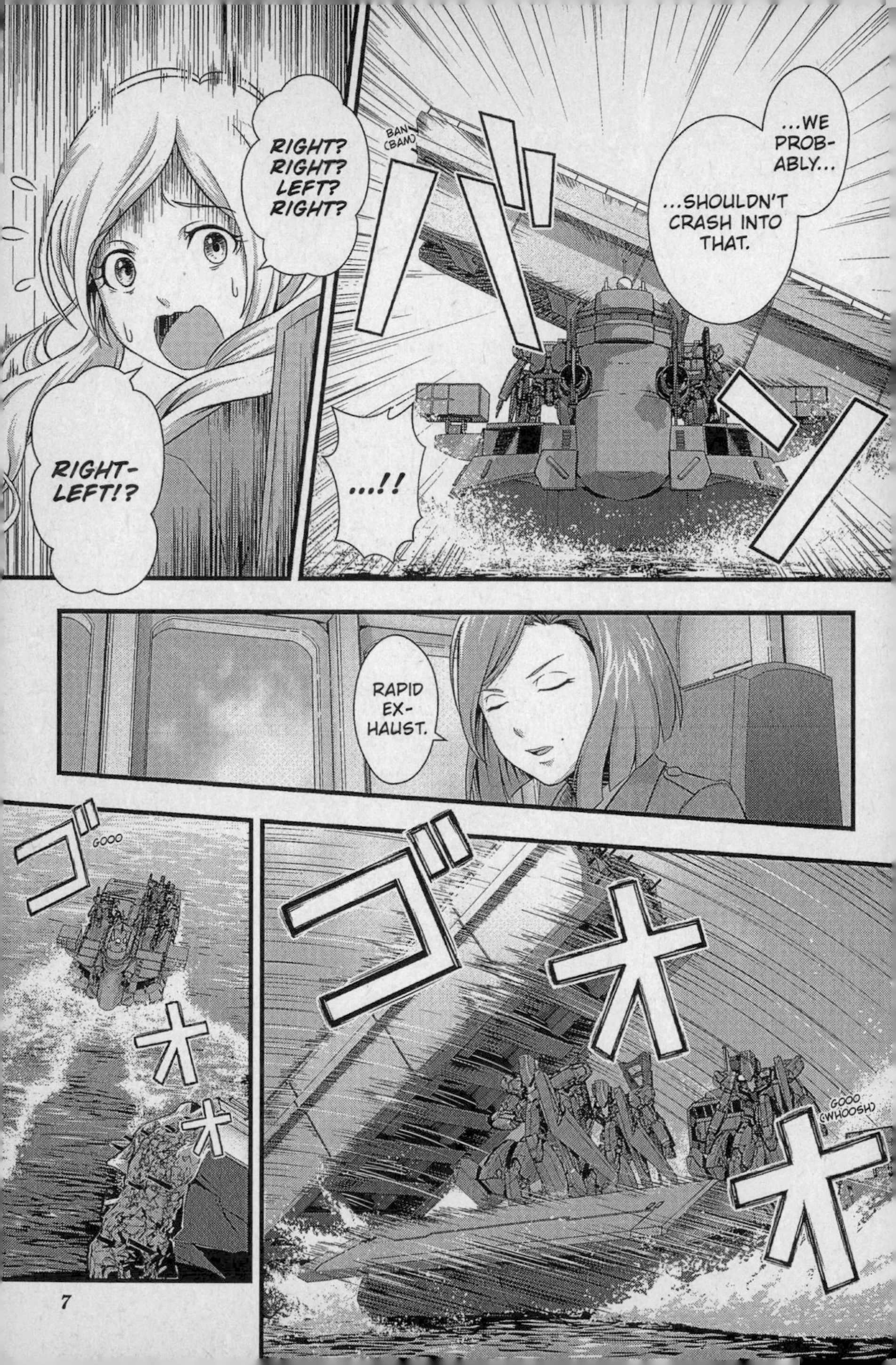
...WE PROBABLY...
...SHOULDN'T CRASH INTO THAT.
BAN (BAM)
...!!
RIGHT? RIGHT? LEFT? RIGHT?
RIGHT-LEFT!?
RAPID EX-HAUST.
GOOO (WHOOSH)
GOOO

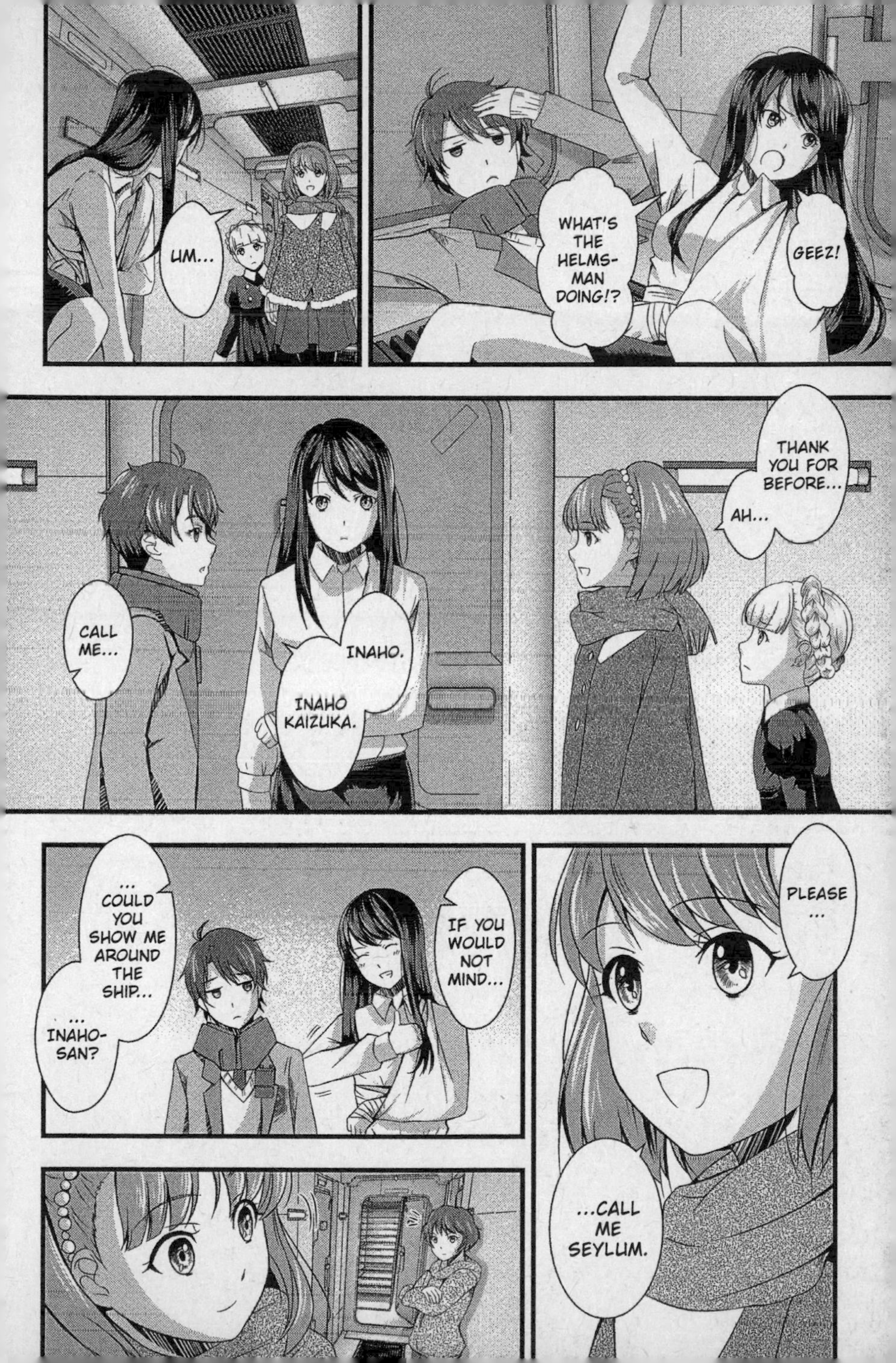
GEEZ!
WHAT'S THE HELMS-MAN DOING!?
UM...
THANK YOU FOR BEFORE...
AH...
INAHO.
INAHO KAIZUKA.
CALL ME...
PLEASE...
...CALL ME SEYLUM.
IF YOU WOULD NOT MIND...
...COULD YOU SHOW ME AROUND THE SHIP...
...INAHO-SAN?

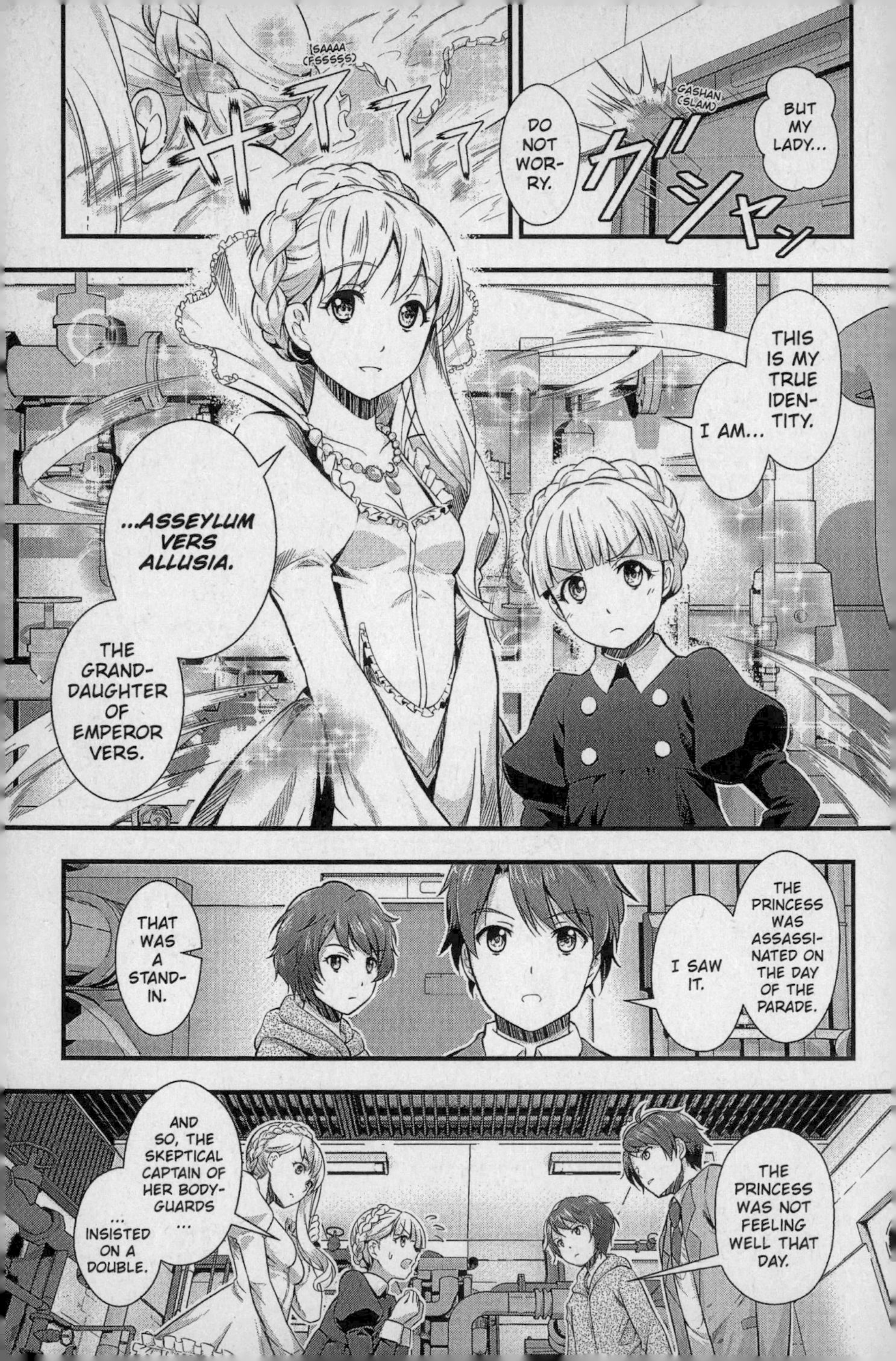
BUT MY LADY...
GASHAN (SLAM)
DO NOT WORRY.
SAAAA (FSSSSS)
THIS IS MY TRUE IDENTITY.
I AM...
...ASSEYLUM VERS ALLUSIA.
THE GRANDDAUGHTER OF EMPEROR VERS.
THE PRINCESS WAS ASSASSINATED ON THE DAY OF THE PARADE.
I SAW IT.
THAT WAS A STAND-IN.
THE PRINCESS WAS NOT FEELING WELL THAT DAY.
AND SO, THE SKEPTICAL CAPTAIN OF HER BODYGUARDS...
...INSISTED ON A DOUBLE.

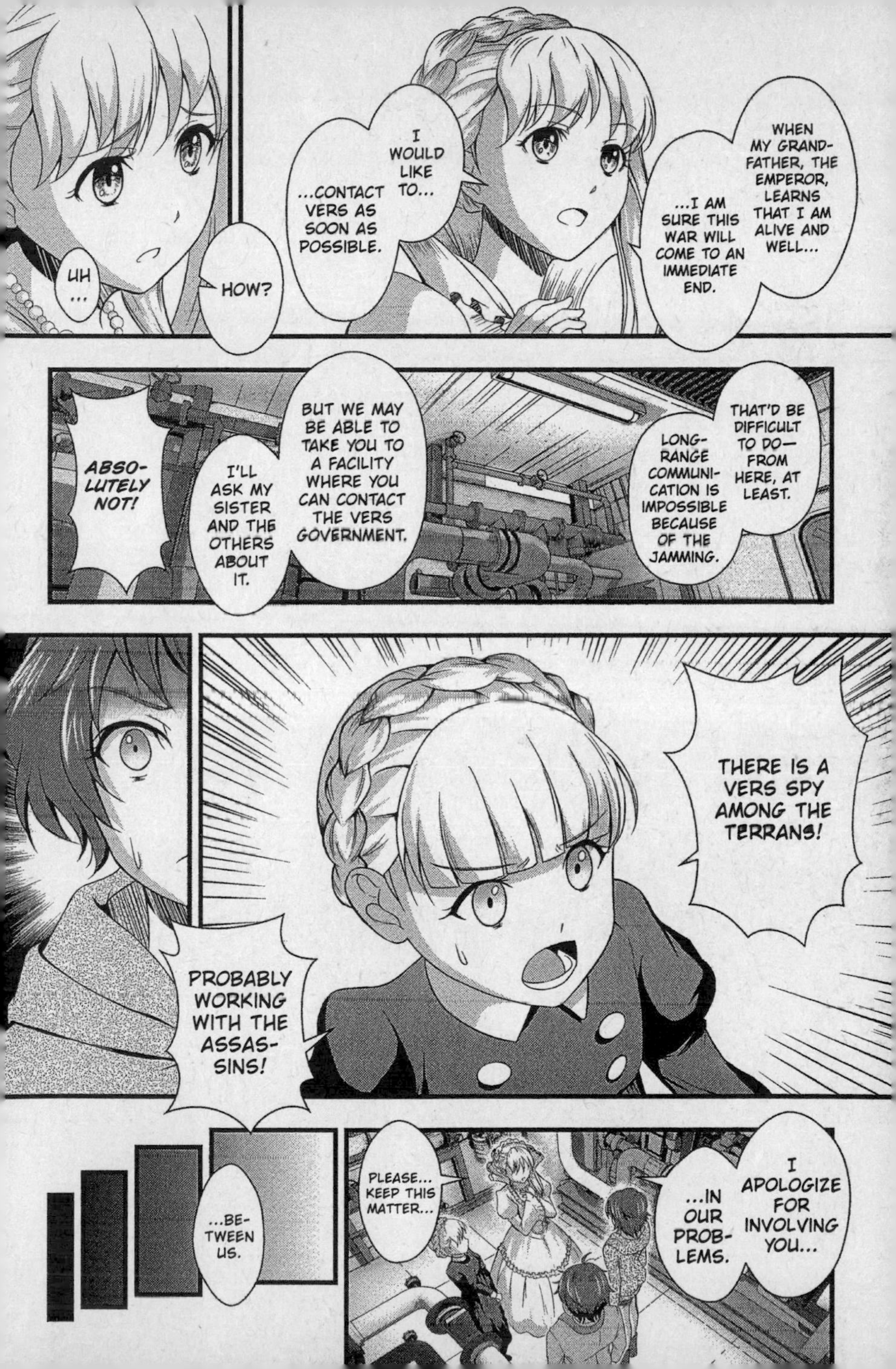
WHEN MY GRANDFATHER, THE EMPEROR, LEARNS THAT I AM ALIVE AND WELL...
...I AM SURE THIS WAR WILL COME TO AN IMMEDIATE END.
I WOULD LIKE TO...
...CONTACT VERS AS SOON AS POSSIBLE.
HOW?
UH ...
THAT'D BE DIFFICULT TO DO—FROM HERE, AT LEAST.
LONG-RANGE COMMUNICATION IS IMPOSSIBLE BECAUSE OF THE JAMMING.
BUT WE MAY BE ABLE TO TAKE YOU TO A FACILITY WHERE YOU CAN CONTACT THE VERS GOVERNMENT.
I'LL ASK MY SISTER AND THE OTHERS ABOUT IT.
ABSOLUTELY NOT!
THERE IS A VERS SPY AMONG THE TERRANS!
PROBABLY WORKING WITH THE ASSASSINS!
I APOLOGIZE FOR INVOLVING YOU...
...IN OUR PROBLEMS.
PLEASE... KEEP THIS MATTER...
...BETWEEN US.

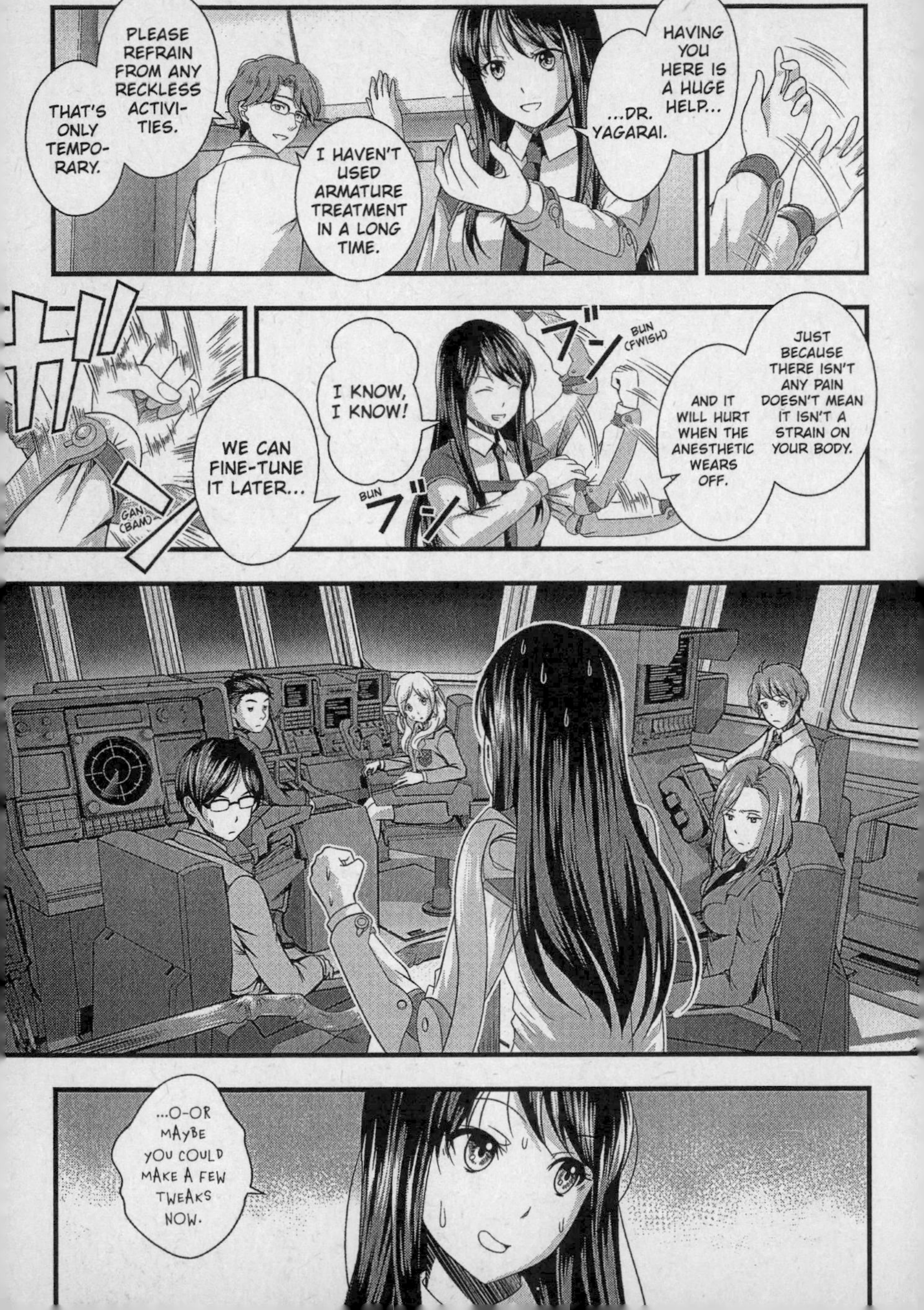
HAVING YOU HERE IS A HUGE HELP...
...DR. YAGARAI.
I HAVEN'T USED ARMATURE TREATMENT IN A LONG TIME.
PLEASE REFRAIN FROM ANY RECKLESS ACTIVITIES.
THAT'S ONLY TEMPORARY.
JUST BECAUSE THERE ISN'T ANY PAIN DOESN'T MEAN IT ISN'T A STRAIN ON YOUR BODY.
AND IT WILL HURT WHEN THE ANESTHETIC WEARS OFF.
BUN (FWISH)
I KNOW, I KNOW!
BUN
WE CAN FINE-TUNE IT LATER...
GAN (BAM)
...O-OR MAYBE YOU COULD MAKE A FEW TWEAKS NOW.

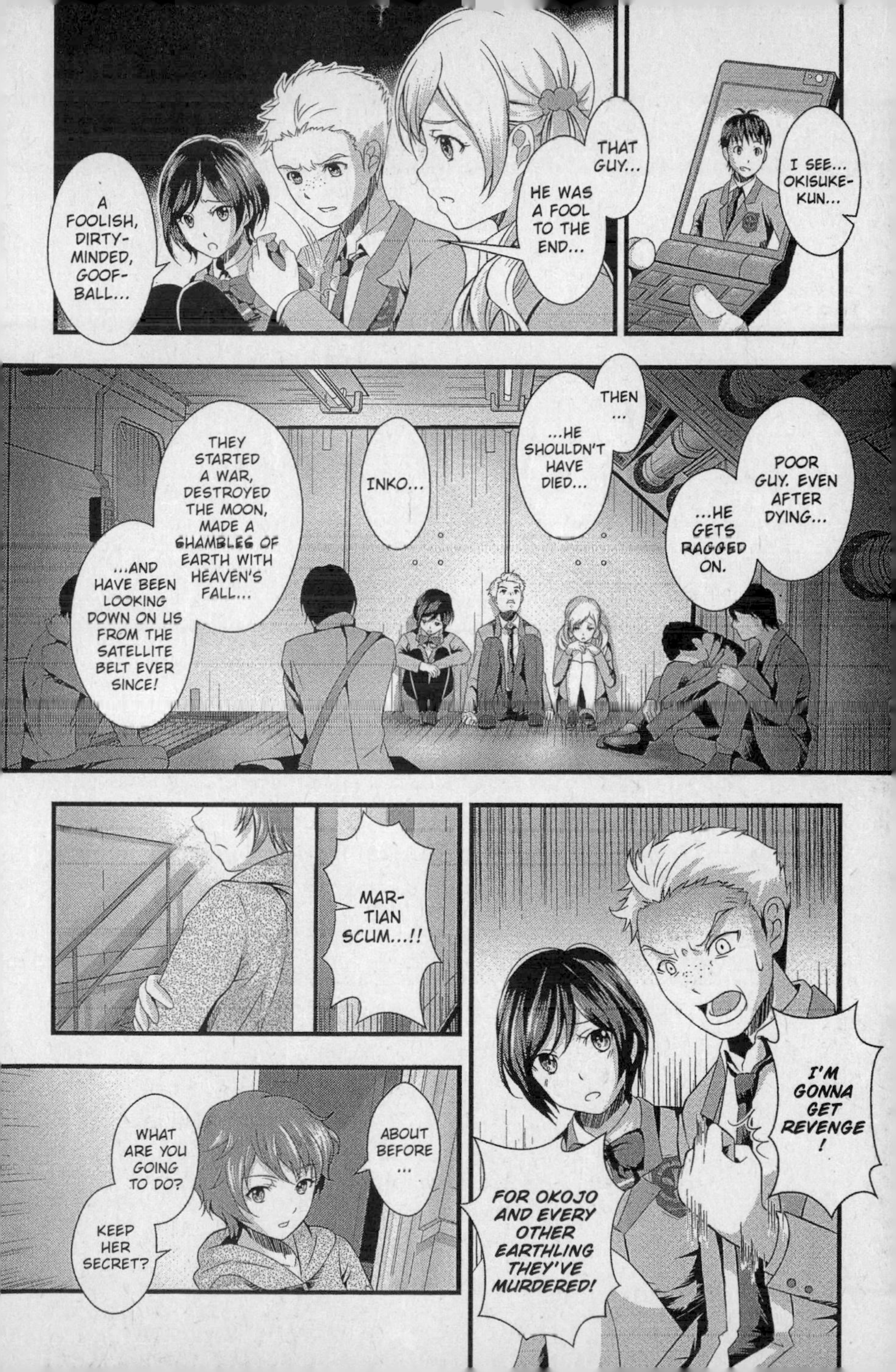
I SEE... OKISUKE-KUN...
THAT GUY...
HE WAS A FOOL TO THE END...
A FOOLISH, DIRTY-MINDED, GOOF-BALL...
POOR GUY. EVEN AFTER DYING...
...HE GETS RAGGED ON.
THEN ...
...HE SHOULDN'T HAVE DIED...
INKO...
THEY STARTED A WAR, DESTROYED THE MOON, MADE A SHAMBLES OF EARTH WITH HEAVEN'S FALL...
...AND HAVE BEEN LOOKING DOWN ON US FROM THE SATELLITE BELT EVER SINCE!
I'M GONNA GET REVENGE!
FOR OKOJO AND EVERY OTHER EARTHLING THEY'VE MURDERED!
MAR-TIAN SCUM...!!
ABOUT BEFORE ...
WHAT ARE YOU GOING TO DO?
KEEP HER SECRET?

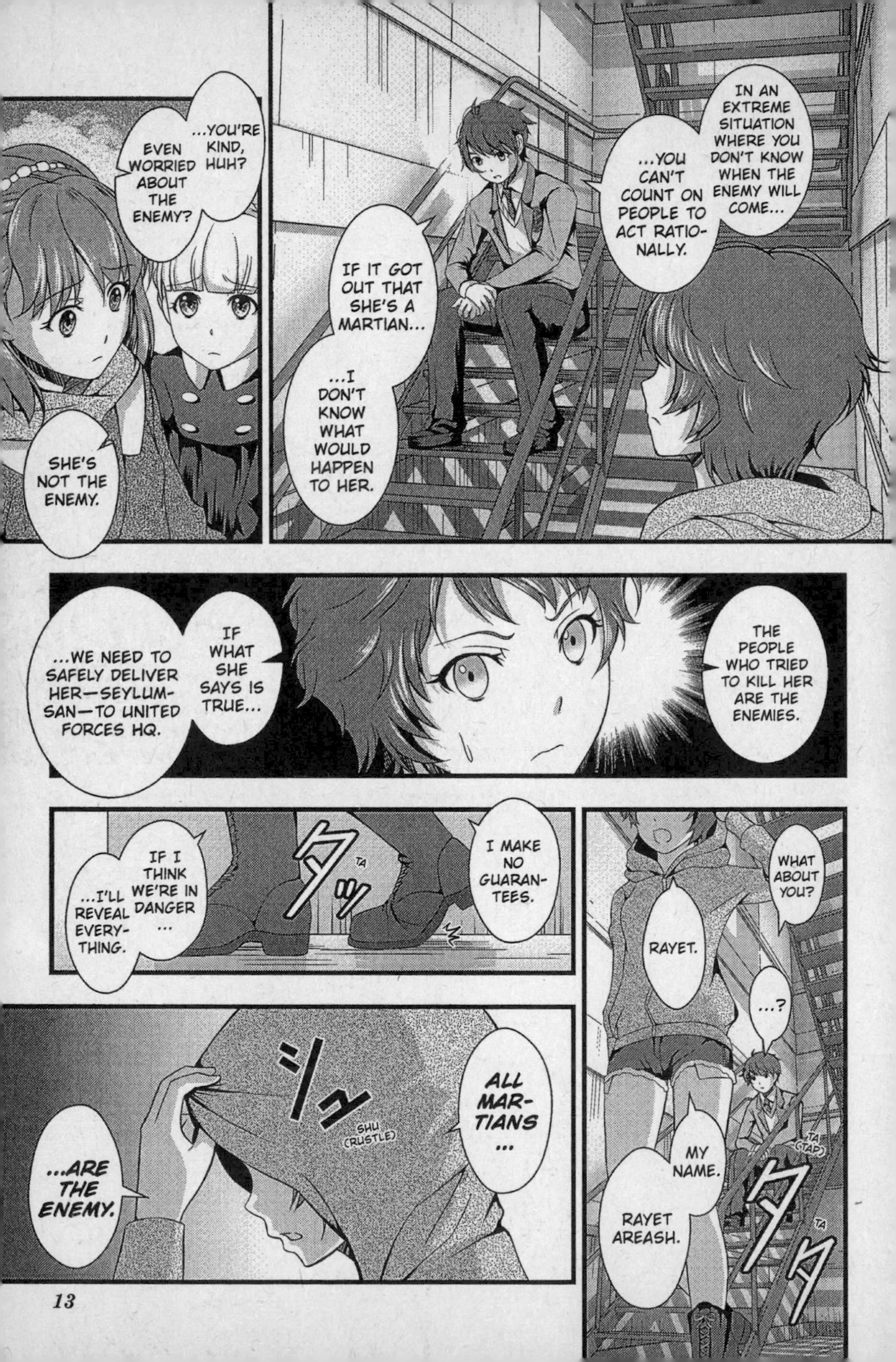
IN AN EXTREME SITUATION WHERE YOU DON'T KNOW WHEN THE ENEMY WILL COME...
...YOU CAN'T COUNT ON PEOPLE TO ACT RATIONALLY.
IF IT GOT OUT THAT SHE'S A MARTIAN...
...I DON'T KNOW WHAT WOULD HAPPEN TO HER.
...YOU'RE KIND, HUH?
EVEN WORRIED ABOUT THE ENEMY?
SHE'S NOT THE ENEMY.
THE PEOPLE WHO TRIED TO KILL HER ARE THE ENEMIES.
IF WHAT SHE SAYS IS TRUE...
...WE NEED TO SAFELY DELIVER HER—SEYLUM-SAN—TO UNITED FORCES HQ.
WHAT ABOUT YOU?
RAYET.
...?
MY NAME.
RAYET AREASH.
TA (TAP)
TA
I MAKE NO GUARANTEES.
TA
IF I THINK WE'RE IN DANGER...
...I'LL REVEAL EVERYTHING.
SHU (RUSTLE)
ALL MARTIANS...
...ARE THE ENEMY.

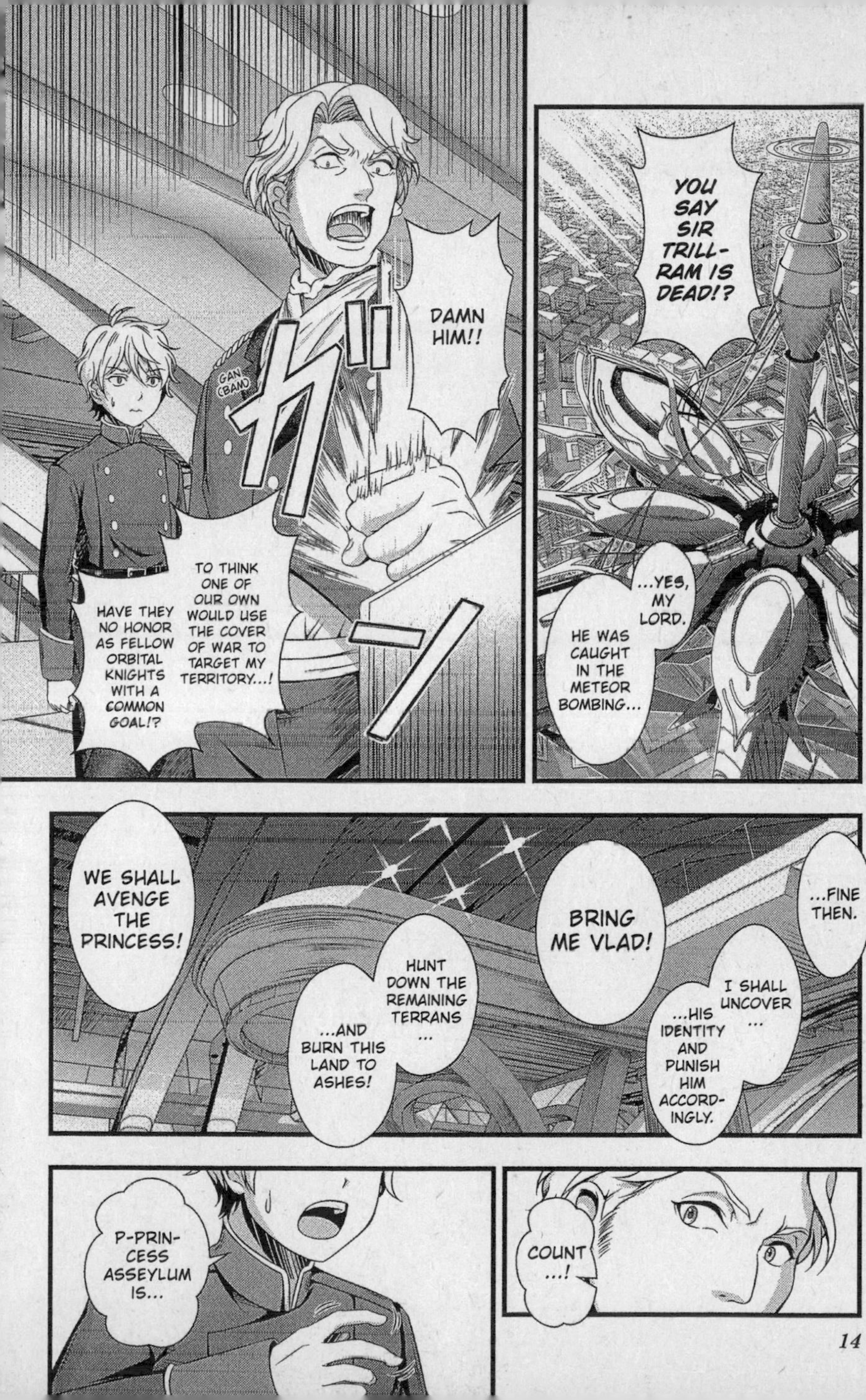
YOU SAY SIR TRILL-RAM IS DEAD!?
...YES, MY LORD.
HE WAS CAUGHT IN THE METEOR BOMBING...
DAMN HIM!!
GAN (BAM)
TO THINK ONE OF OUR OWN WOULD USE THE COVER OF WAR TO TARGET MY TERRITORY...!
HAVE THEY NO HONOR AS FELLOW ORBITAL KNIGHTS WITH A COMMON GOAL!?
...FINE THEN.
I SHALL UNCOVER...
...HIS IDENTITY AND PUNISH HIM ACCORD-INGLY.
BRING ME VLAD!
HUNT DOWN THE REMAINING TERRANS...
...AND BURN THIS LAND TO ASHES!
WE SHALL AVENGE THE PRINCESS!
COUNT...!
P-PRIN-CESS ASSEYLUM IS...

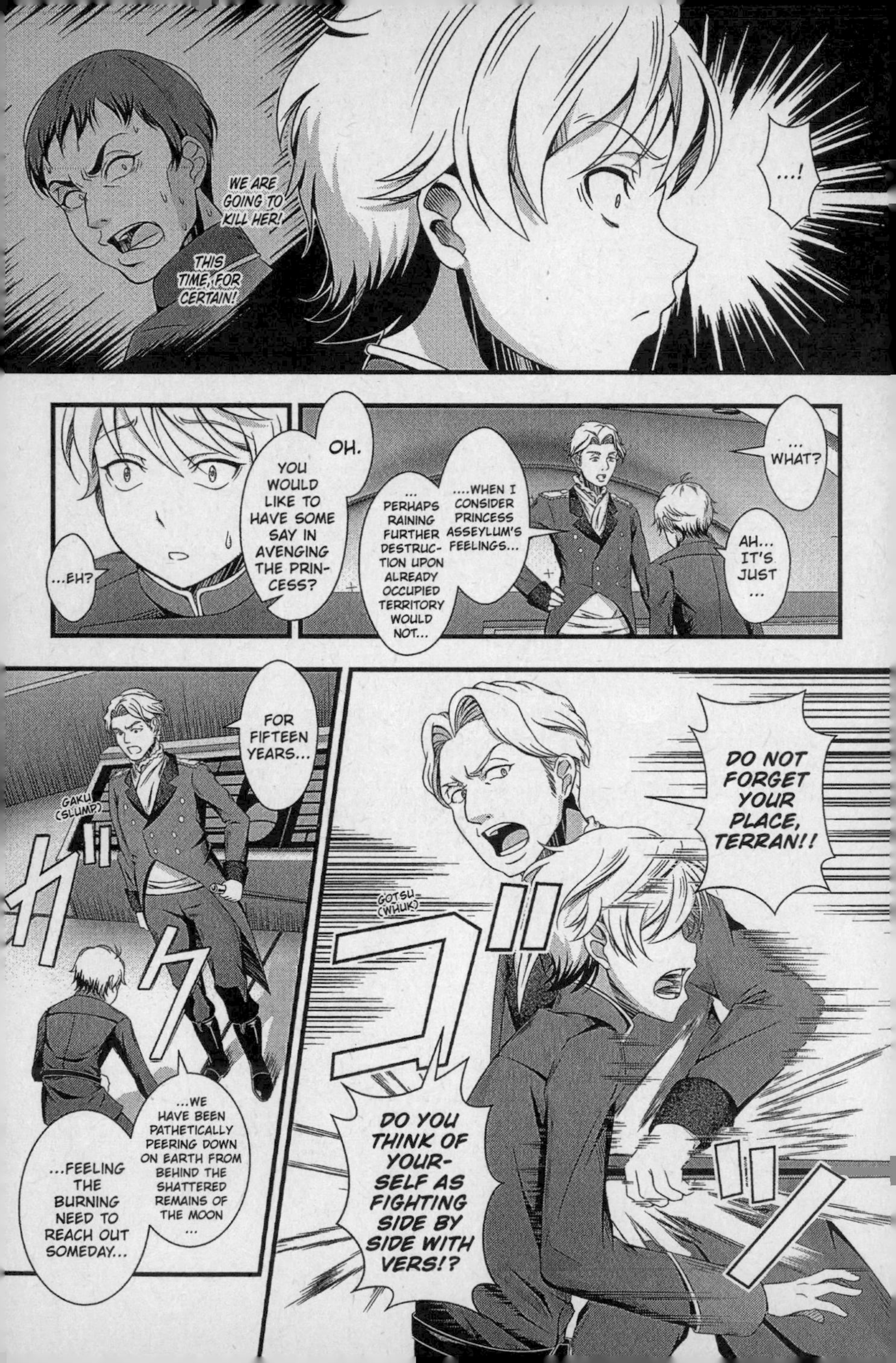
...!
WE ARE GOING TO KILL HER!
THIS TIME, FOR CERTAIN!
... WHAT?
AH... IT'S JUST ...
....WHEN I CONSIDER PRINCESS ASSEYLUM'S FEELINGS...
... PERHAPS RAINING FURTHER DESTRUCTION UPON ALREADY OCCUPIED TERRITORY WOULD NOT...
OH.
YOU WOULD LIKE TO HAVE SOME SAY IN AVENGING THE PRINCESS?
...EH?
DO NOT FORGET YOUR PLACE, TERRAN!!
GOTSU (WHUK)
DO YOU THINK OF YOURSELF AS FIGHTING SIDE BY SIDE WITH VERS!?
FOR FIFTEEN YEARS...
GAKU (SLUMP)
...WE HAVE BEEN PATHETICALLY PEERING DOWN ON EARTH FROM BEHIND THE SHATTERED REMAINS OF THE MOON ...
...FEELING THE BURNING NEED TO REACH OUT SOMEDAY...

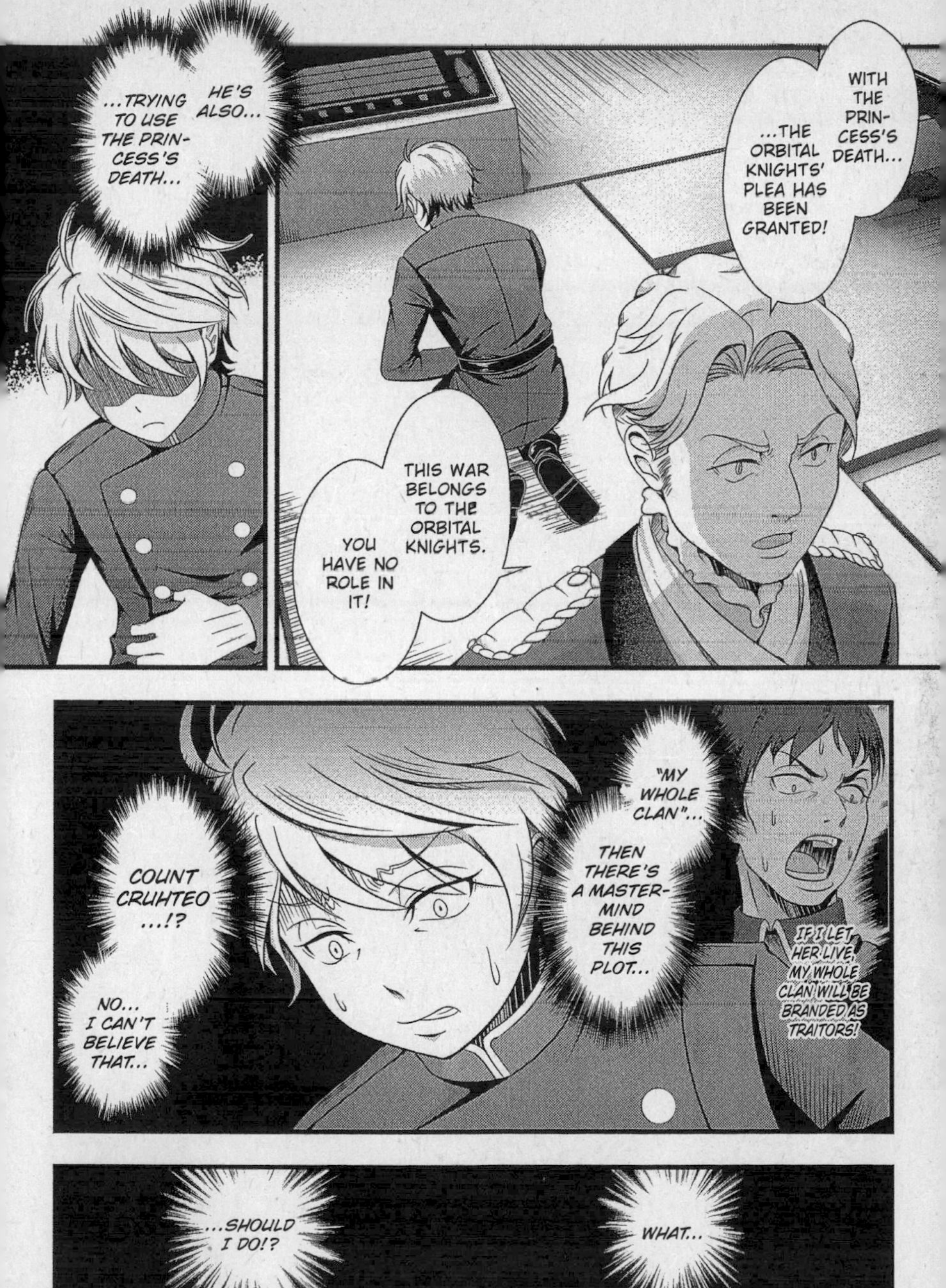
WITH THE PRINCESS'S DEATH...
...THE ORBITAL KNIGHTS' PLEA HAS BEEN GRANTED!
THIS WAR BELONGS TO THE ORBITAL KNIGHTS.
YOU HAVE NO ROLE IN IT!
HE'S ALSO...
...TRYING TO USE THE PRINCESS'S DEATH...
IF I LET HER LIVE, MY WHOLE CLAN WILL BE BRANDED AS TRAITORS!
"MY WHOLE CLAN"...
THEN THERE'S A MASTERMIND BEHIND THIS PLOT...
COUNT CRUHTEO ...!?
NO... I CAN'T BELIEVE THAT...
WHAT...
...SHOULD I DO!?

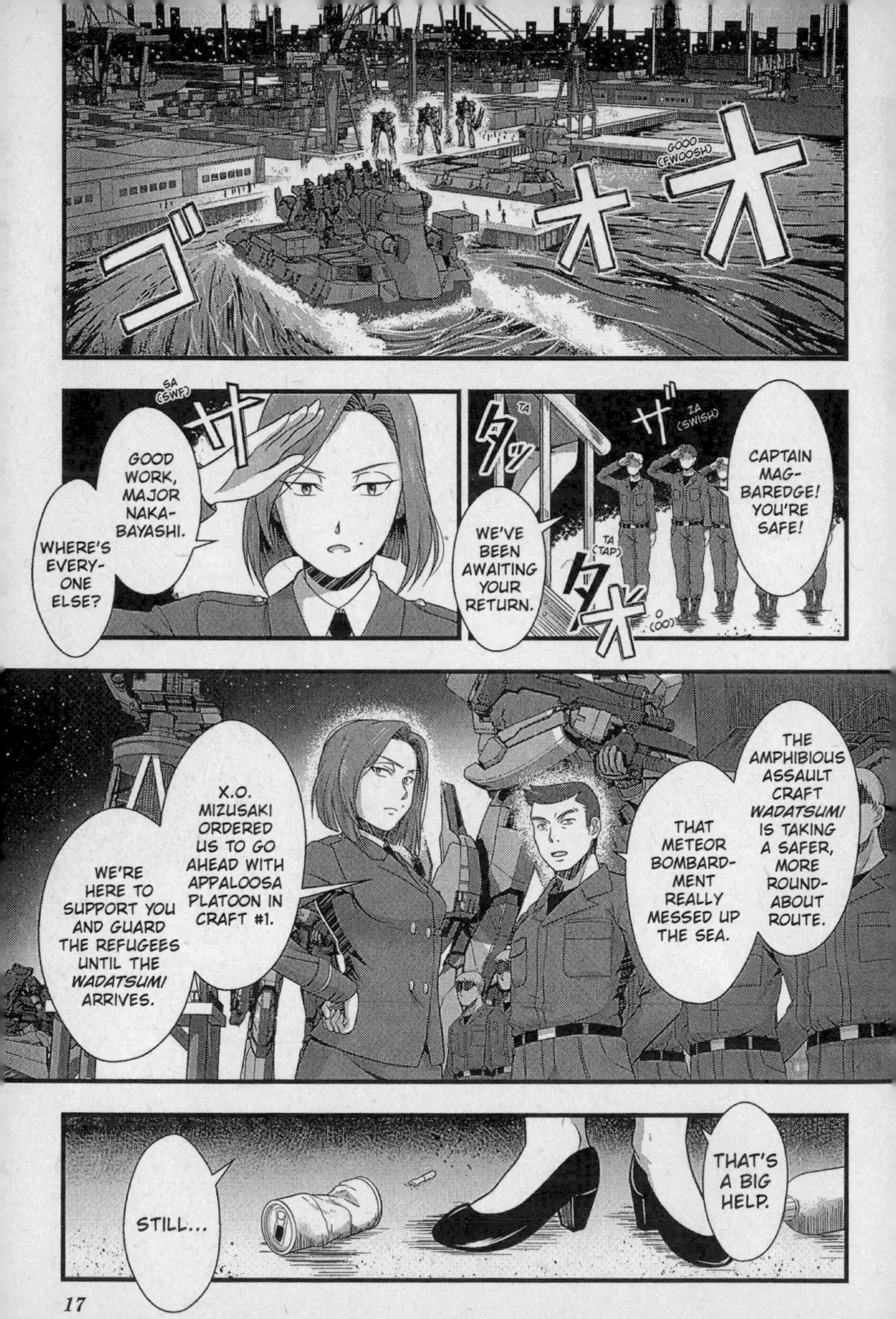

GOOO (FWOOSH)
ZA (SWISH)
CAPTAIN MAGBAREDGE! YOU'RE SAFE!
TA
TA (TAP)
O (OO)
WE'VE BEEN AWAITING YOUR RETURN.
SA (SWF)
GOOD WORK, MAJOR NAKABAYASHI.
WHERE'S EVERYONE ELSE?
THE AMPHIBIOUS ASSAULT CRAFT *WADATSUMI* IS TAKING A SAFER, MORE ROUNDABOUT ROUTE.
THAT METEOR BOMBARDMENT REALLY MESSED UP THE SEA.
X.O. MIZUSAKI ORDERED US TO GO AHEAD WITH APPALOOSA PLATOON IN CRAFT #1.
WE'RE HERE TO SUPPORT YOU AND GUARD THE REFUGEES UNTIL THE *WADATSUMI* ARRIVES.
THAT'S A BIG HELP.
STILL...

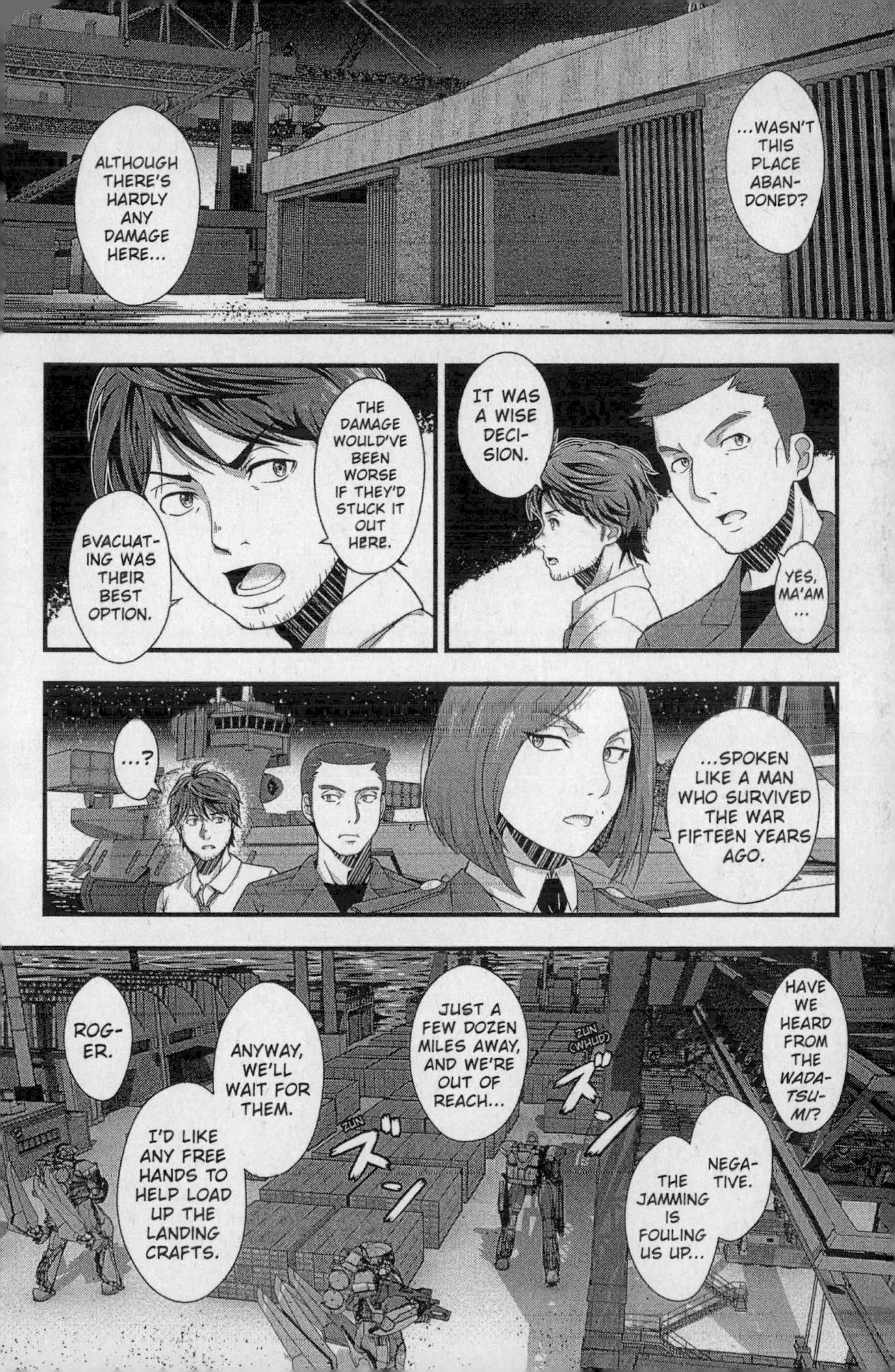
...WASN'T THIS PLACE ABANDONED?
ALTHOUGH THERE'S HARDLY ANY DAMAGE HERE...
IT WAS A WISE DECISION.
YES, MA'AM...
THE DAMAGE WOULD'VE BEEN WORSE IF THEY'D STUCK IT OUT HERE.
EVACUATING WAS THEIR BEST OPTION.
...SPOKEN LIKE A MAN WHO SURVIVED THE WAR FIFTEEN YEARS AGO.
...?
HAVE WE HEARD FROM THE *WADATSUMI*?
NEGATIVE.
THE JAMMING IS FOULING US UP...
ZUN (WHUD)
JUST A FEW DOZEN MILES AWAY, AND WE'RE OUT OF REACH...
ZUN
ANYWAY, WE'LL WAIT FOR THEM.
I'D LIKE ANY FREE HANDS TO HELP LOAD UP THE LANDING CRAFTS.
ROGER.

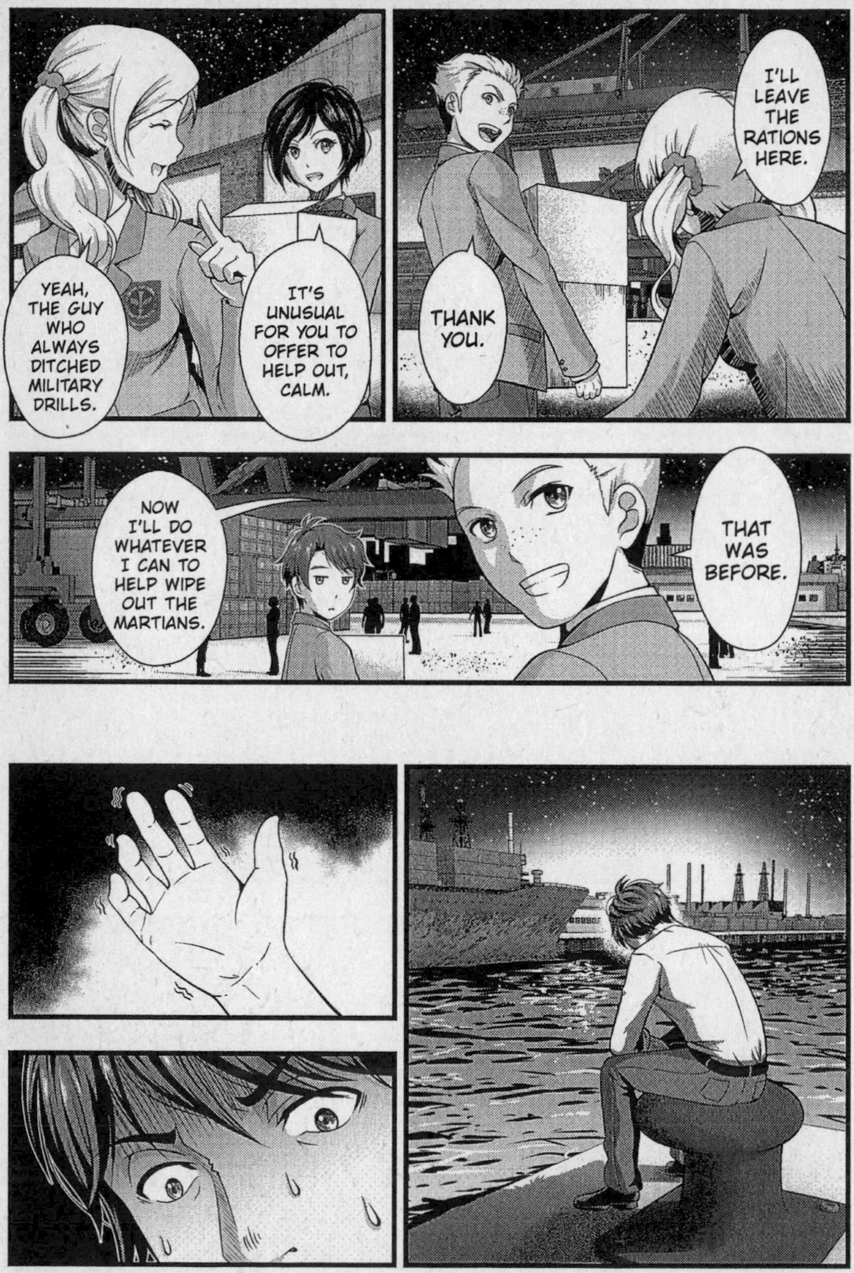
I'LL LEAVE THE RATIONS HERE.
THANK YOU.
IT'S UNUSUAL FOR YOU TO OFFER TO HELP OUT, CALM.
YEAH, THE GUY WHO ALWAYS DITCHED MILITARY DRILLS.
THAT WAS BEFORE.
NOW I'LL DO WHATEVER I CAN TO HELP WIPE OUT THE MARTIANS.

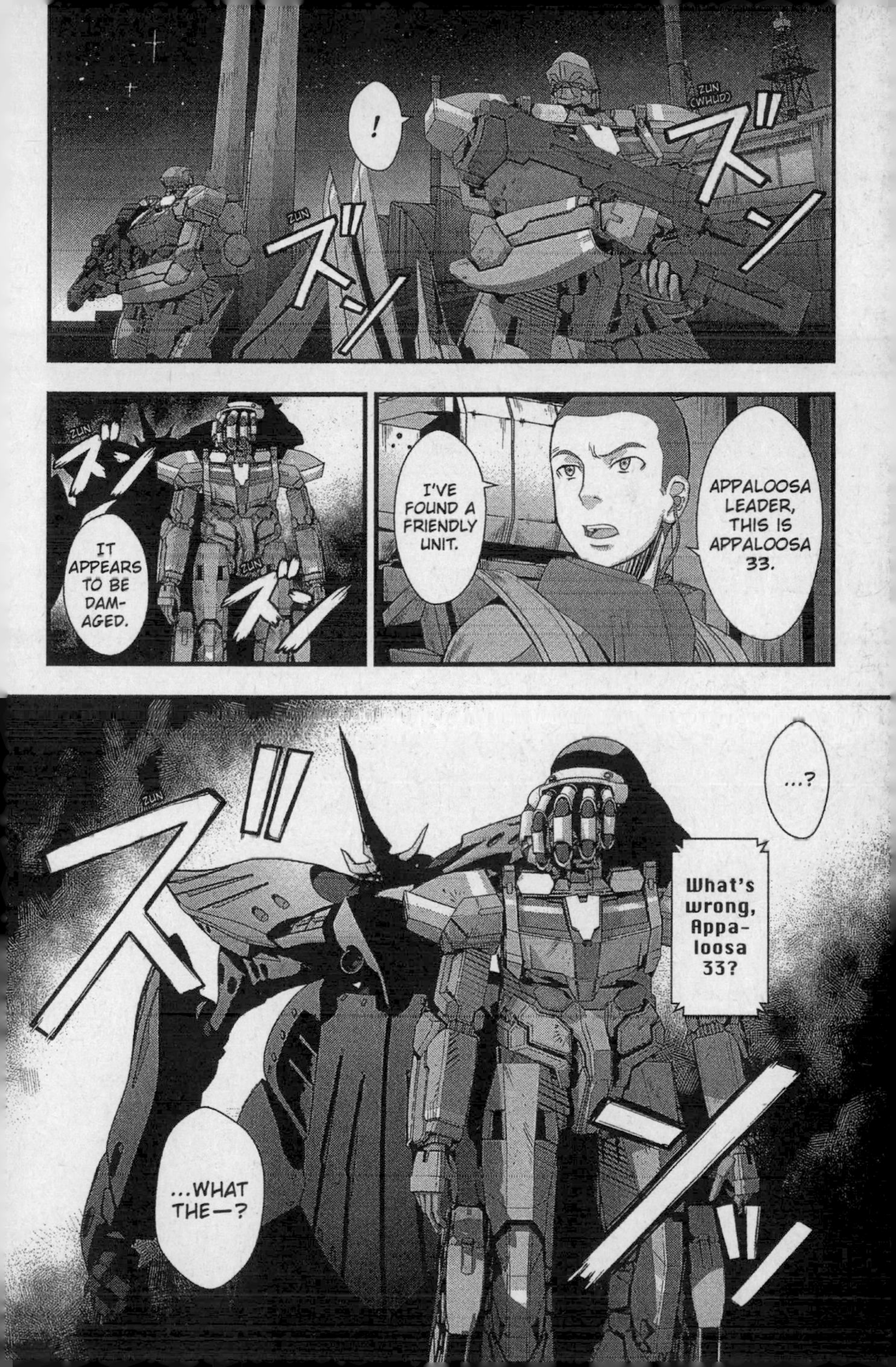
ZUN (WHUD)
ズーン
!
ZUN
ズーン
APPALOOSA LEADER, THIS IS APPALOOSA 33.
I'VE FOUND A FRIENDLY UNIT.
ZUN
ZUN
IT APPEARS TO BE DAMAGED.
...?
What's wrong, Appaloosa 33?
ZUN
ズーン
...WHAT THE—?

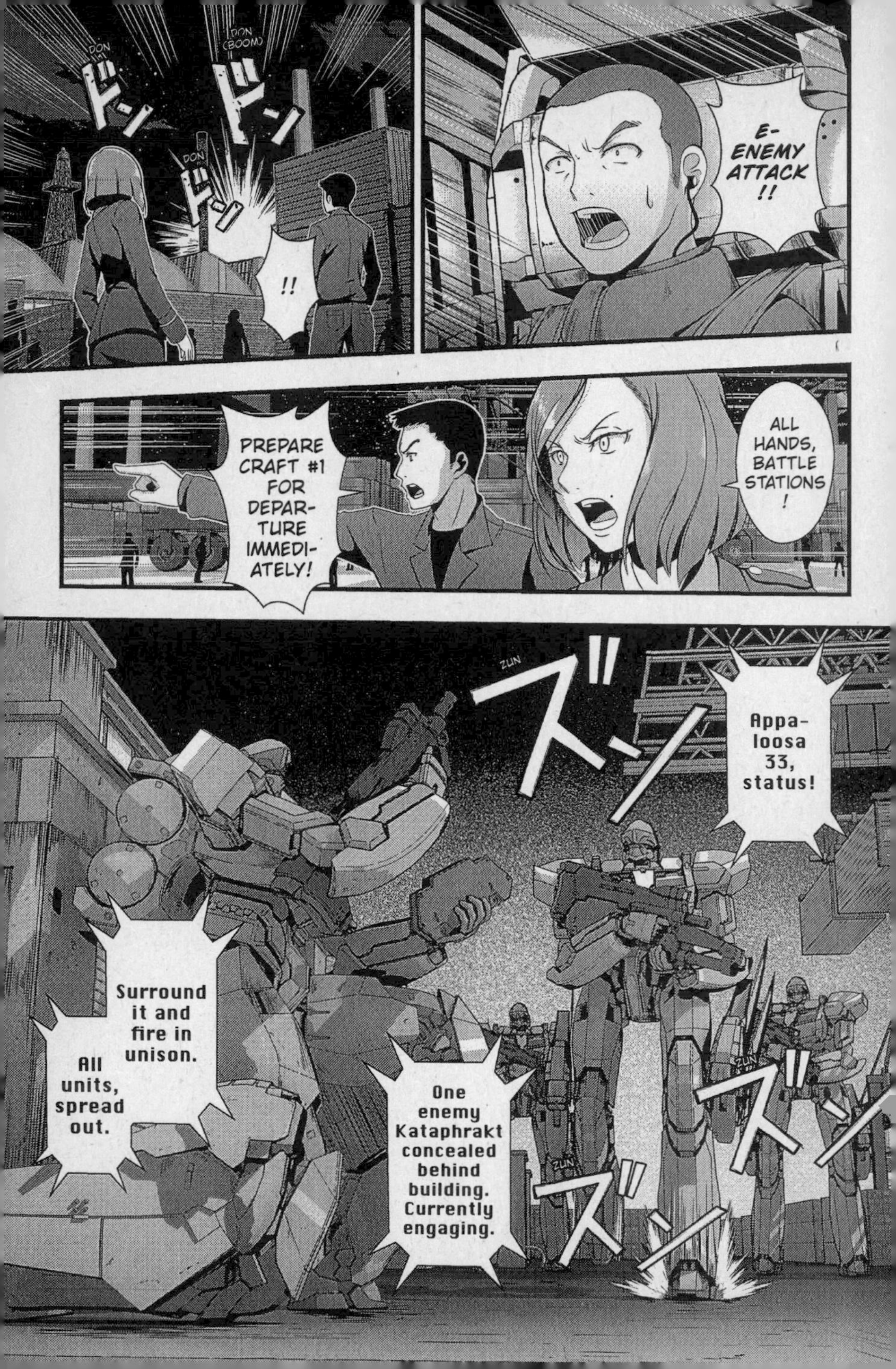
E-ENEMY ATTACK!!
DON (BOOM)
DON
DON
!!
ALL HANDS, BATTLE STATIONS!
PREPARE CRAFT #1 FOR DEPARTURE IMMEDIATELY!
Appaloosa 33, status!
ZUN
One enemy Kataphrakt concealed behind building. Currently engaging.
Surround it and fire in unison.
All units, spread out.
ZUN
ZUN

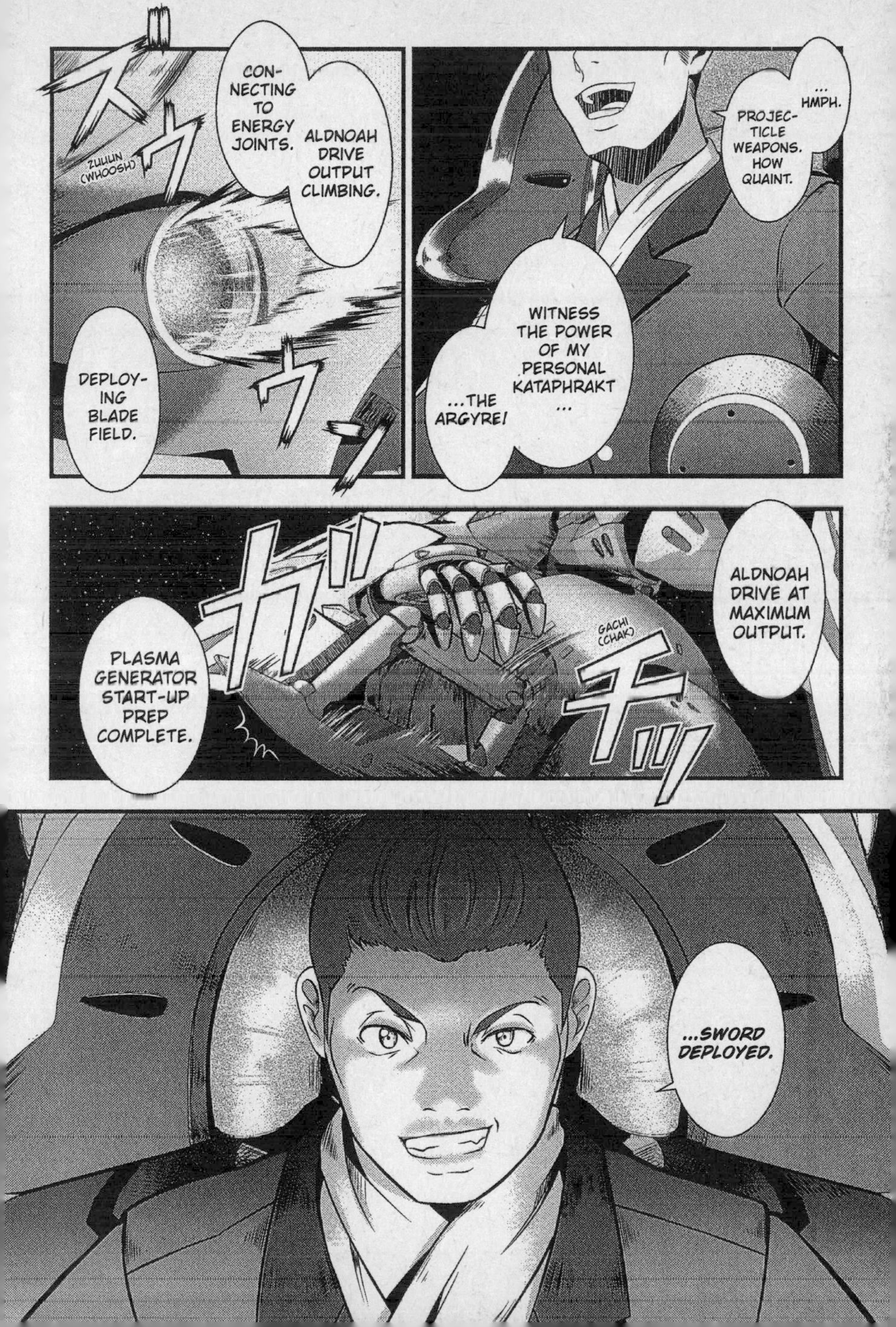
...HMPH.
PROJEC-TICLE WEAPONS. HOW QUAINT.
WITNESS THE POWER OF MY PERSONAL KATAPHRAKT...
...THE ARGYRE!
CON-NECTING TO ENERGY JOINTS.
ALDNOAH DRIVE OUTPUT CLIMBING.
ZUUUN (WHOOSH)
DEPLOY-ING BLADE FIELD.
ALDNOAH DRIVE AT MAXIMUM OUTPUT.
GACHI (CHAK)
PLASMA GENERATOR START-UP PREP COMPLETE.
...SWORD DEPLOYED.

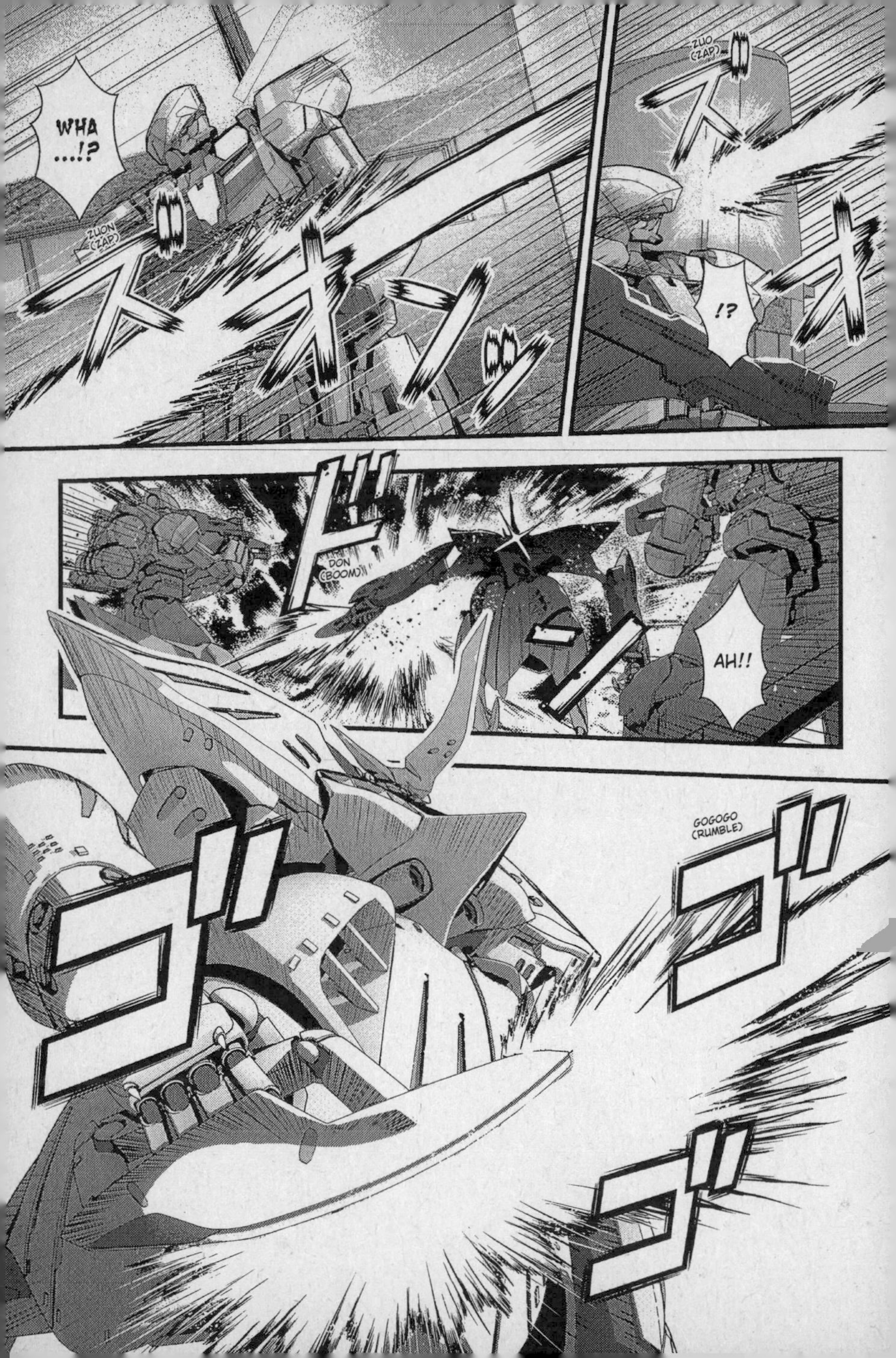
ズオ
ZUO (ZAP)
!?
WHA ...!?
ズオンッ
ZUON (ZAP)
AH!!
ド
DON (BOOM)
ゴゴゴ
GOGOGO (RUMBLE)

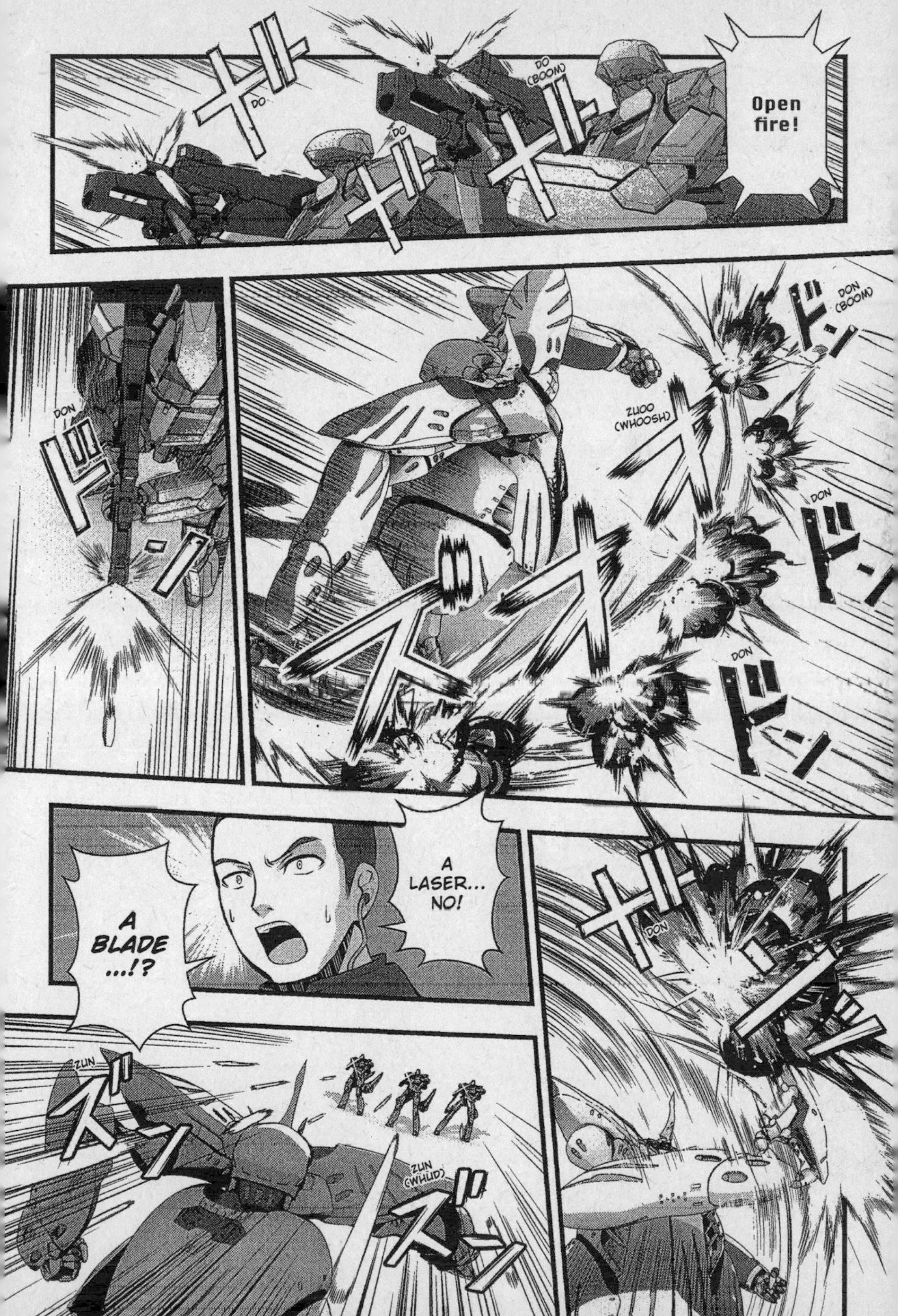
Open fire!
DO (BOOM)
DO
DO
DON (BOOM)
ZUOO (WHOOSH)
DON
DON
DON
DON
A LASER... NO!
A BLADE ...!?
ZUN (WHUD)
ZUN

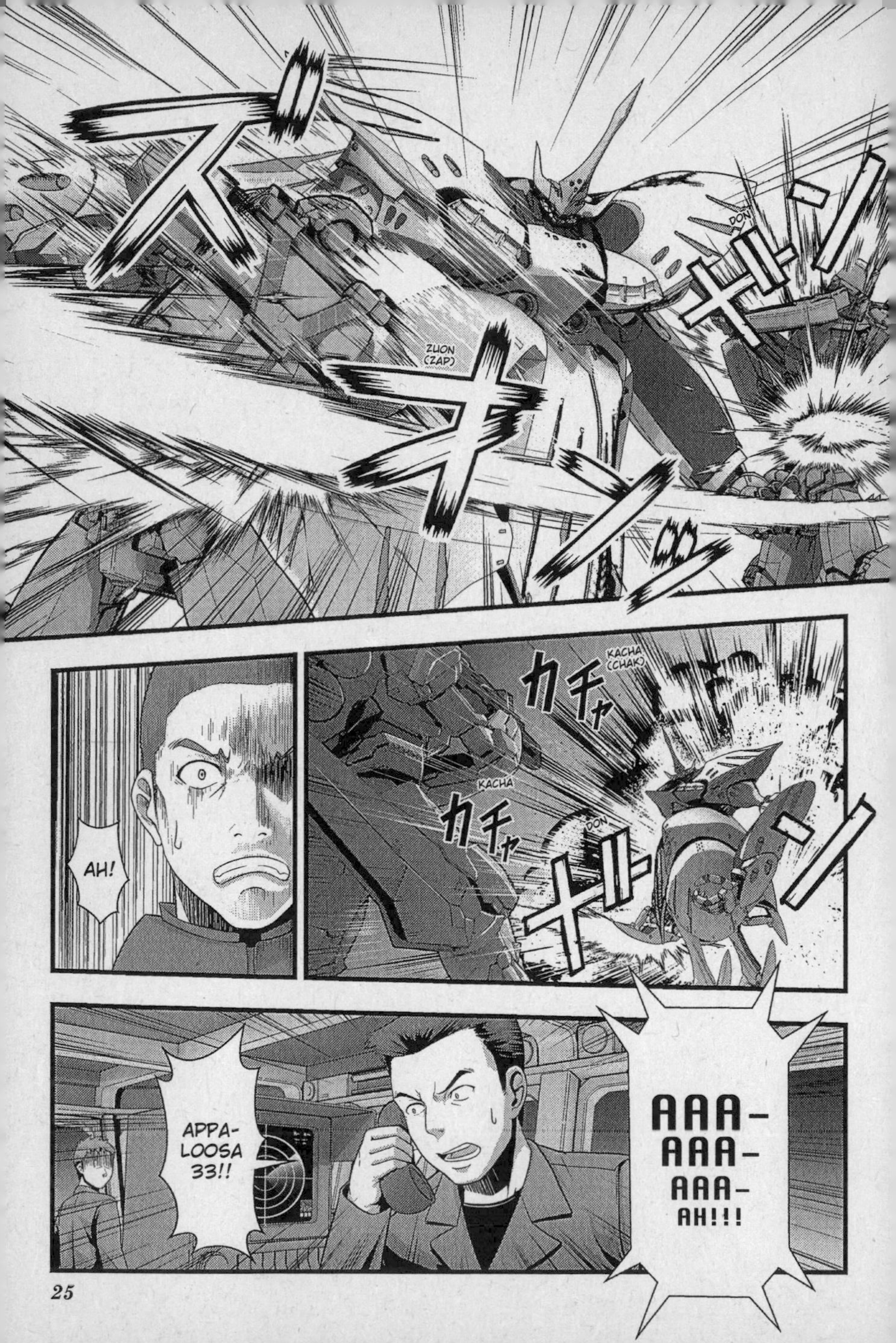
DON
ZUON (ZAP)
KACHA (CHAK)
KACHA
DON
AH!
AAA-AAA-AAA-AH!!!
APPA-LOOSA 33!!

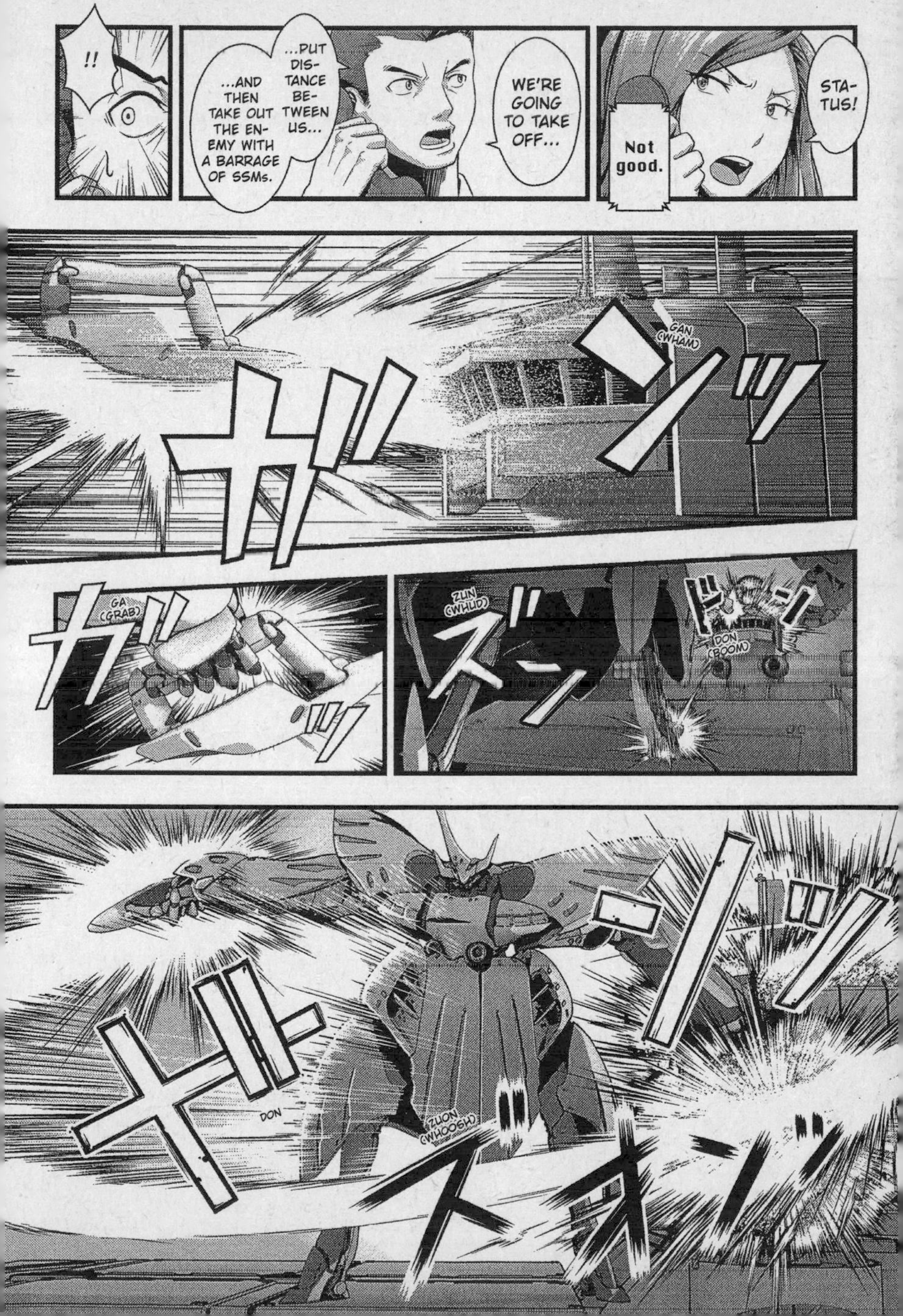
STA-TUS!
Not good.
WE'RE GOING TO TAKE OFF...
...PUT DIS-TANCE BE-TWEEN US...
...AND THEN TAKE OUT THE EN-EMY WITH A BARRAGE OF SSMs.
!!
GAN (WHAM)
DON (BOOM)
ZUN (WHUD)
GA (GRAB)
DON
ZUON (WHOOSH)

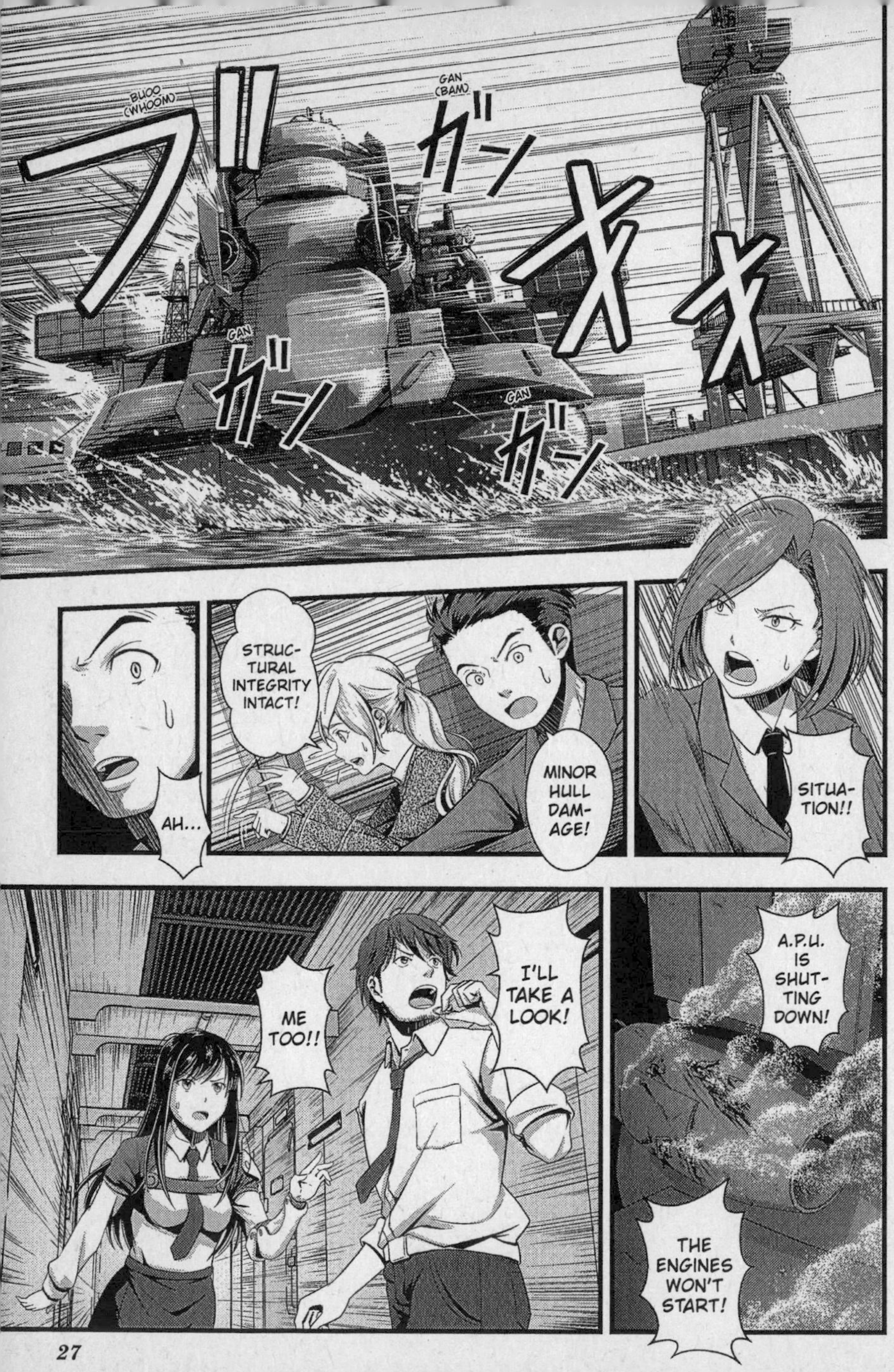
GAN (BAM)
BUOO (WHOOM)
GAN
GAN
SITUA-TION!!
MINOR HULL DAM-AGE!
STRUC-TURAL INTEGRITY INTACT!
AH...
A.P.U. IS SHUT-TING DOWN!
THE ENGINES WON'T START!
I'LL TAKE A LOOK!
ME TOO!!

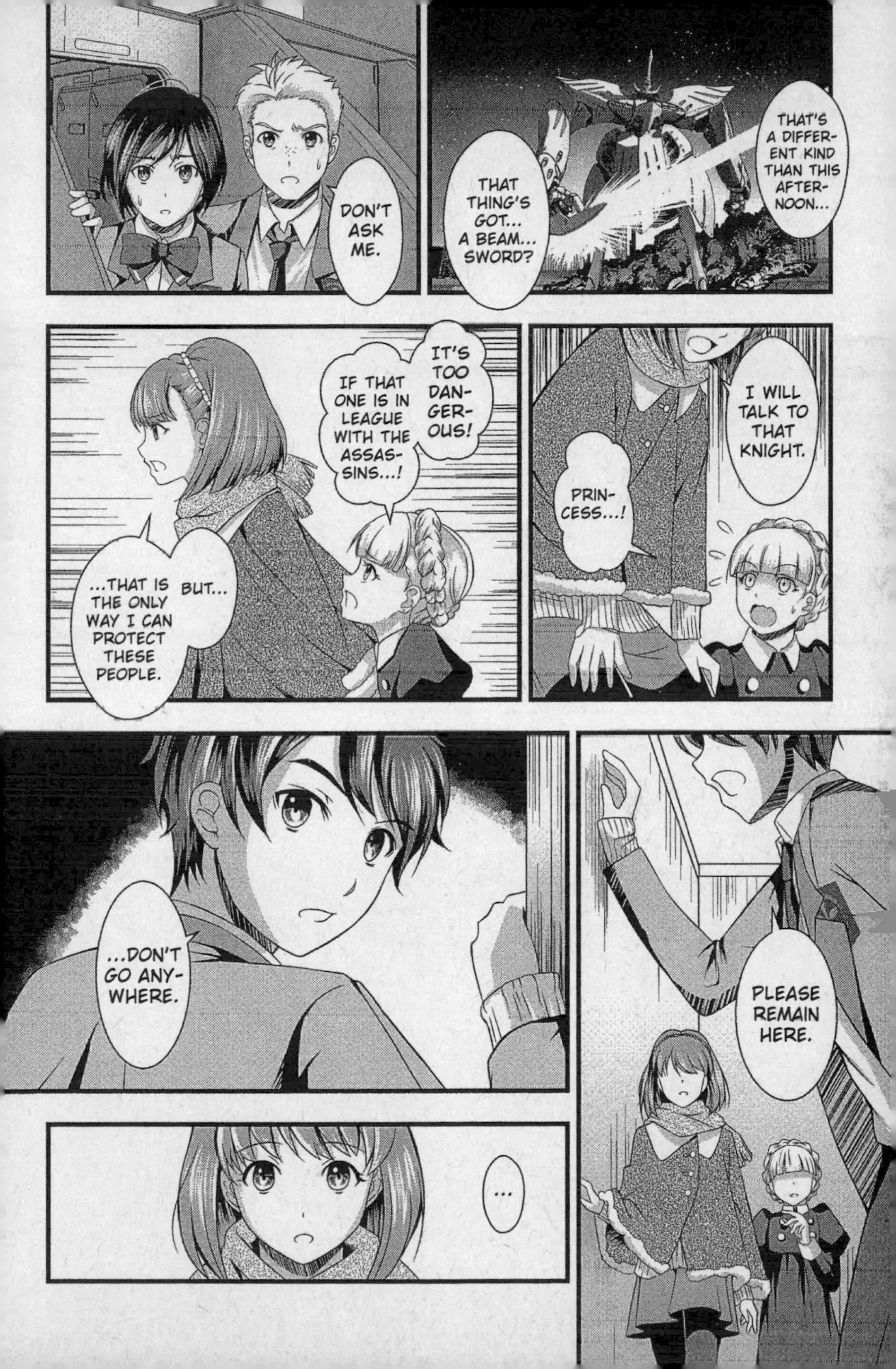
THAT'S A DIFFERENT KIND THAN THIS AFTERNOON...
THAT THING'S GOT... A BEAM... SWORD?
DON'T ASK ME.
I WILL TALK TO THAT KNIGHT.
PRINCESS...!
IT'S TOO DANGEROUS!
IF THAT ONE IS IN LEAGUE WITH THE ASSASSINS...!
BUT...
...THAT IS THE ONLY WAY I CAN PROTECT THESE PEOPLE.
PLEASE REMAIN HERE.
...DON'T GO ANYWHERE.
...

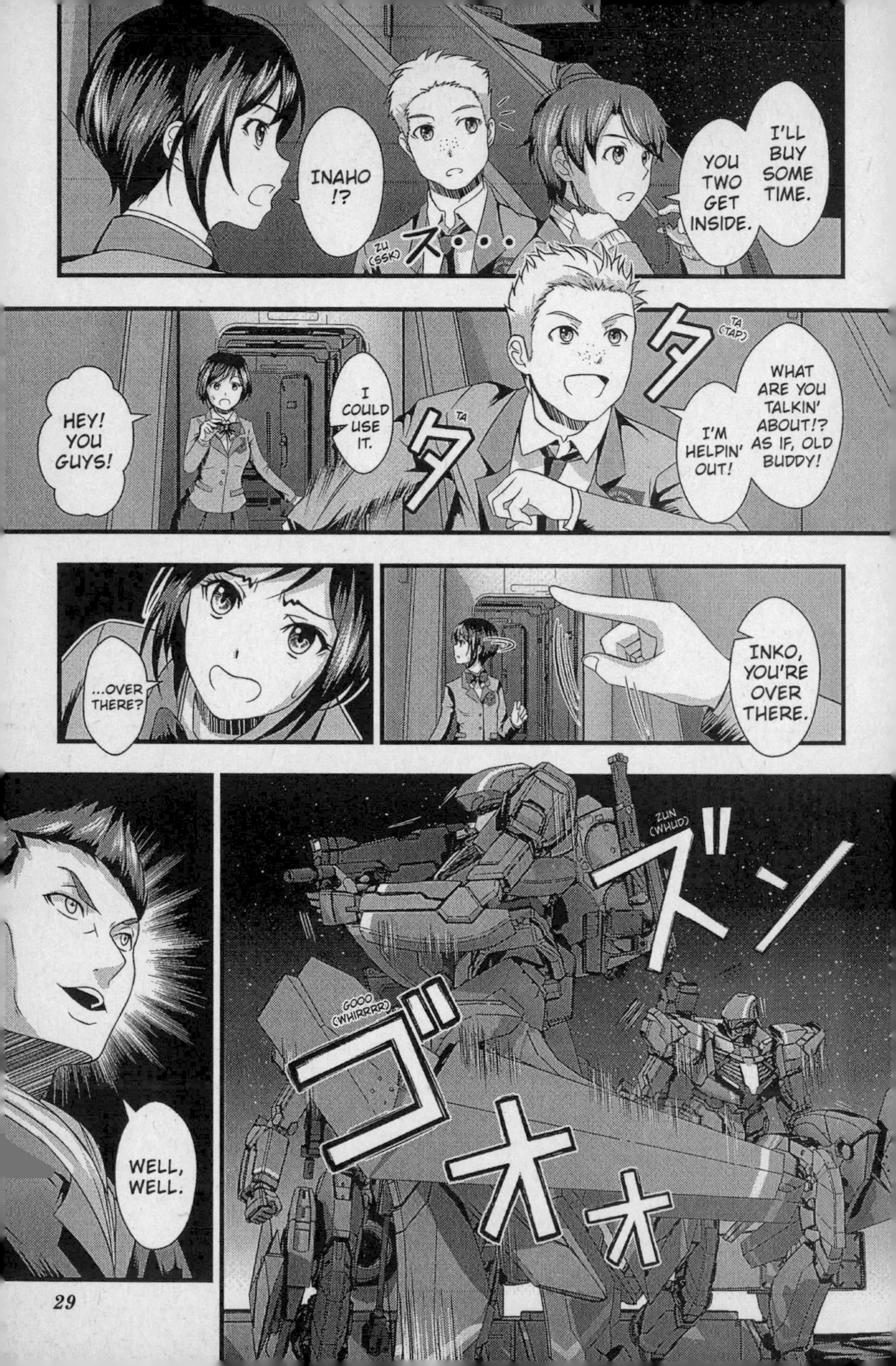
I'LL BUY SOME TIME.
YOU TWO GET INSIDE.
ZU (SSK)
ス・・・
INAHO !?
TA (TAP)
タ
WHAT ARE YOU TALKIN' ABOUT!? AS IF, OLD BUDDY!
I'M HELPIN' OUT!
TA
タ
I COULD USE IT.
HEY! YOU GUYS!
INKO, YOU'RE OVER THERE.
...OVER THERE?
ZUN (WHUD)
ズン
GOOO (WHIRRRR)
ゴオォ
WELL, WELL.

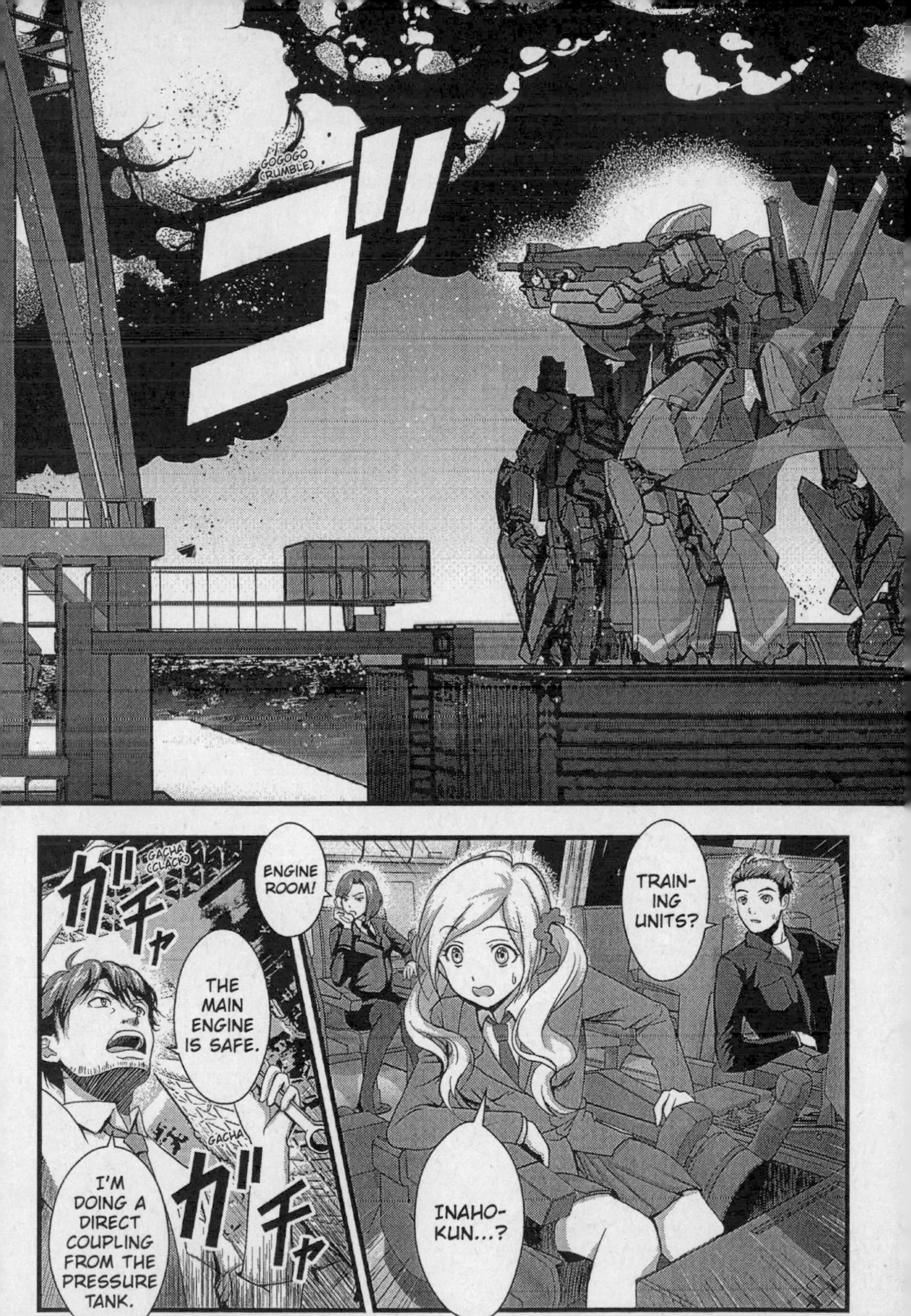
GOGOGO (RUMBLE)
TRAIN-ING UNITS?
ENGINE ROOM!
INAHO-KUN...?
GACHA (CLACK)
THE MAIN ENGINE IS SAFE.
GACHA
I'M DOING A DIRECT COUPLING FROM THE PRESSURE TANK.

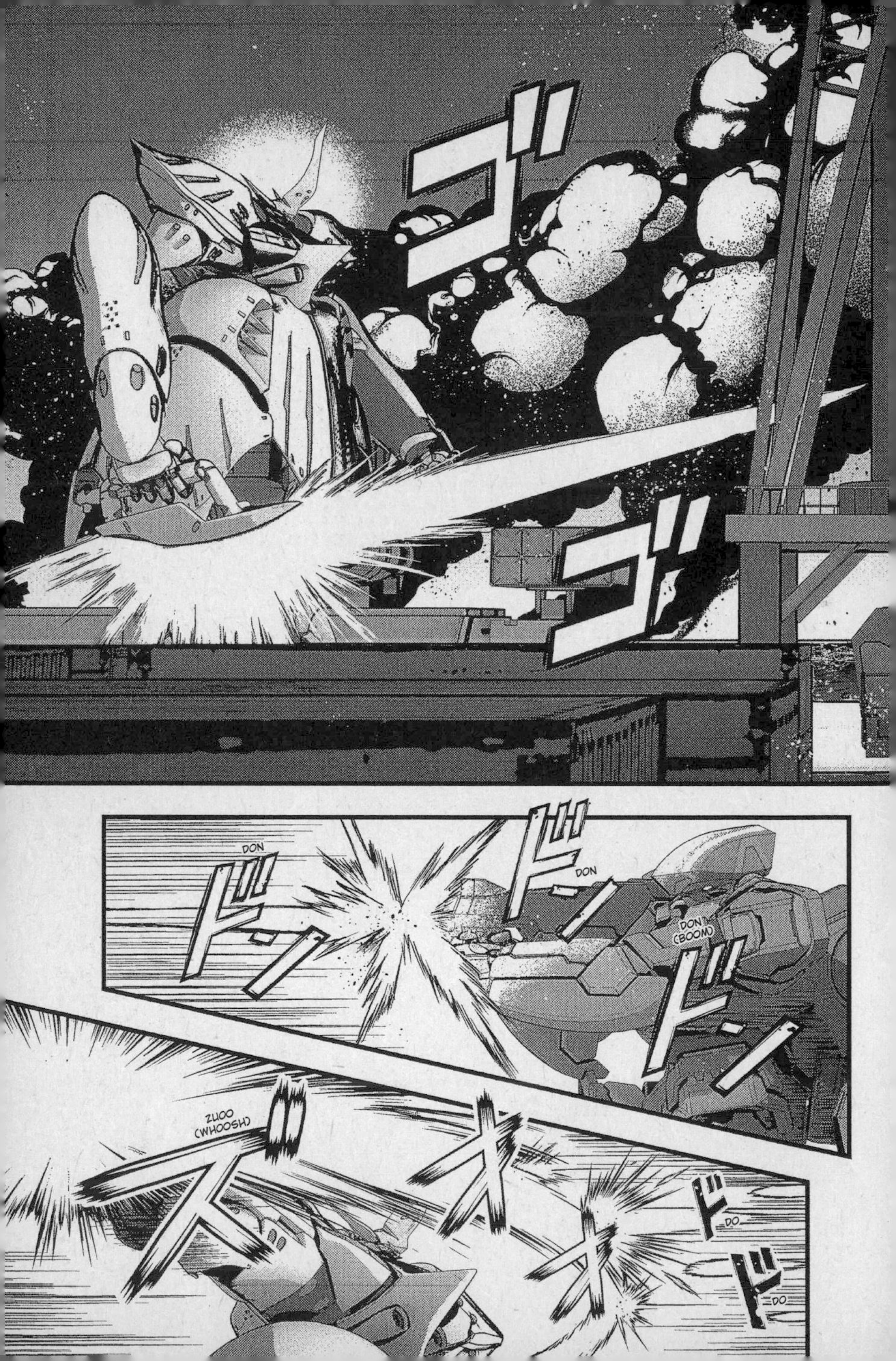

DON (BOOM)
DON
DON
DO
DO
ZUOO (WHOOSH)

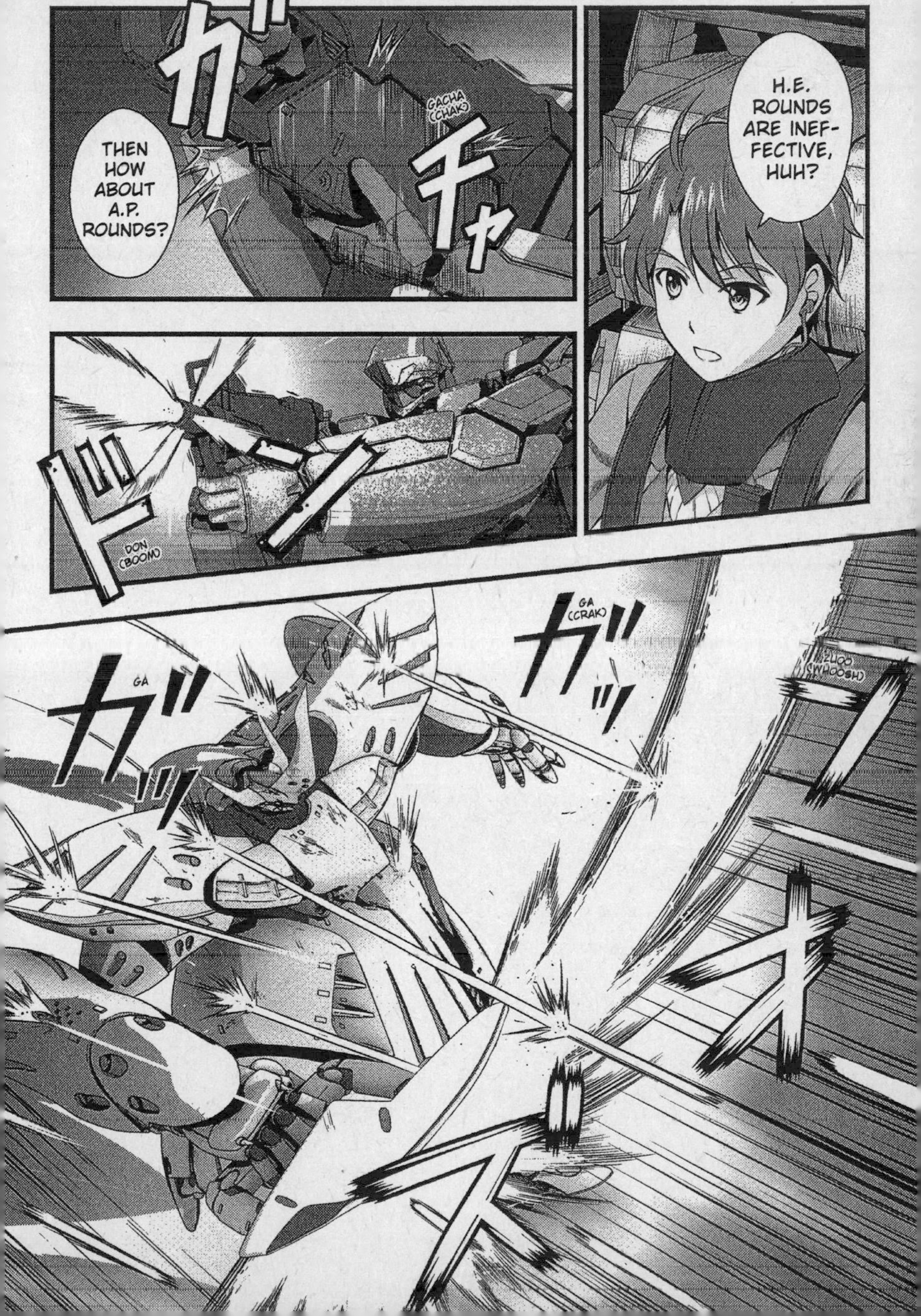
H.E. ROUNDS ARE INEF-FECTIVE, HUH?
GACHA (CHAK)
THEN HOW ABOUT A.P. ROUNDS?
DON (BOOM)
ZUOO (WHOOSH)
GA (CRAK)
GA

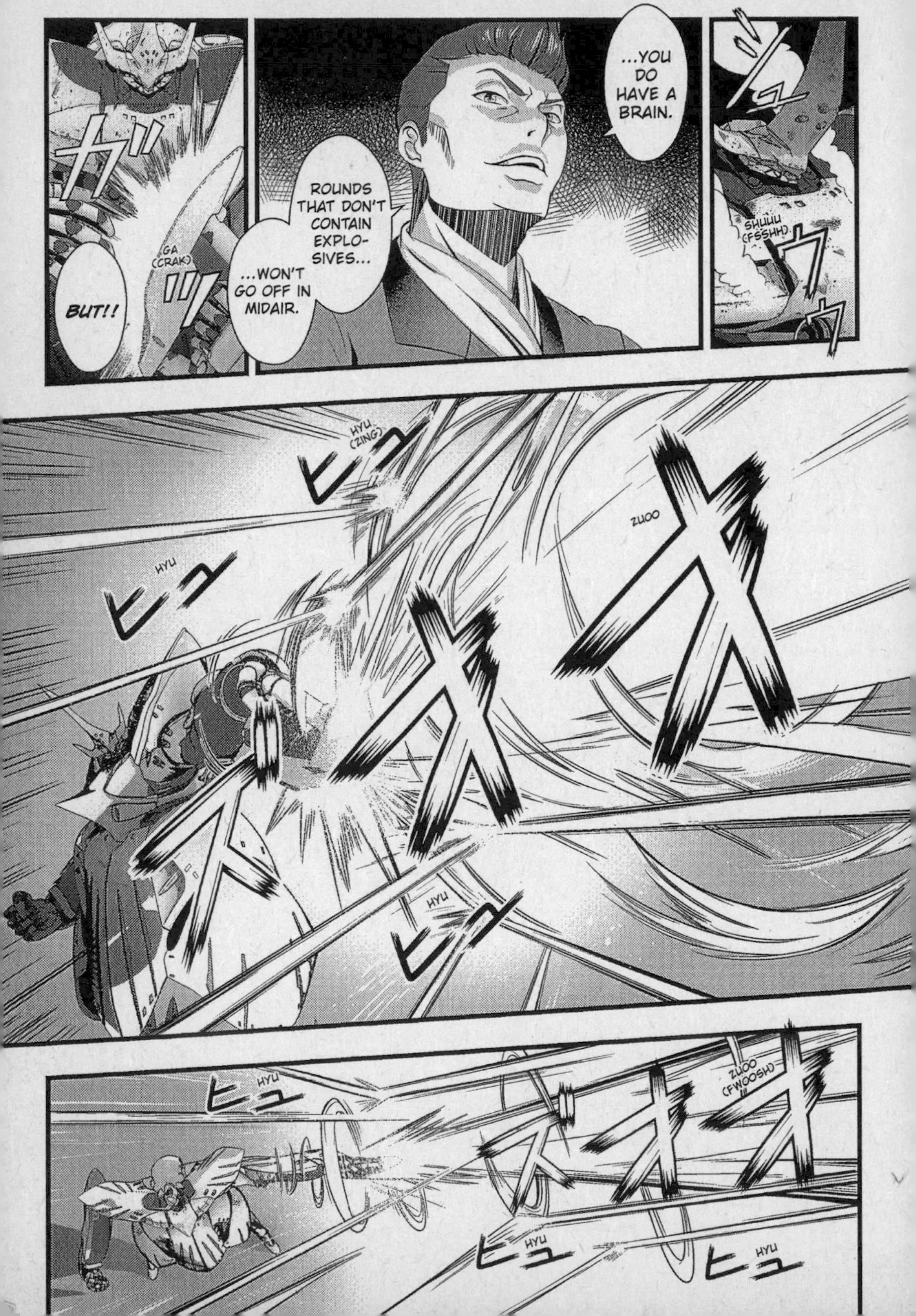
SHUUU (FSSHH)
...YOU DO HAVE A BRAIN.
ROUNDS THAT DON'T CONTAIN EXPLOSIVES...
...WON'T GO OFF IN MIDAIR.
GA (CRAK)
BUT!!
ZUOO
HYU (ZING)
HYU
HYU
ZUOO (FWOOSH)
HYU
HYU
HYU

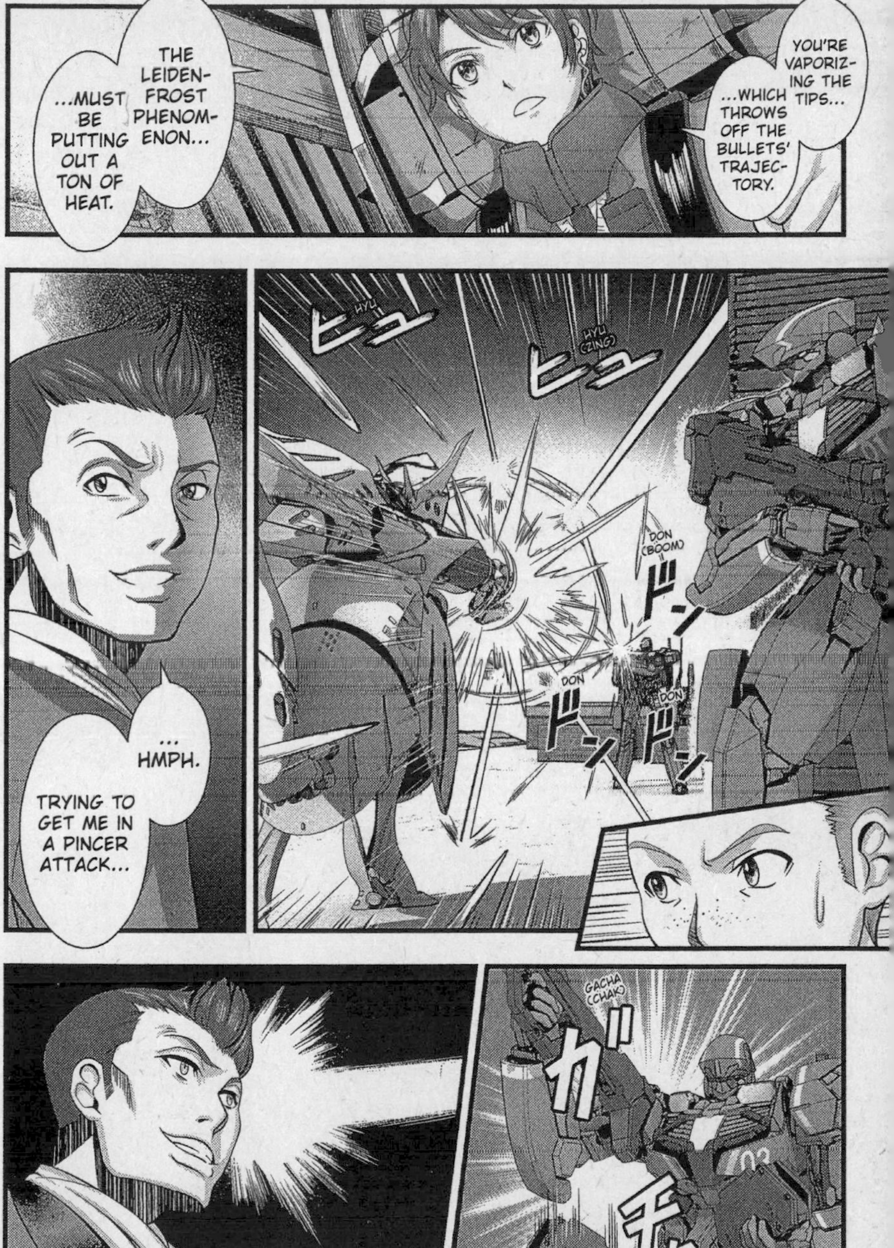
YOU'RE VAPORIZING THE TIPS...
...WHICH THROWS OFF THE BULLETS' TRAJECTORY.
THE LEIDENFROST PHENOMENON...
...MUST BE PUTTING OUT A TON OF HEAT.
ヒュ HYU
ヒュ HYU (ZING)
ドン DON (BOOM)
ドン DON
ドン DON
...HMPH.
TRYING TO GET ME IN A PINCER ATTACK...
ガチャ GACHA (CHAK)

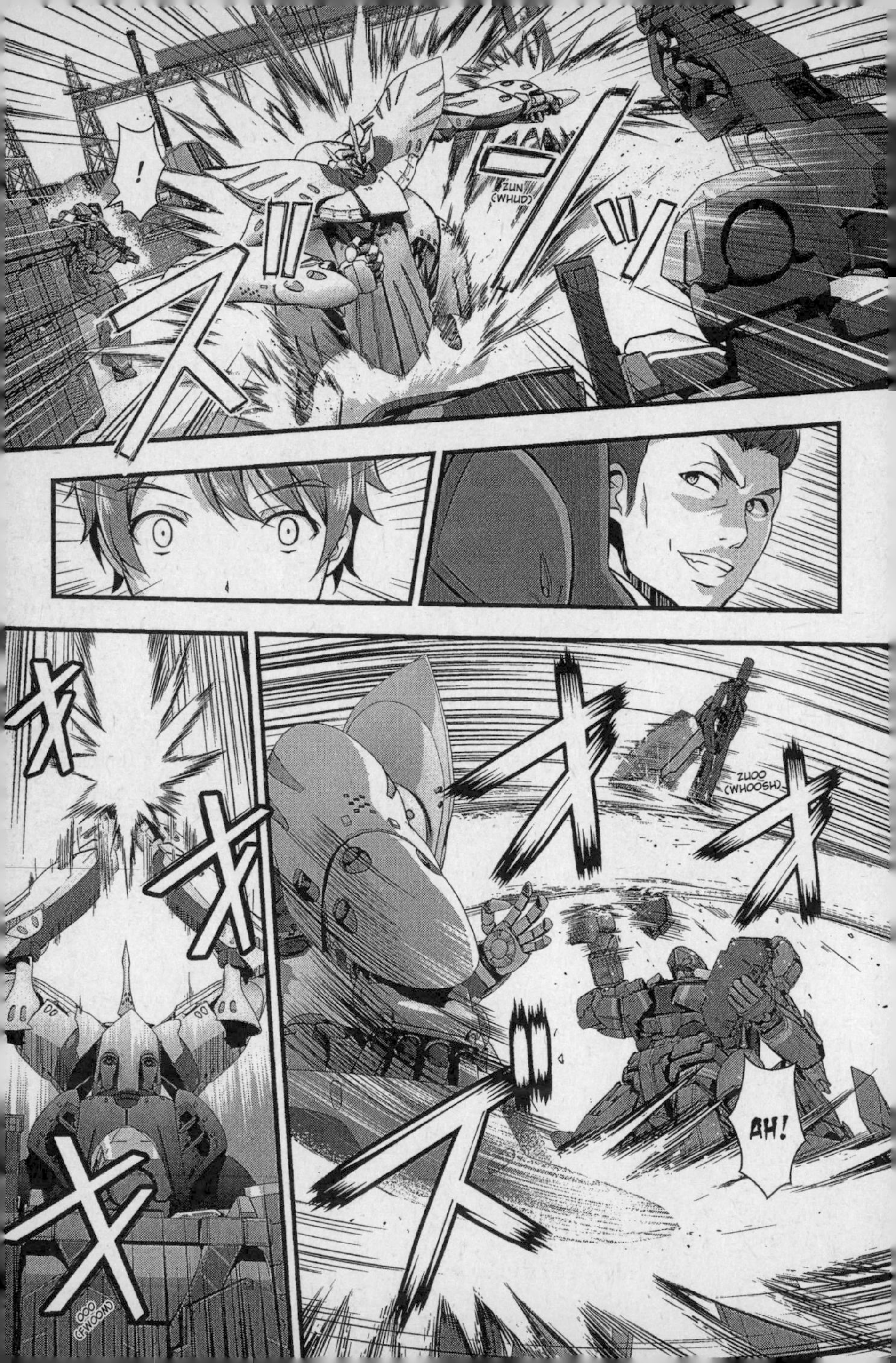
ZUN
(WHUD)
!
ZUOO
(WHOOSH)
AH!
OOO
(FWOOM)

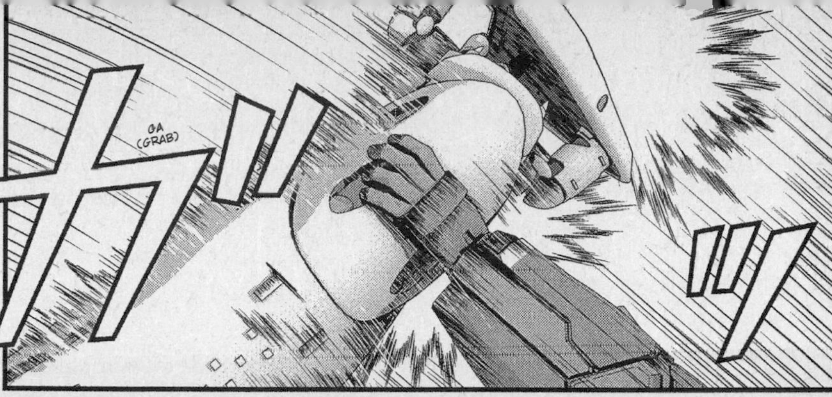
ガッ
GA
(GRAB)

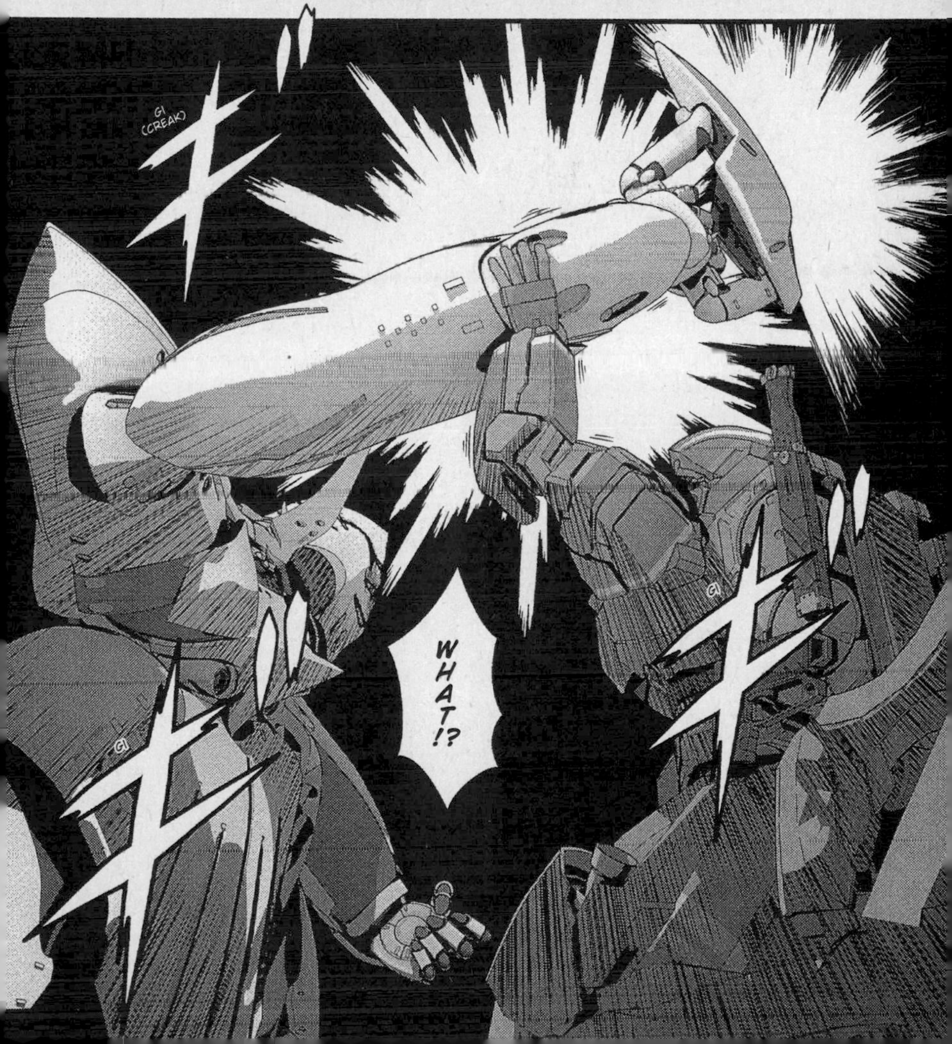
ギ
GI
(CREAK)
ギ
GI
ギ
GI
WHAT!?

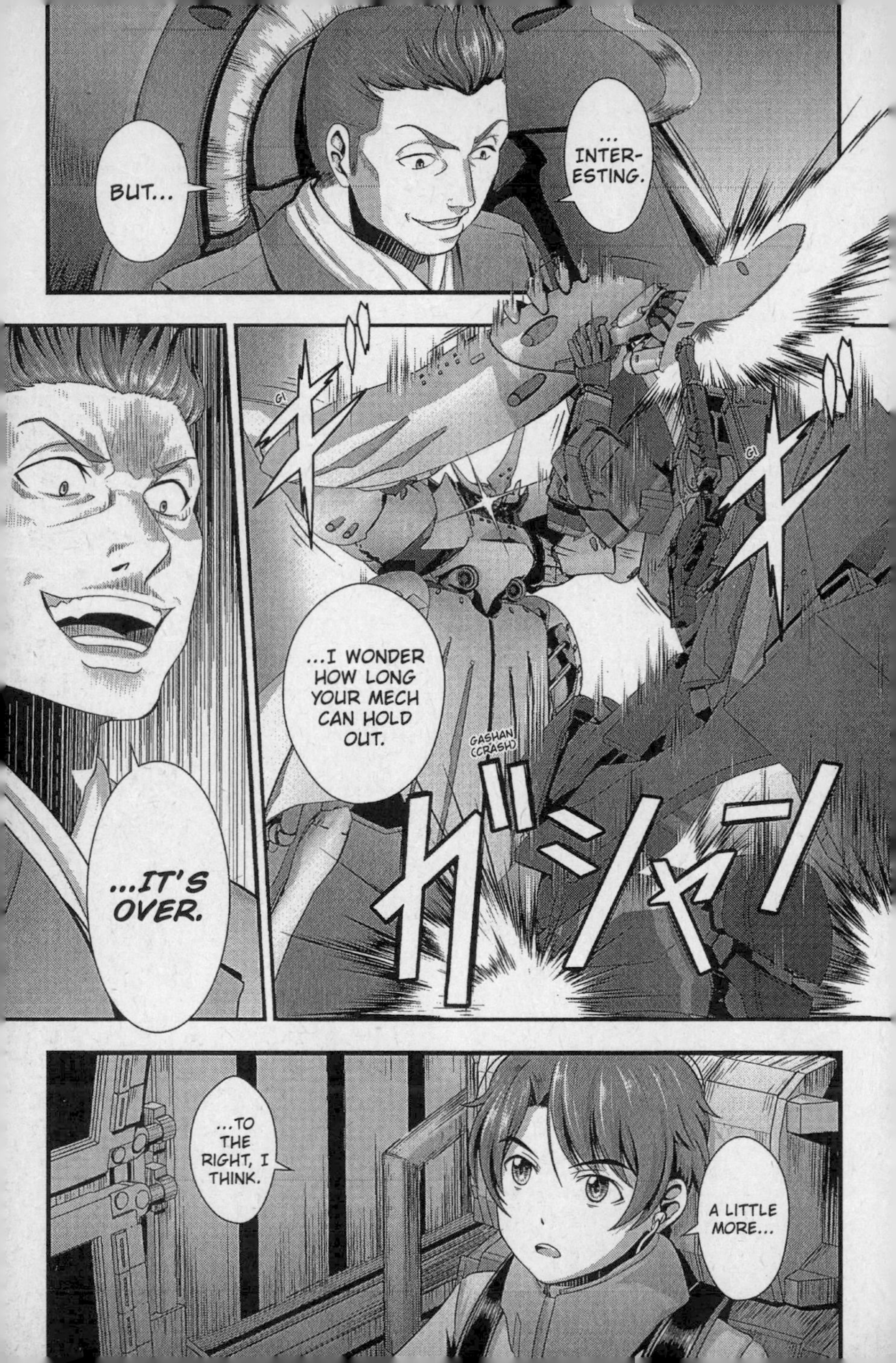
...INTERESTING.
BUT...
GI
GI
...I WONDER HOW LONG YOUR MECH CAN HOLD OUT.
GASHAN (CRASH)
...IT'S OVER.
A LITTLE MORE...
...TO THE RIGHT, I THINK.

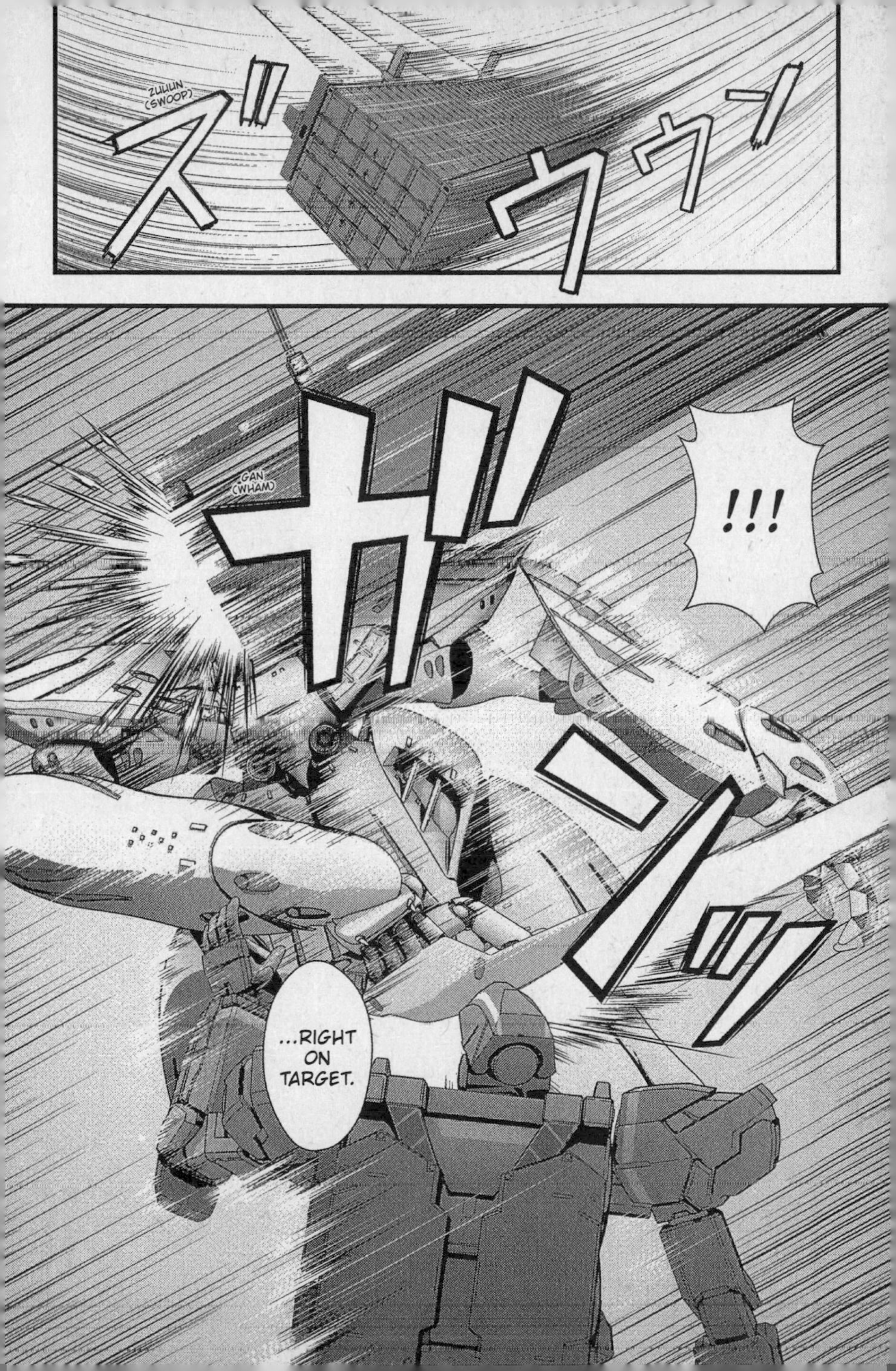
ZUUUN
(SWOOP)
ズウウン
GAN
(WHAM)
ガンッ
!!!
...RIGHT ON TARGET.

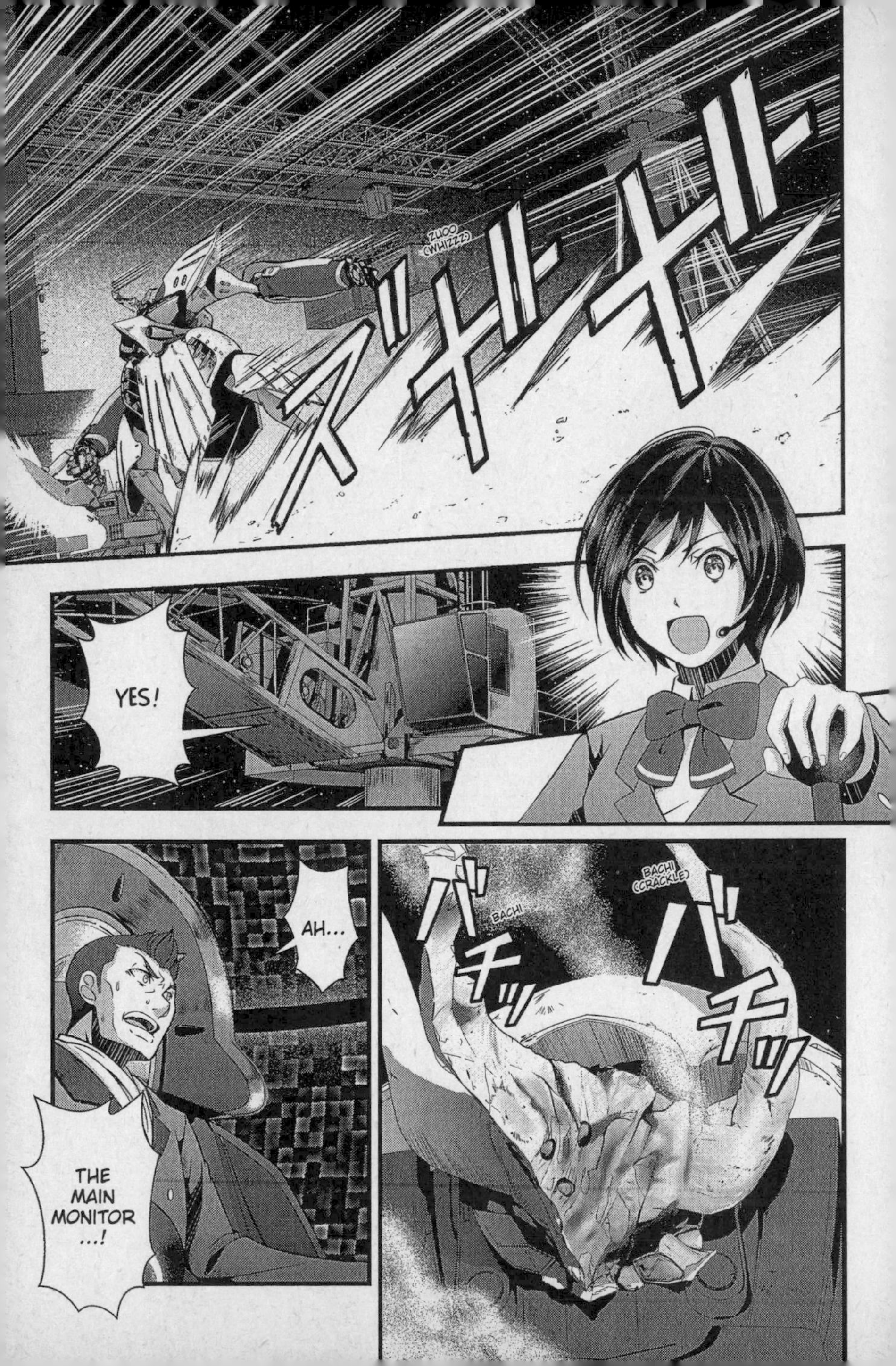
ZUOO (WHIZZZ)
YES!
BACHI (CRACKLE)
BACHI
AH...
THE MAIN MONITOR ...!

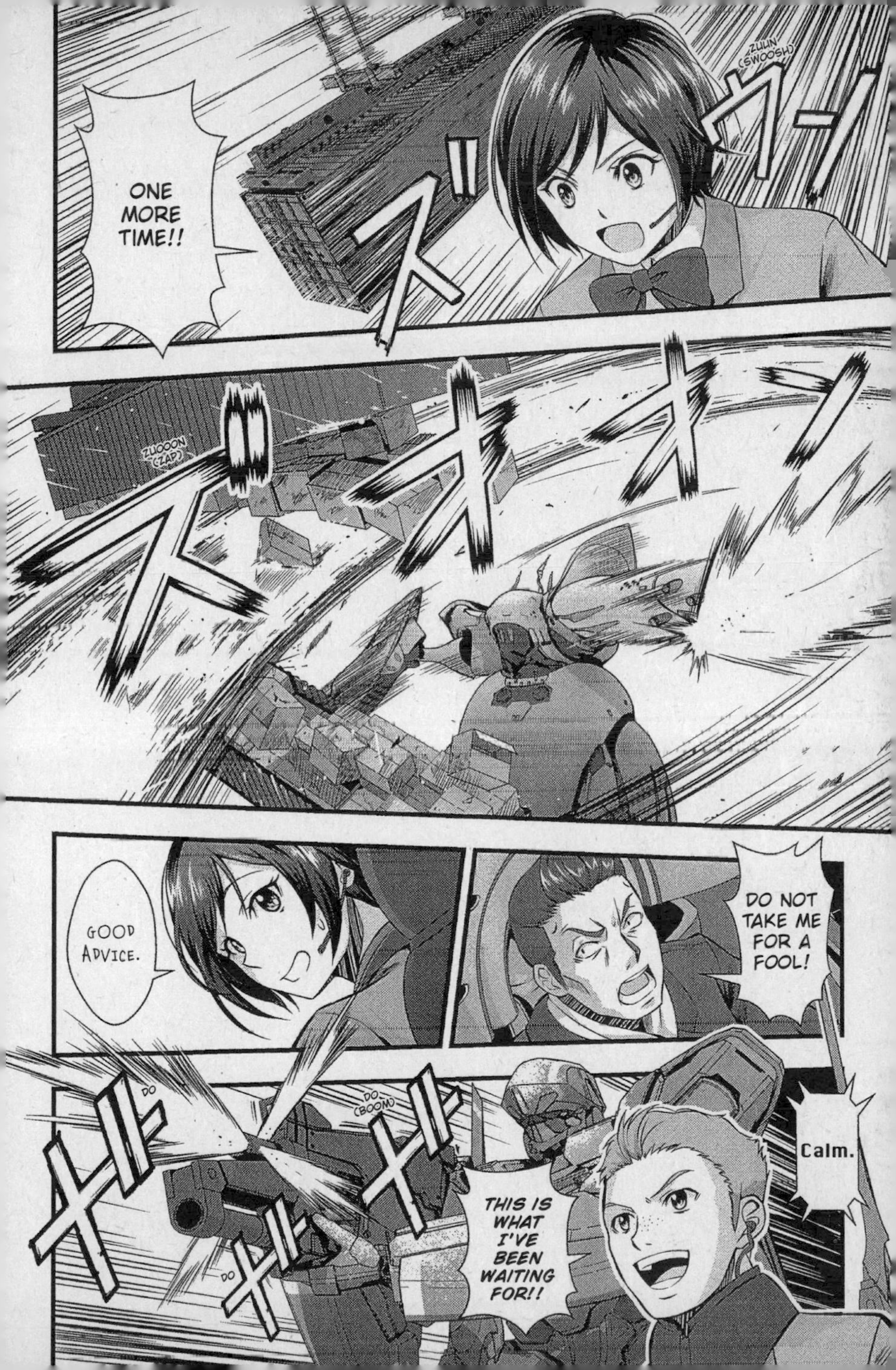
ZUUN (SWOOSH)
ONE MORE TIME!!
ZUOOON (ZAP)
DO NOT TAKE ME FOR A FOOL!
GOOD ADVICE.
Calm.
THIS IS WHAT I'VE BEEN WAITING FOR!!
DO (BOOM)
DO
DO

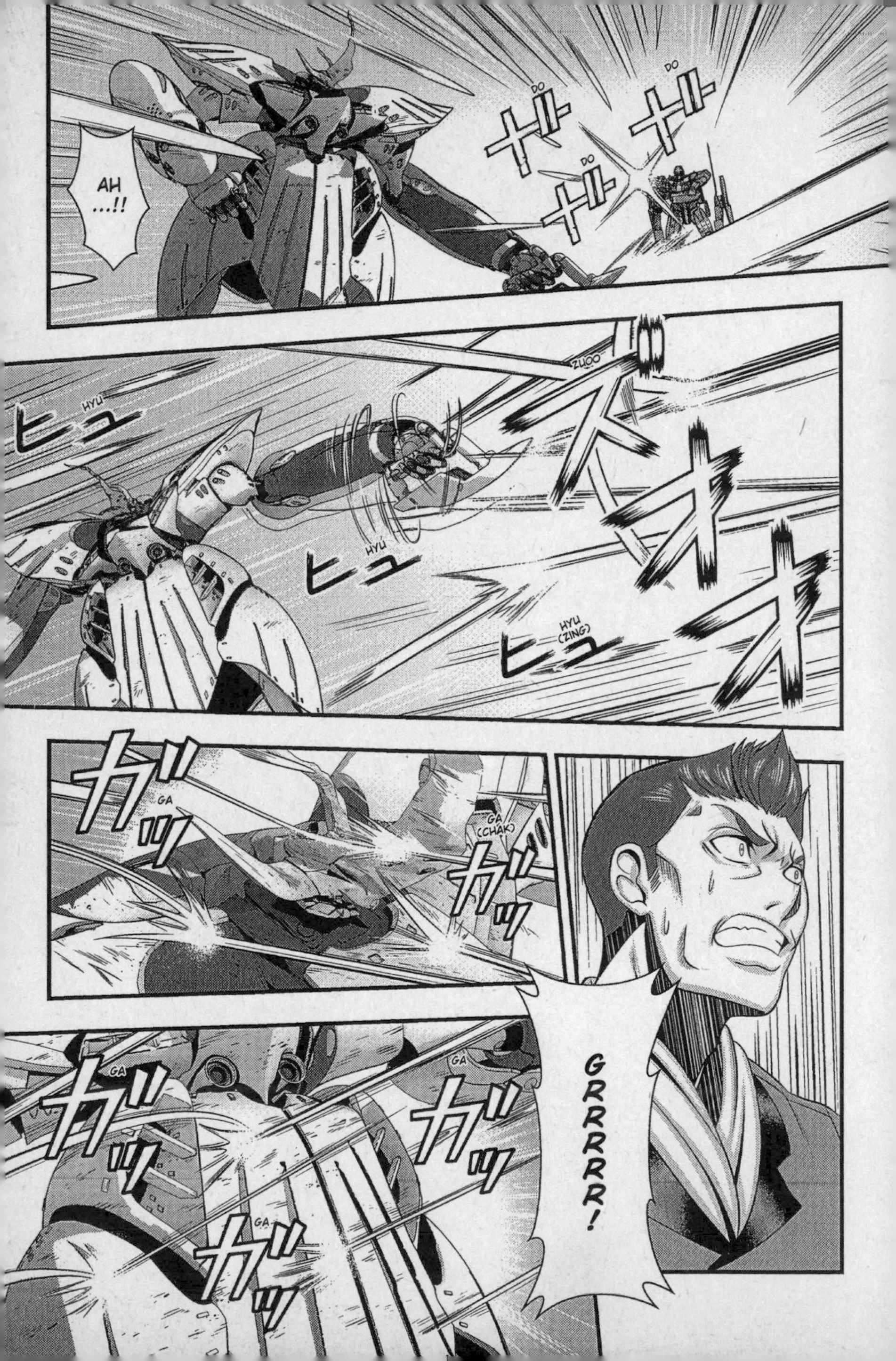

DO
ドド
DO
ドド
DO
ドド
AH ...!!
ZUOO
ズオオ
HYU (ZING)
ヒュ
HYU
ヒュ
HYU
ヒュ
GRRRRR!
GA (CHAK)
ガッ
GA
ガッ
GA
ガッ
GA
ガッ
GA
ガッ

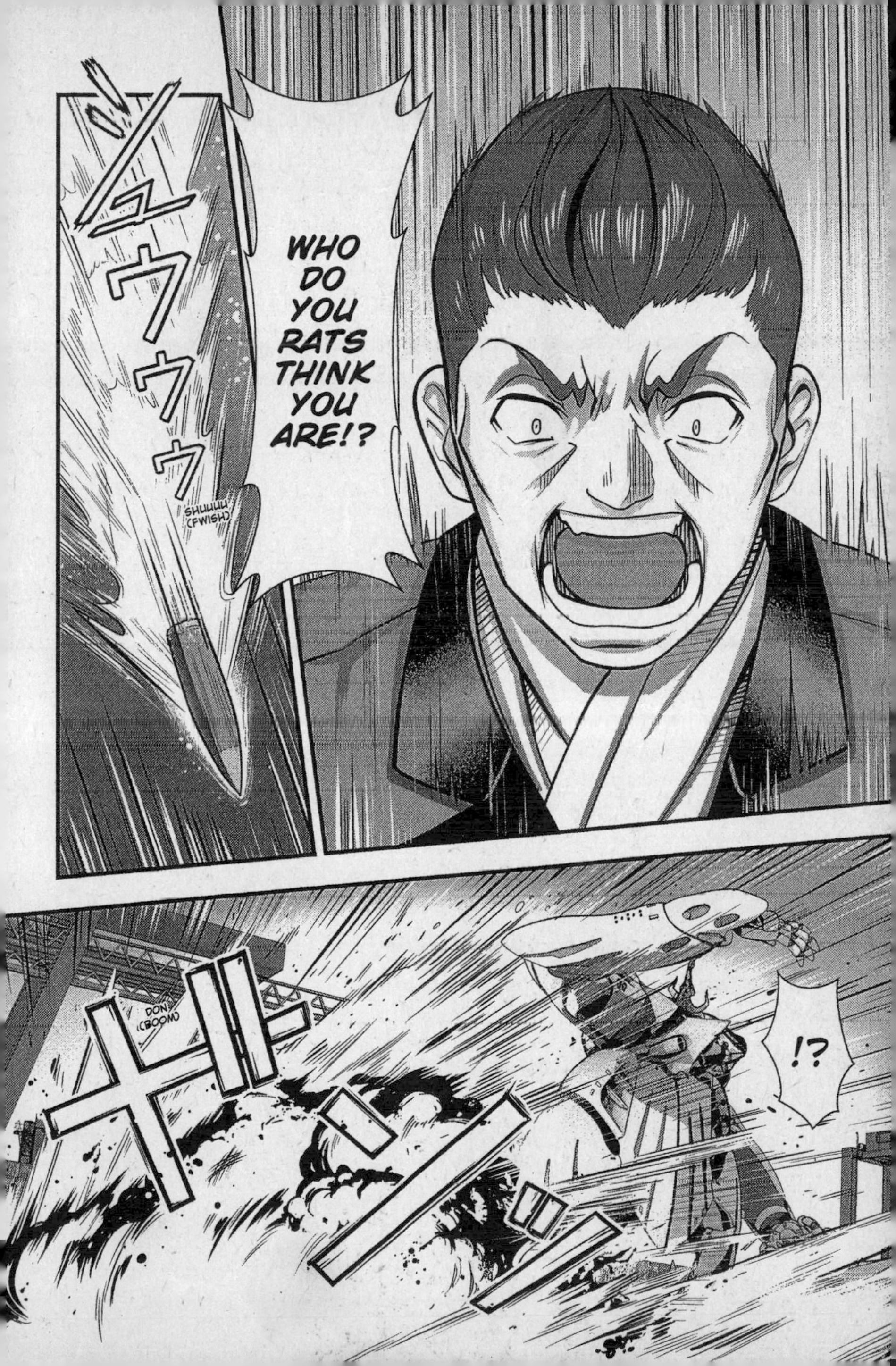
WHO DO YOU RATS THINK YOU ARE!?
SHUUUU (FWISH)
!?
DON (BOOM)

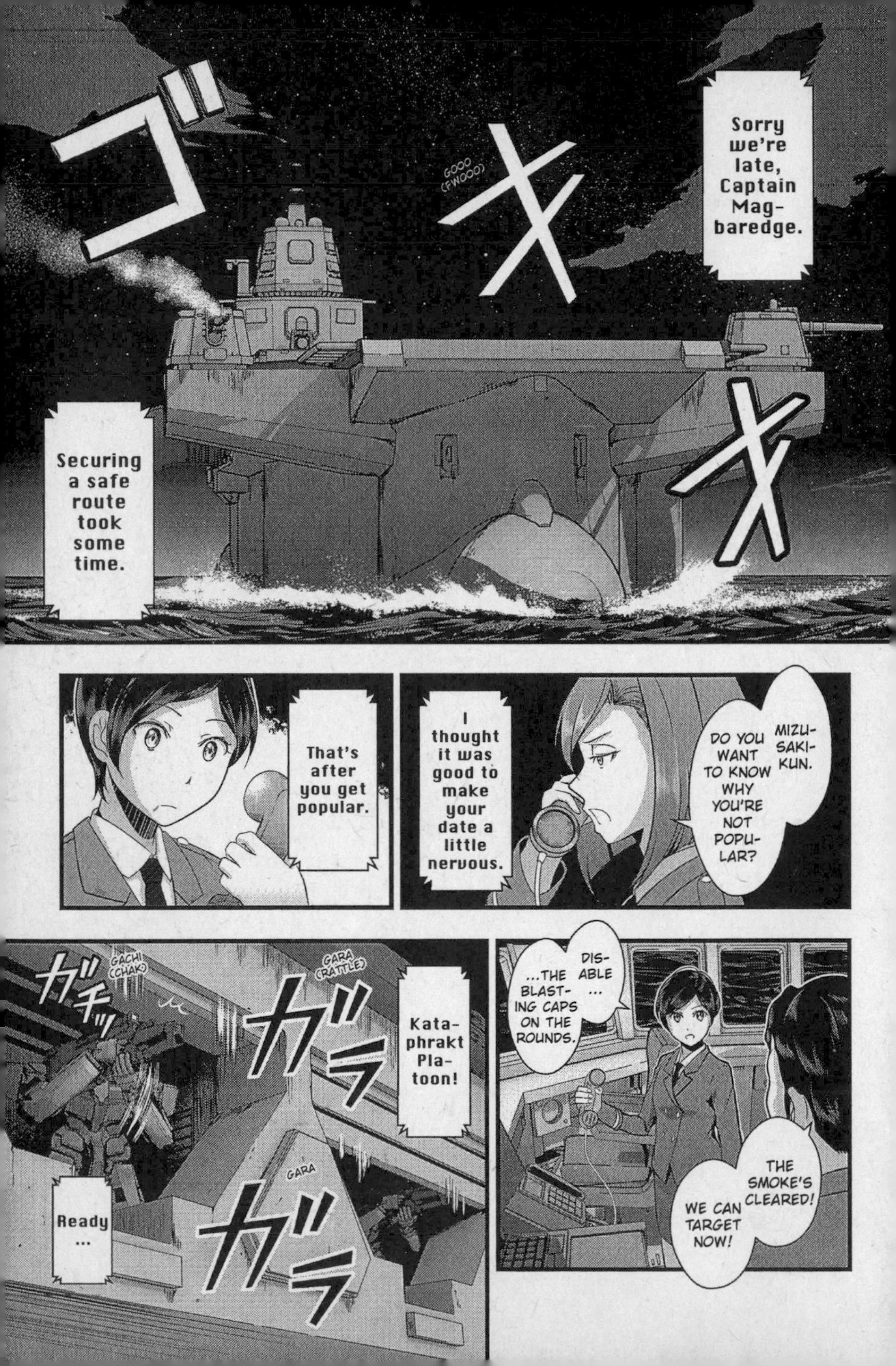
Sorry we're late, Captain Magbaredge.
GOOO (FWOOO)
Securing a safe route took some time.
MIZUSAKI-KUN.
DO YOU WANT TO KNOW WHY YOU'RE NOT POPULAR?
I thought it was good to make your date a little nervous.
That's after you get popular.
DISABLE...
...THE BLASTING CAPS ON THE ROUNDS.
THE SMOKE'S CLEARED!
WE CAN TARGET NOW!
Kataphrakt Platoon!
GARA (RATTLE)
ガラ
GACHI (CHAK)
ガチッ
GARA
ガラ
Ready...

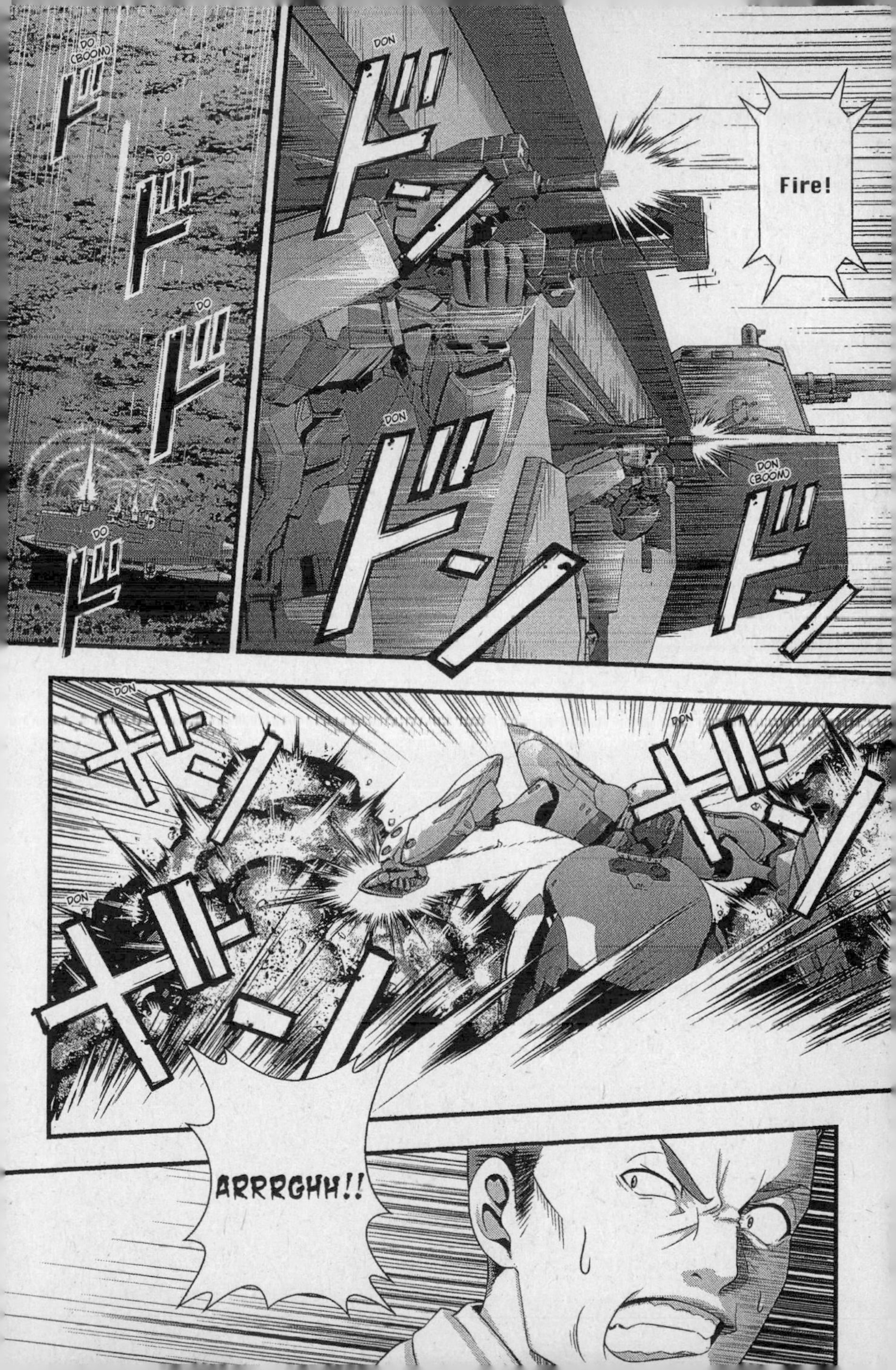

Fire!
DON
DON (BOOM)
DON
DO (BOOM)
DO
DO
DO
DON
DON
DON
ARRRGHH!!

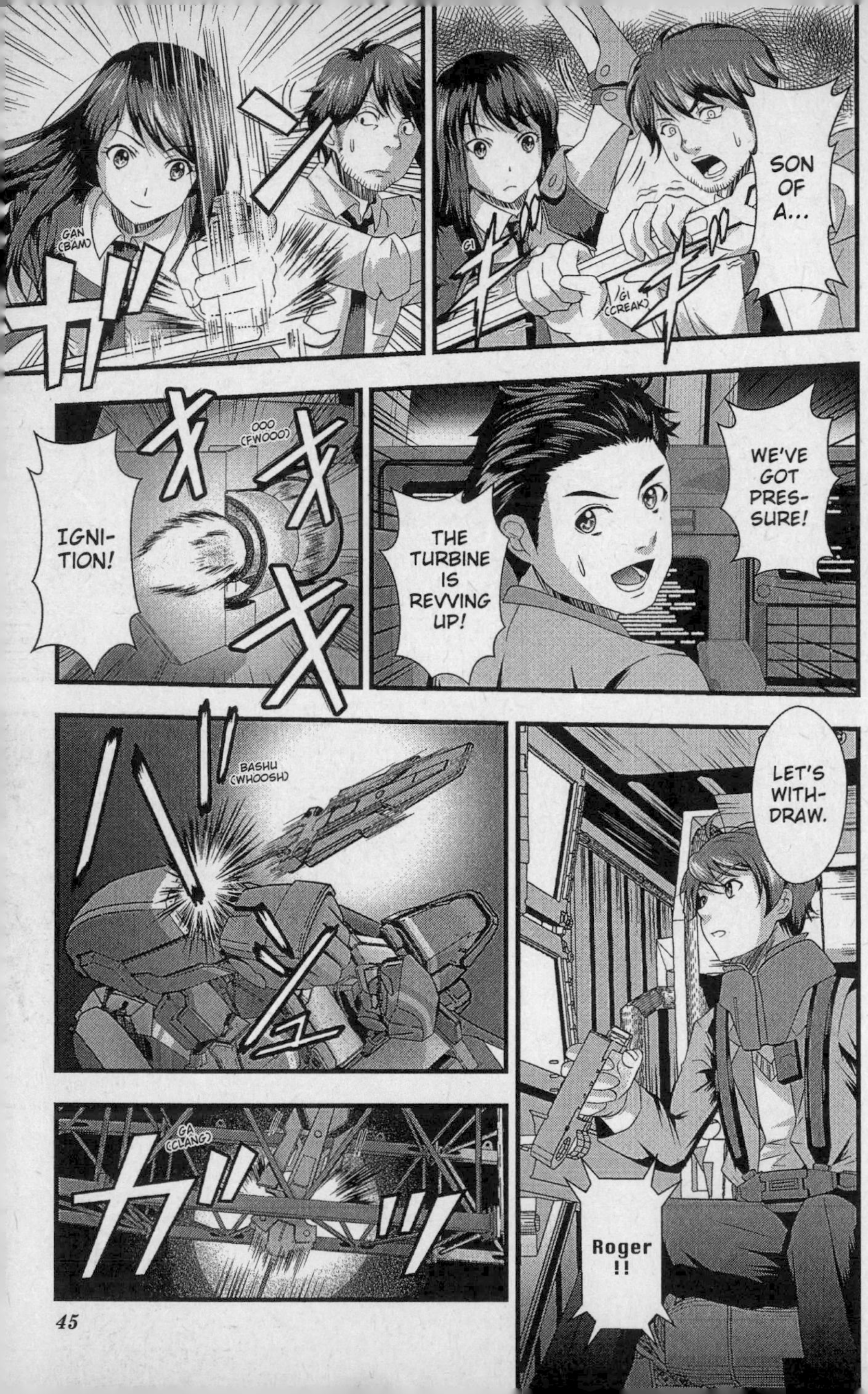
SON OF A...
GI
GI (CREAK)
GAN (BAM)
WE'VE GOT PRES-SURE!
THE TURBINE IS REVVING UP!
OOO (FWOOO)
IGNI-TION!
LET'S WITH-DRAW.
Roger !!
BASHU (WHOOSH)
GA (CLANG)

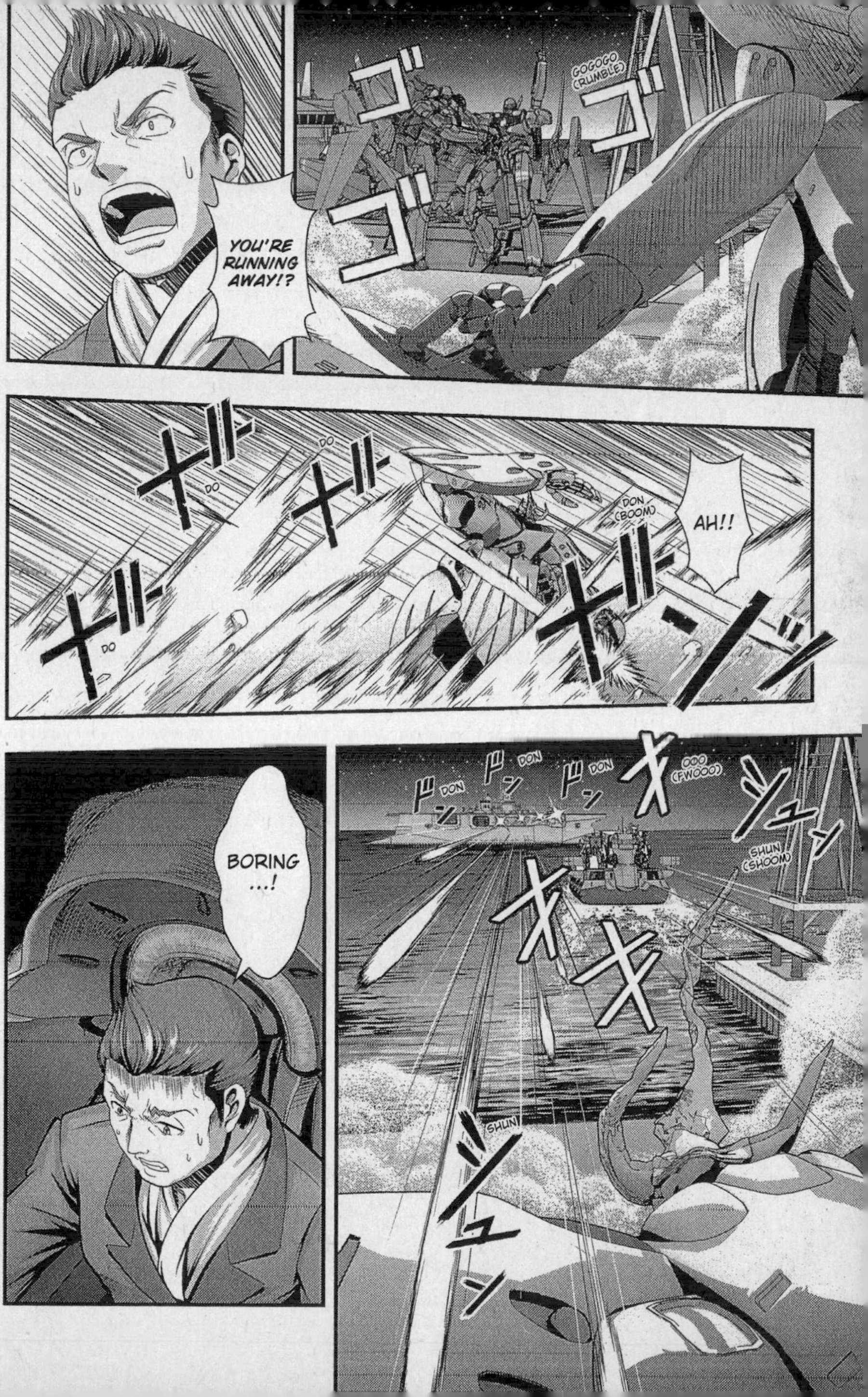
GOGOGO (RUMBLE)
YOU'RE RUNNING AWAY!?
AH!!
DON (BOOM)
DO
DO
DO
SHUN (SHOOM)
OOO (FWOOO)
DON
DON
DON
SHUN
BORING ...!

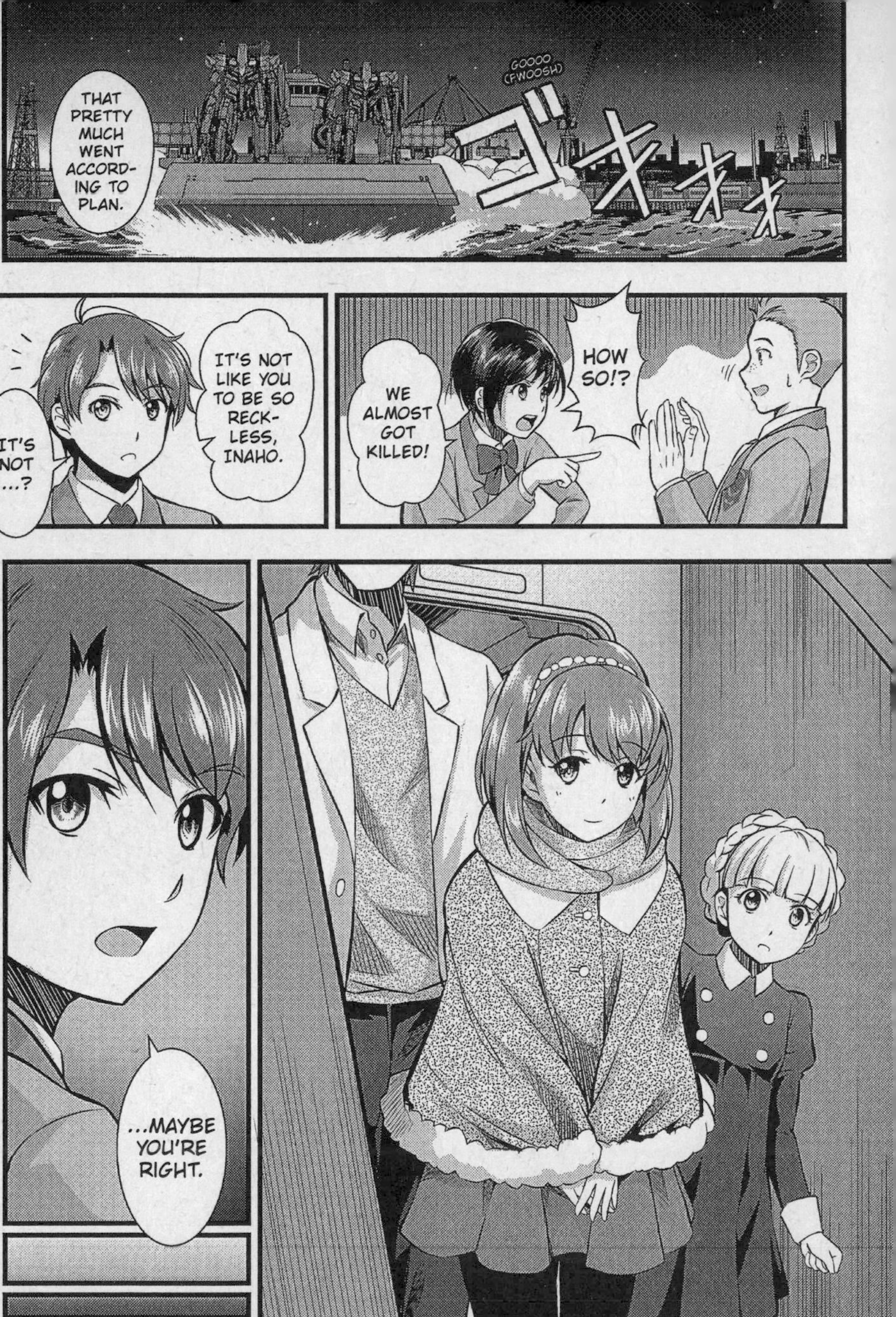
GOOOO (FWOOSH)
ゴォォォ
THAT PRETTY MUCH WENT ACCORDING TO PLAN.
HOW SO!?
WE ALMOST GOT KILLED!
IT'S NOT LIKE YOU TO BE SO RECKLESS, INAHO.
IT'S NOT ...?
...MAYBE YOU'RE RIGHT.

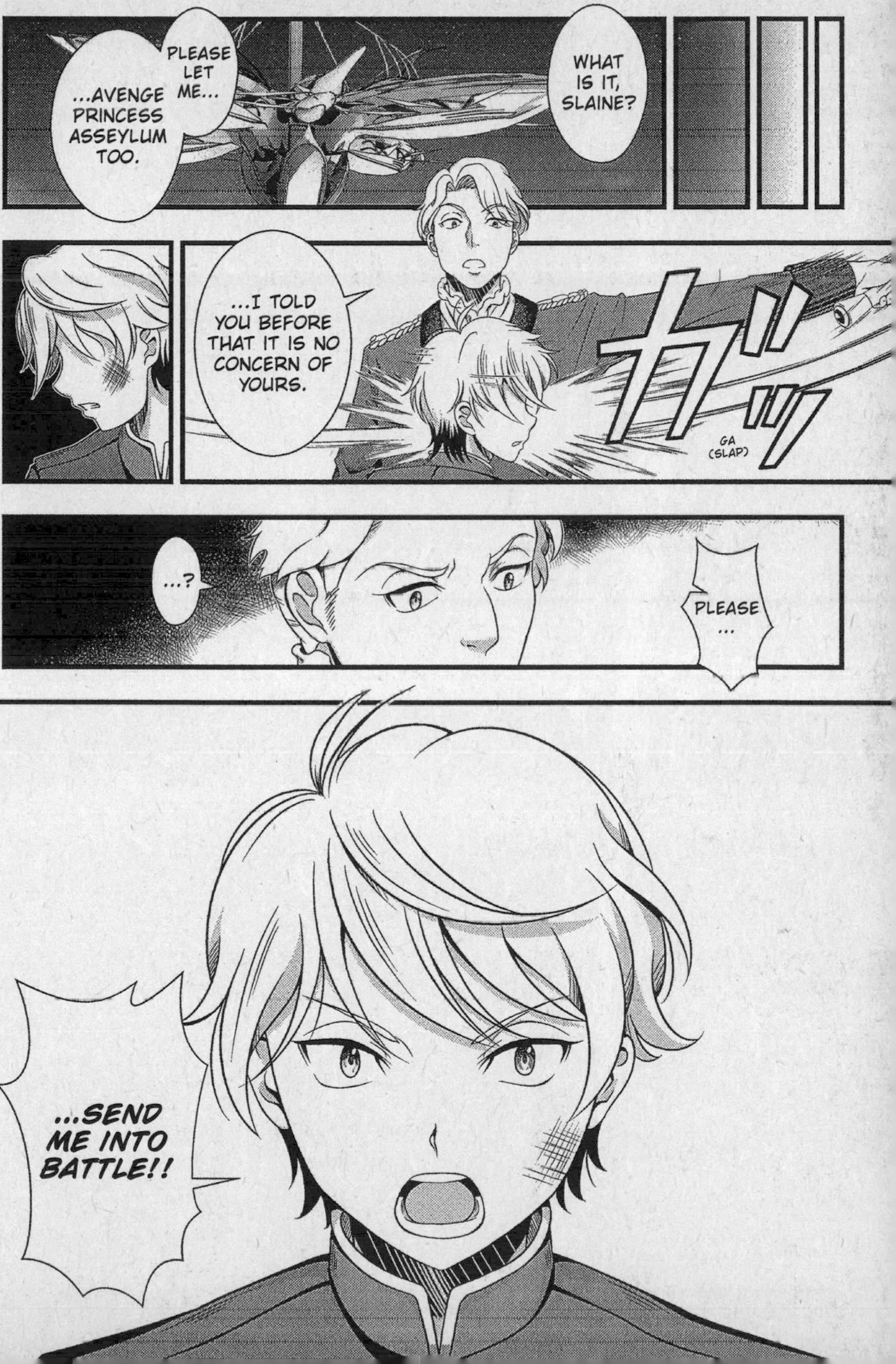
WHAT IS IT, SLAINE?
PLEASE LET ME...
...AVENGE PRINCESS ASSEYLUM TOO.
ガッ
GA (SLAP)
...I TOLD YOU BEFORE THAT IT IS NO CONCERN OF YOURS.
PLEASE ...
...?
...SEND ME INTO BATTLE!!

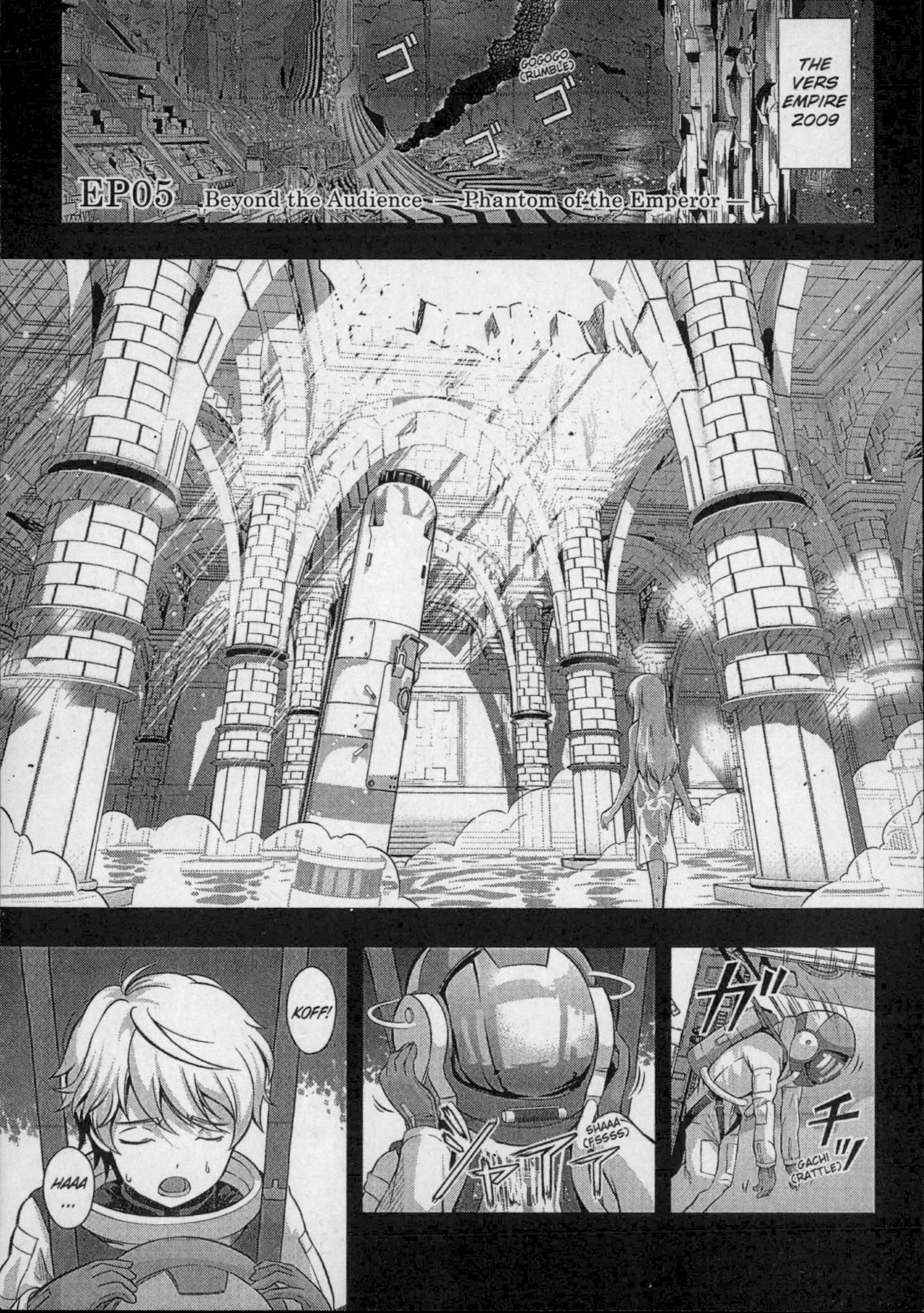

THE VERS EMPIRE 2009
ゴゴゴ
GOGOGO (RUMBLE)
EP05 Beyond the Audience —Phantom of the Emperor—
ガチッ
GACHI (RATTLE)
シャアア
SHAAA (FSSSS)
KOFF!
HAAA ...

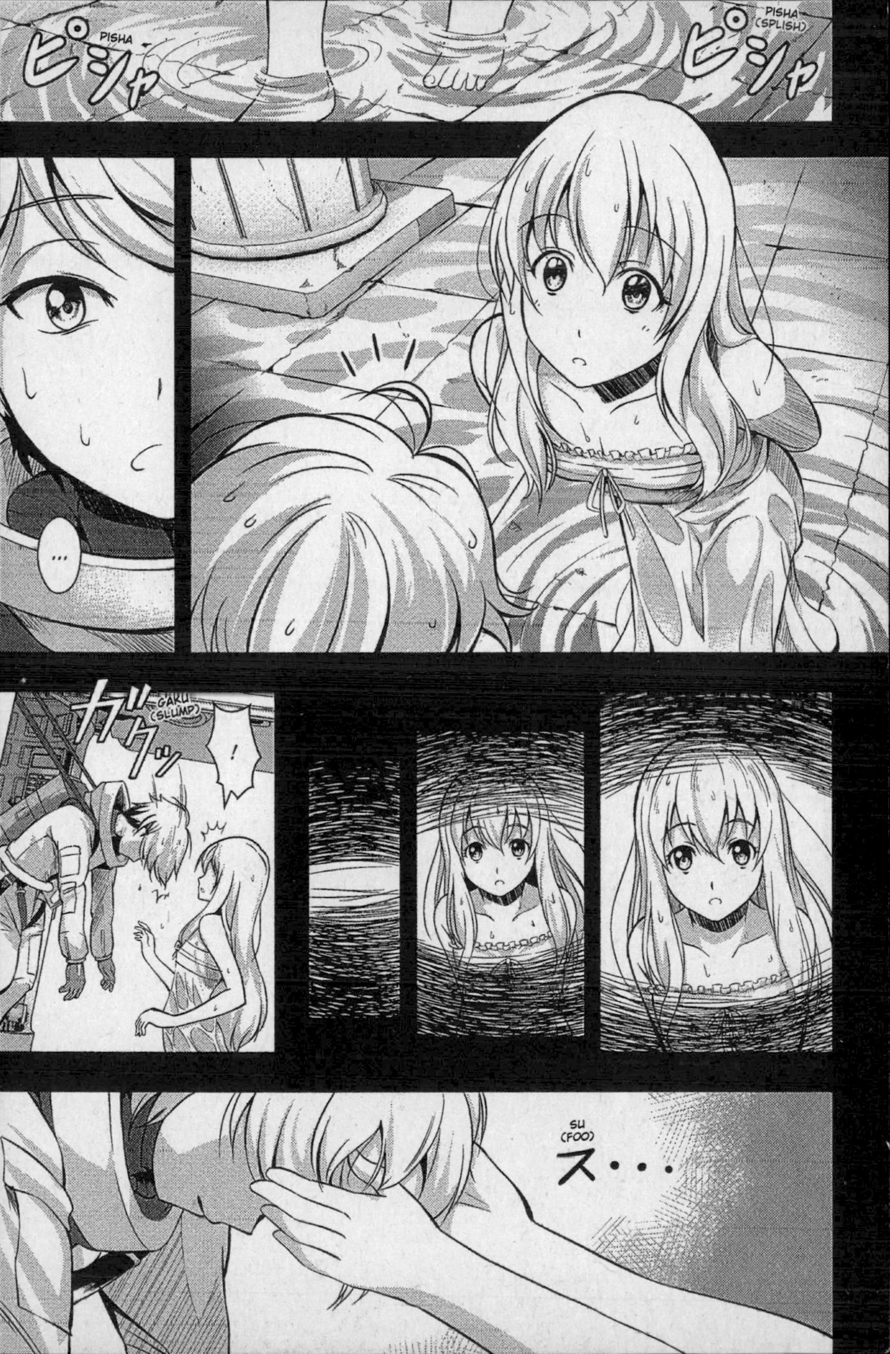
PISHA (SPLISH)
ピシャ
ピシャ
PISHA
...
GAKU (SLUMP)
ガクッ
!
SU (FOO)
ス・・・

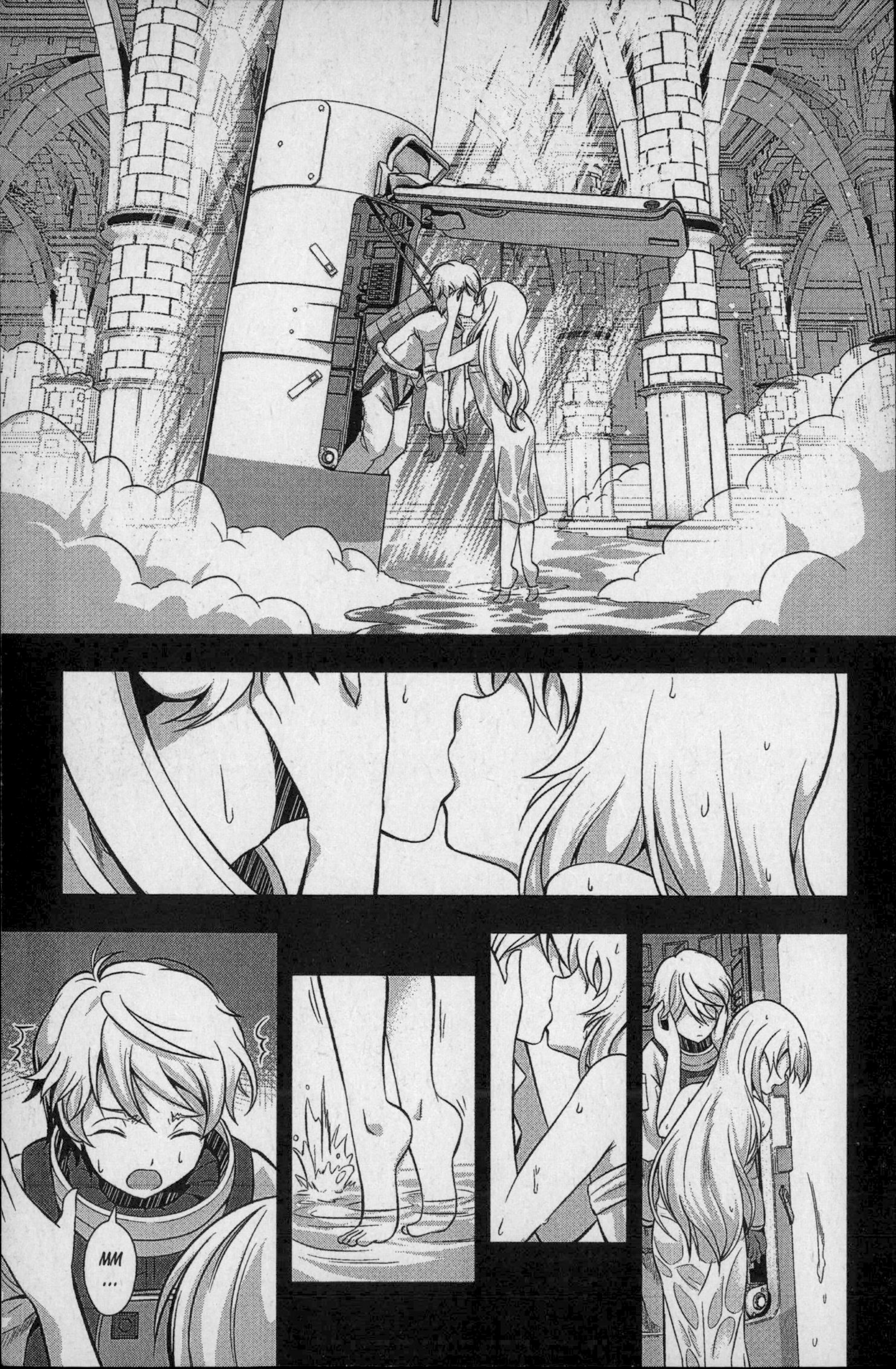
MM...

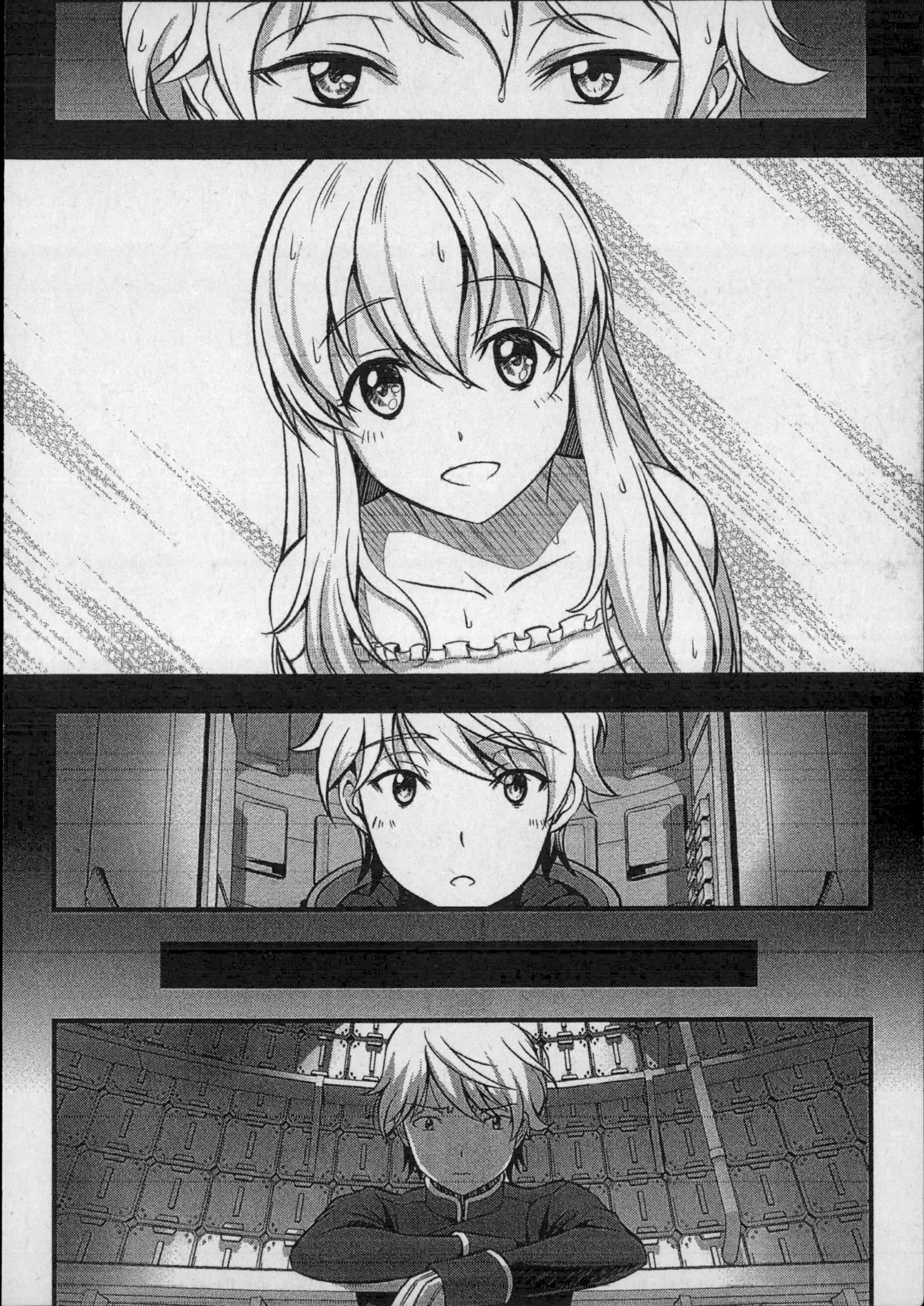

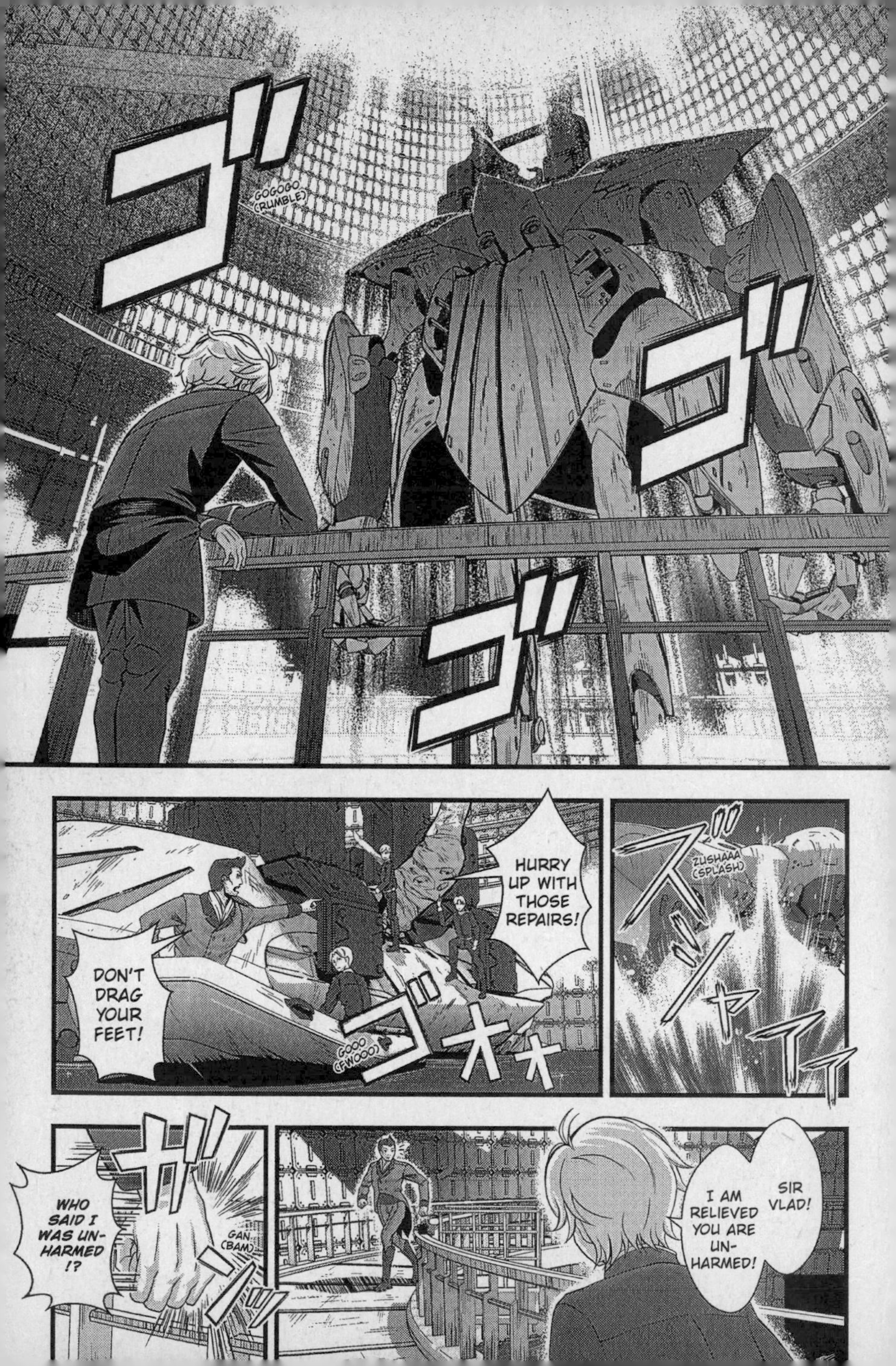

GOGOGO (RUMBLE)
ZUSHAAA (SPLASH)
HURRY UP WITH THOSE REPAIRS!
DON'T DRAG YOUR FEET!
GOOO (FWOOO)
SIR VLAD!
I AM RELIEVED YOU ARE UN-HARMED!
GAN (BAM)
WHO SAID I WAS UN-HARMED!?

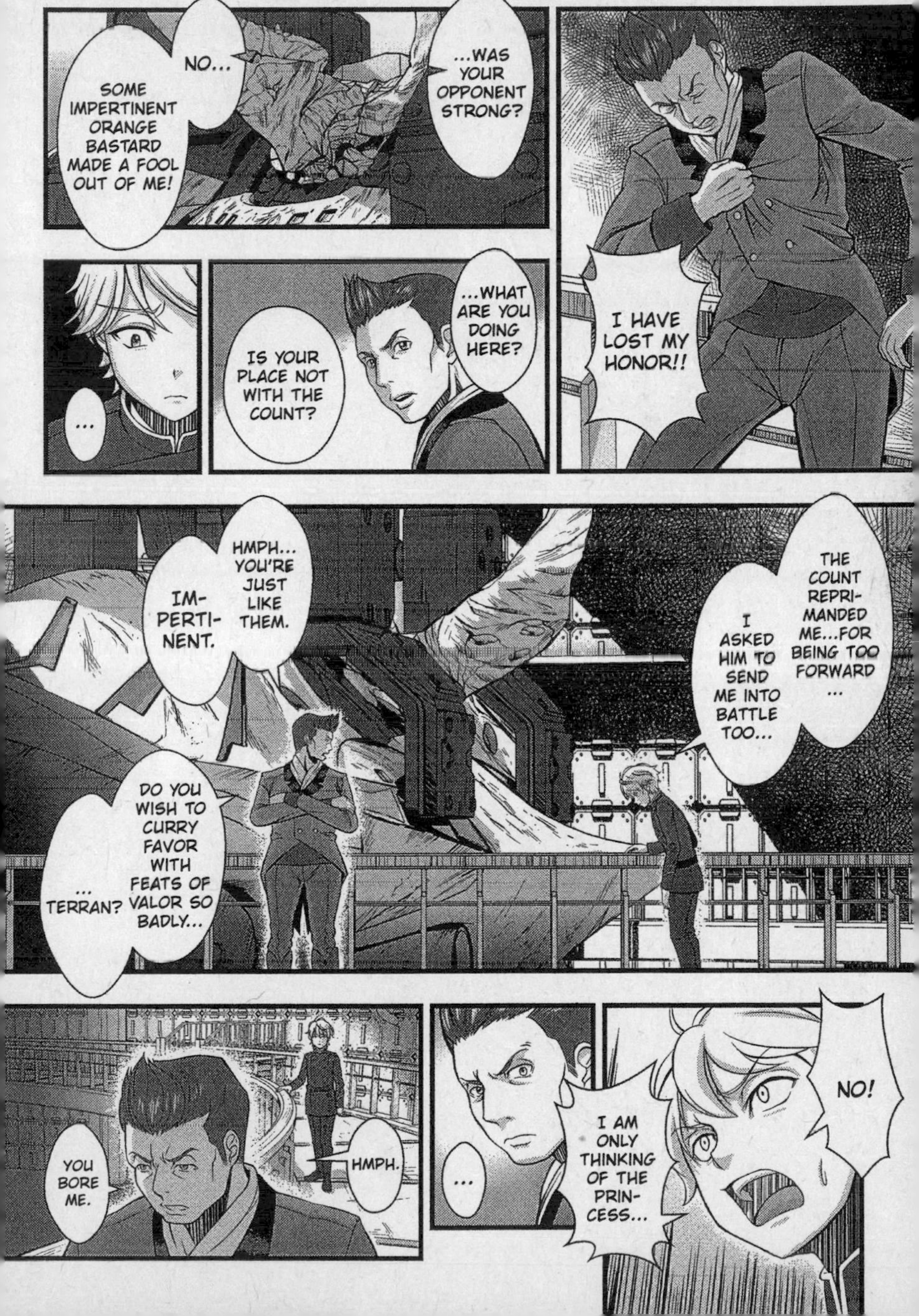
I HAVE LOST MY HONOR!!
...WAS YOUR OPPONENT STRONG?
NO...
SOME IMPERTINENT ORANGE BASTARD MADE A FOOL OUT OF ME!
...WHAT ARE YOU DOING HERE?
IS YOUR PLACE NOT WITH THE COUNT?
...
THE COUNT REPRIMANDED ME...FOR BEING TOO FORWARD...
I ASKED HIM TO SEND ME INTO BATTLE TOO...
HMPH... YOU'RE JUST LIKE THEM.
IMPERTINENT.
DO YOU WISH TO CURRY FAVOR WITH FEATS OF VALOR SO BADLY...
...TERRAN?
NO!
I AM ONLY THINKING OF THE PRINCESS...
...
HMPH.
YOU BORE ME.

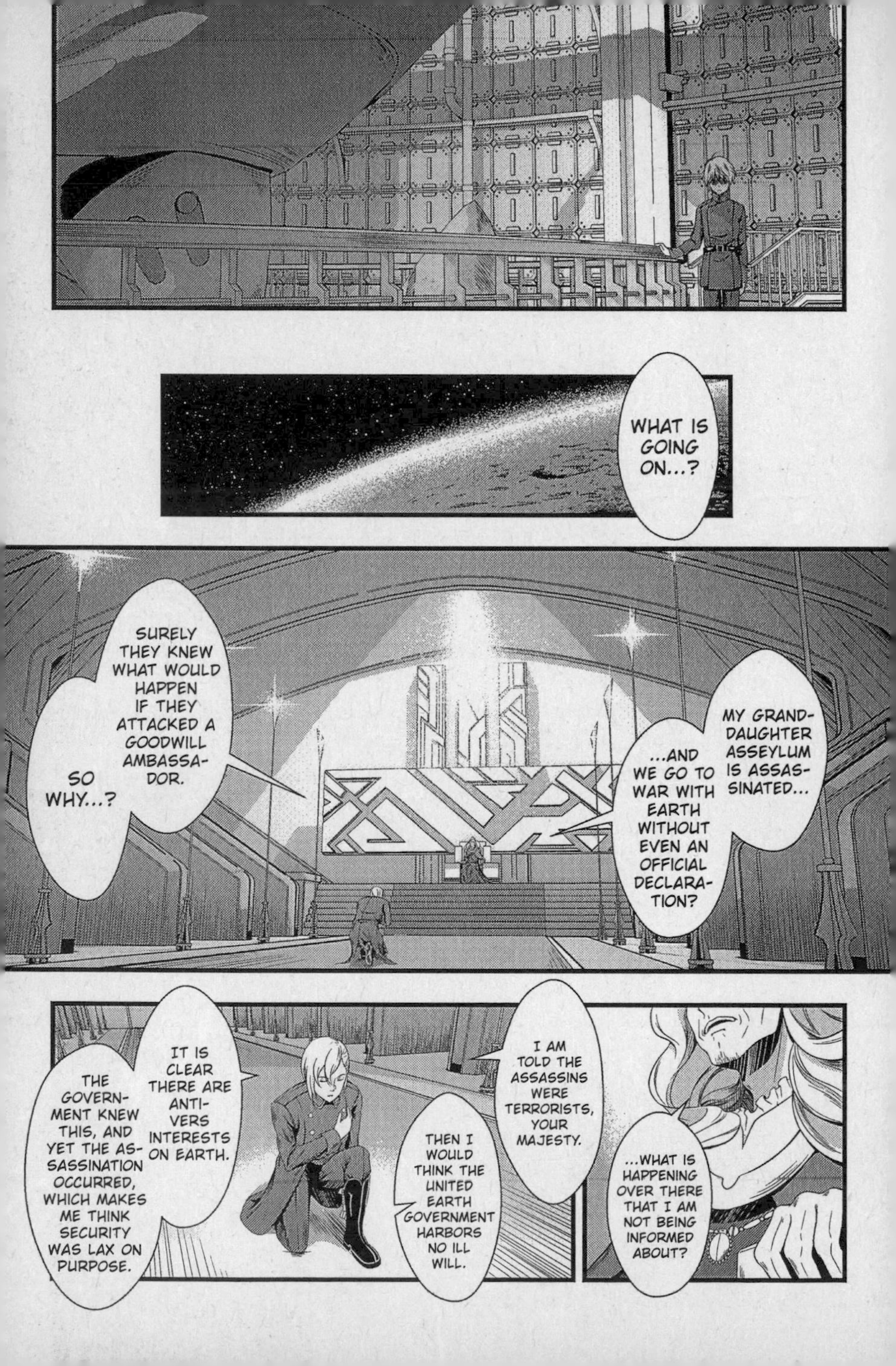
WHAT IS GOING ON...?
MY GRAND-DAUGHTER ASSEYLUM IS ASSASSINATED...
...AND WE GO TO WAR WITH EARTH WITHOUT EVEN AN OFFICIAL DECLARATION?
SURELY THEY KNEW WHAT WOULD HAPPEN IF THEY ATTACKED A GOODWILL AMBASSADOR.
SO WHY...?
...WHAT IS HAPPENING OVER THERE THAT I AM NOT BEING INFORMED ABOUT?
I AM TOLD THE ASSASSINS WERE TERRORISTS, YOUR MAJESTY.
THEN I WOULD THINK THE UNITED EARTH GOVERNMENT HARBORS NO ILL WILL.
IT IS CLEAR THERE ARE ANTI-VERS INTERESTS ON EARTH.
THE GOVERNMENT KNEW THIS, AND YET THE ASSASSINATION OCCURRED, WHICH MAKES ME THINK SECURITY WAS LAX ON PURPOSE.

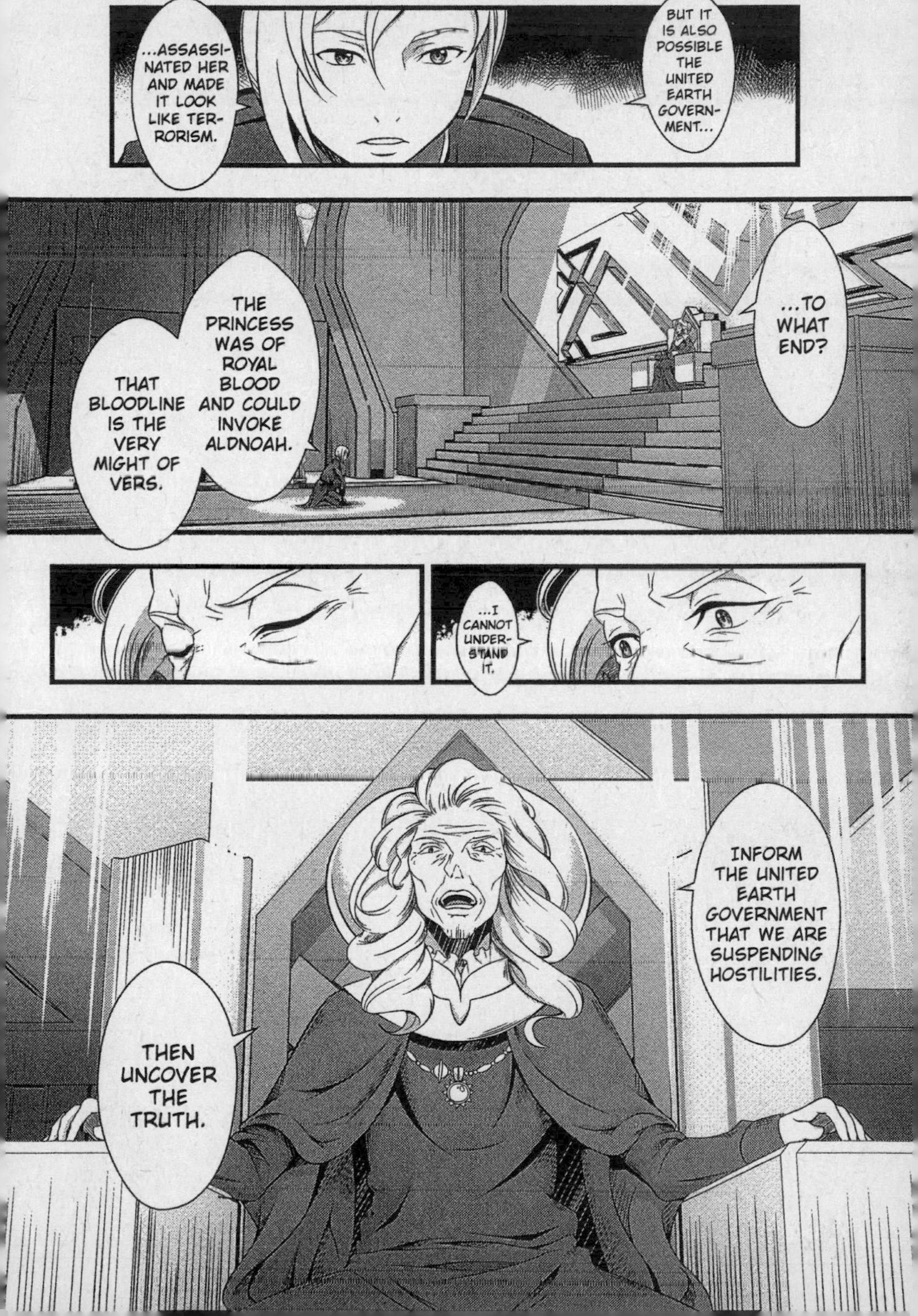
BUT IT IS ALSO POSSIBLE THE UNITED EARTH GOVERNMENT...
...ASSASSINATED HER AND MADE IT LOOK LIKE TERRORISM.
...TO WHAT END?
THE PRINCESS WAS OF ROYAL BLOOD AND COULD INVOKE ALDNOAH.
THAT BLOODLINE IS THE VERY MIGHT OF VERS.
...I CANNOT UNDERSTAND IT.
INFORM THE UNITED EARTH GOVERNMENT THAT WE ARE SUSPENDING HOSTILITIES.
THEN UNCOVER THE TRUTH.

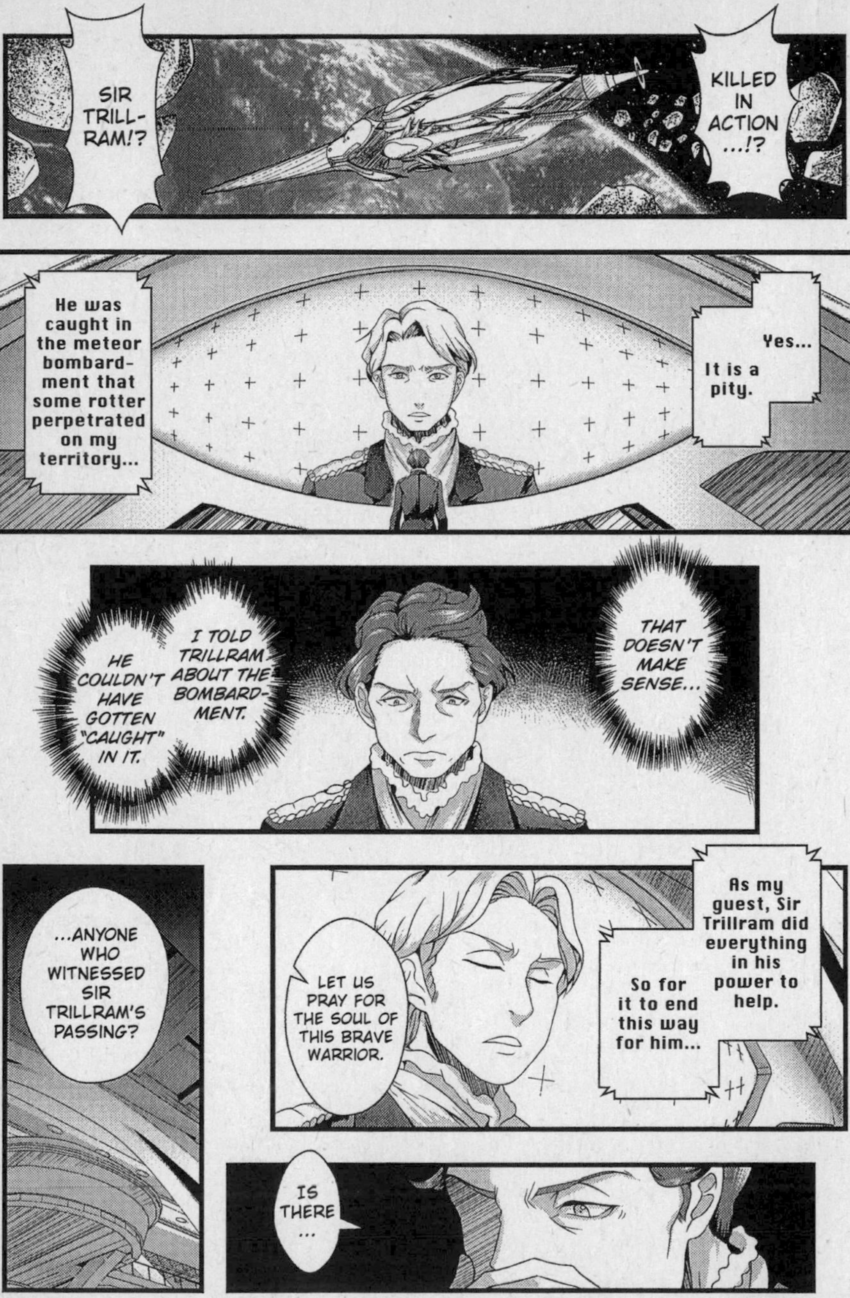
KILLED IN ACTION ...!?
SIR TRILL-RAM!?
Yes... It is a pity.
He was caught in the meteor bombard-ment that some rotter perpetrated on my territory...
THAT DOESN'T MAKE SENSE...
I TOLD TRILLRAM ABOUT THE BOMBARD-MENT.
HE COULDN'T HAVE GOTTEN "CAUGHT" IN IT.
As my guest, Sir Trillram did everything in his power to help.
So for it to end this way for him...
LET US PRAY FOR THE SOUL OF THIS BRAVE WARRIOR.
IS THERE ...
...ANYONE WHO WITNESSED SIR TRILLRAM'S PASSING?

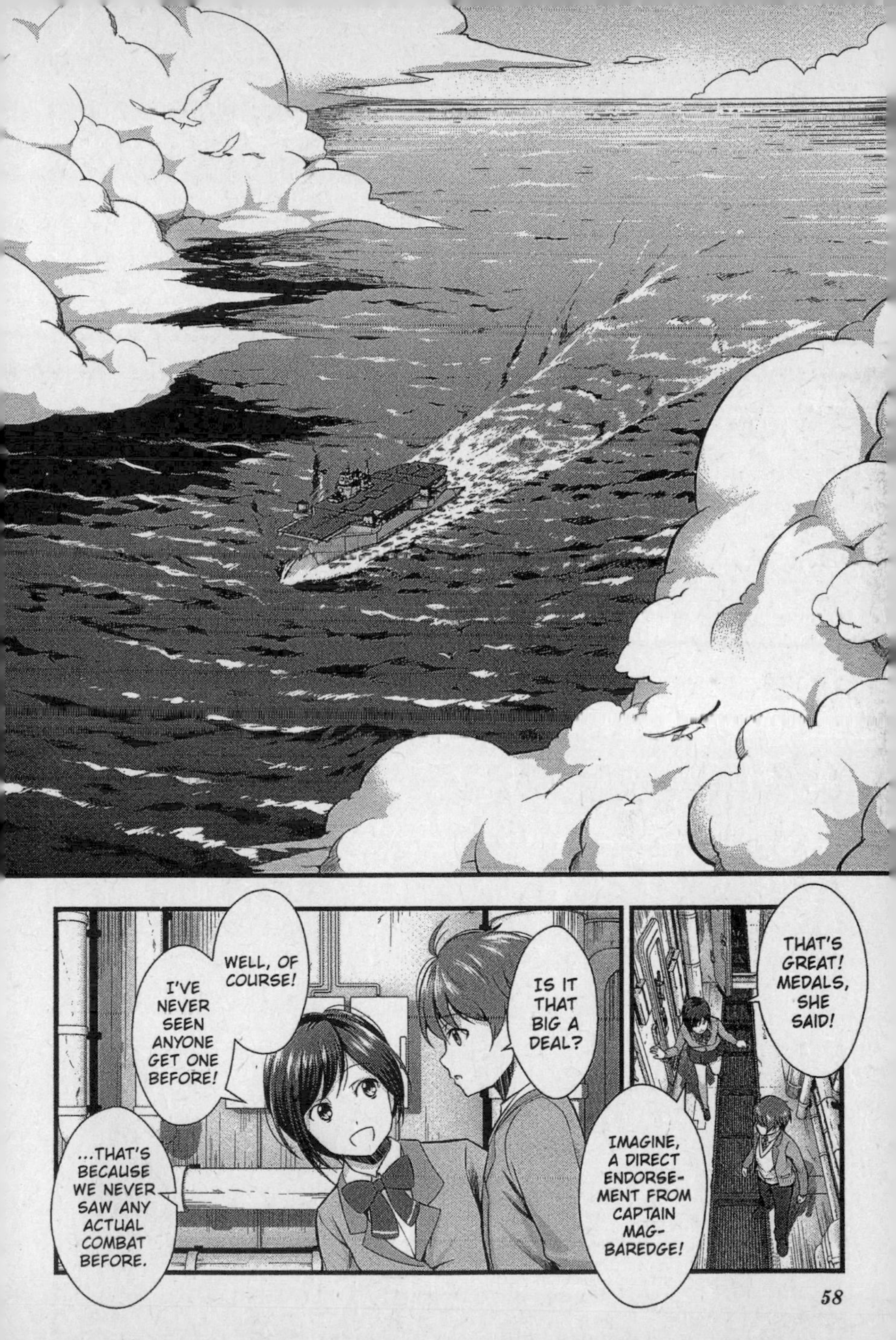
THAT'S GREAT! MEDALS, SHE SAID!
IMAGINE, A DIRECT ENDORSEMENT FROM CAPTAIN MAG-BAREDGE!
IS IT THAT BIG A DEAL?
WELL, OF COURSE!
I'VE NEVER SEEN ANYONE GET ONE BEFORE!
...THAT'S BECAUSE WE NEVER SAW ANY ACTUAL COMBAT BEFORE.

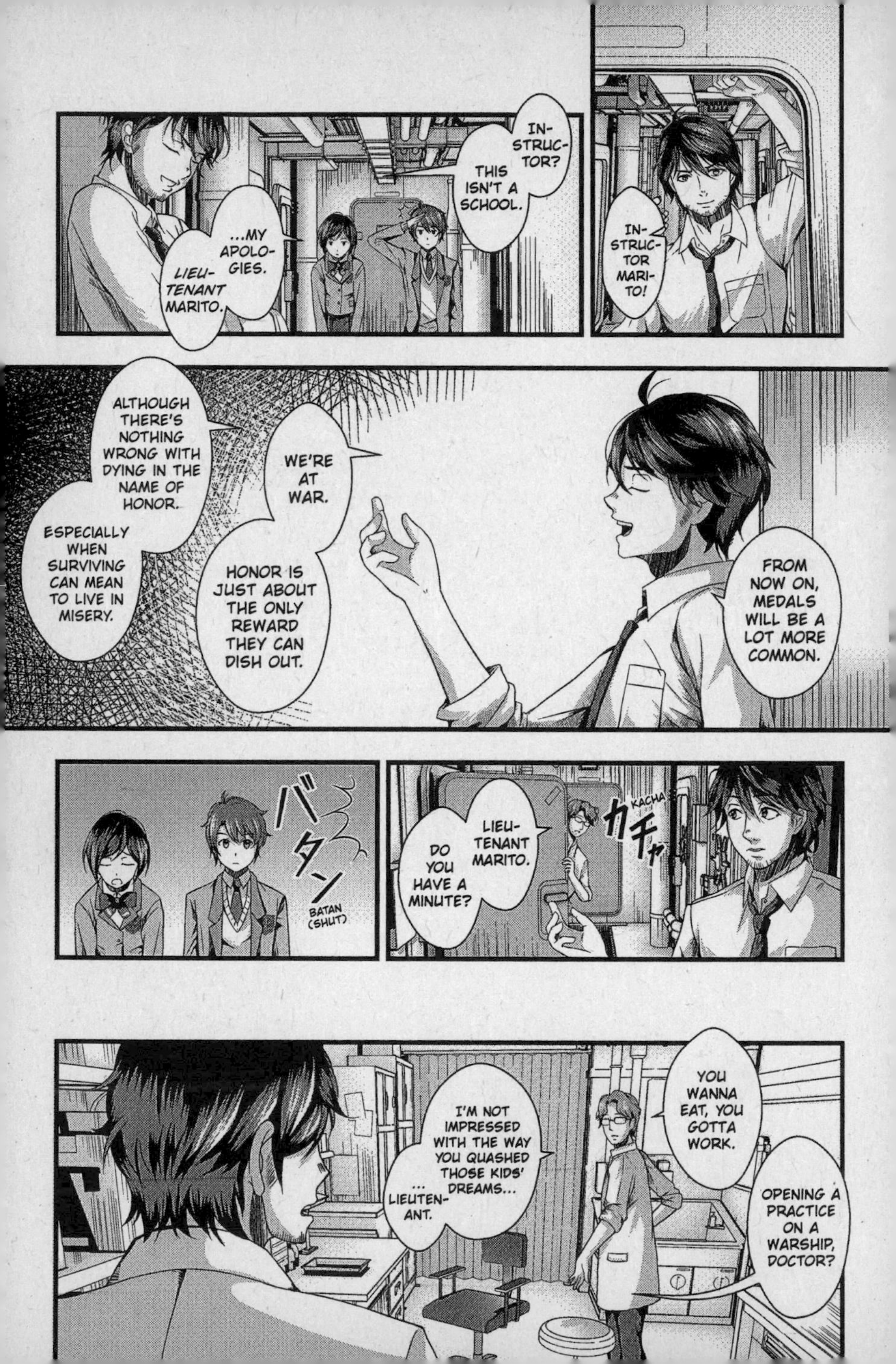
INSTRUCTOR MARITO!
INSTRUCTOR? THIS ISN'T A SCHOOL.
...MY APOLOGIES. LIEUTENANT MARITO.
FROM NOW ON, MEDALS WILL BE A LOT MORE COMMON.
WE'RE AT WAR.
HONOR IS JUST ABOUT THE ONLY REWARD THEY CAN DISH OUT.
ALTHOUGH THERE'S NOTHING WRONG WITH DYING IN THE NAME OF HONOR.
ESPECIALLY WHEN SURVIVING CAN MEAN TO LIVE IN MISERY.
カチャ KACHA
LIEUTENANT MARITO.
DO YOU HAVE A MINUTE?
バタン BATAN (SHUT)
YOU WANNA EAT, YOU GOTTA WORK.
OPENING A PRACTICE ON A WARSHIP, DOCTOR?
I'M NOT IMPRESSED WITH THE WAY YOU QUASHED THOSE KIDS' DREAMS...
...LIEUTENANT.

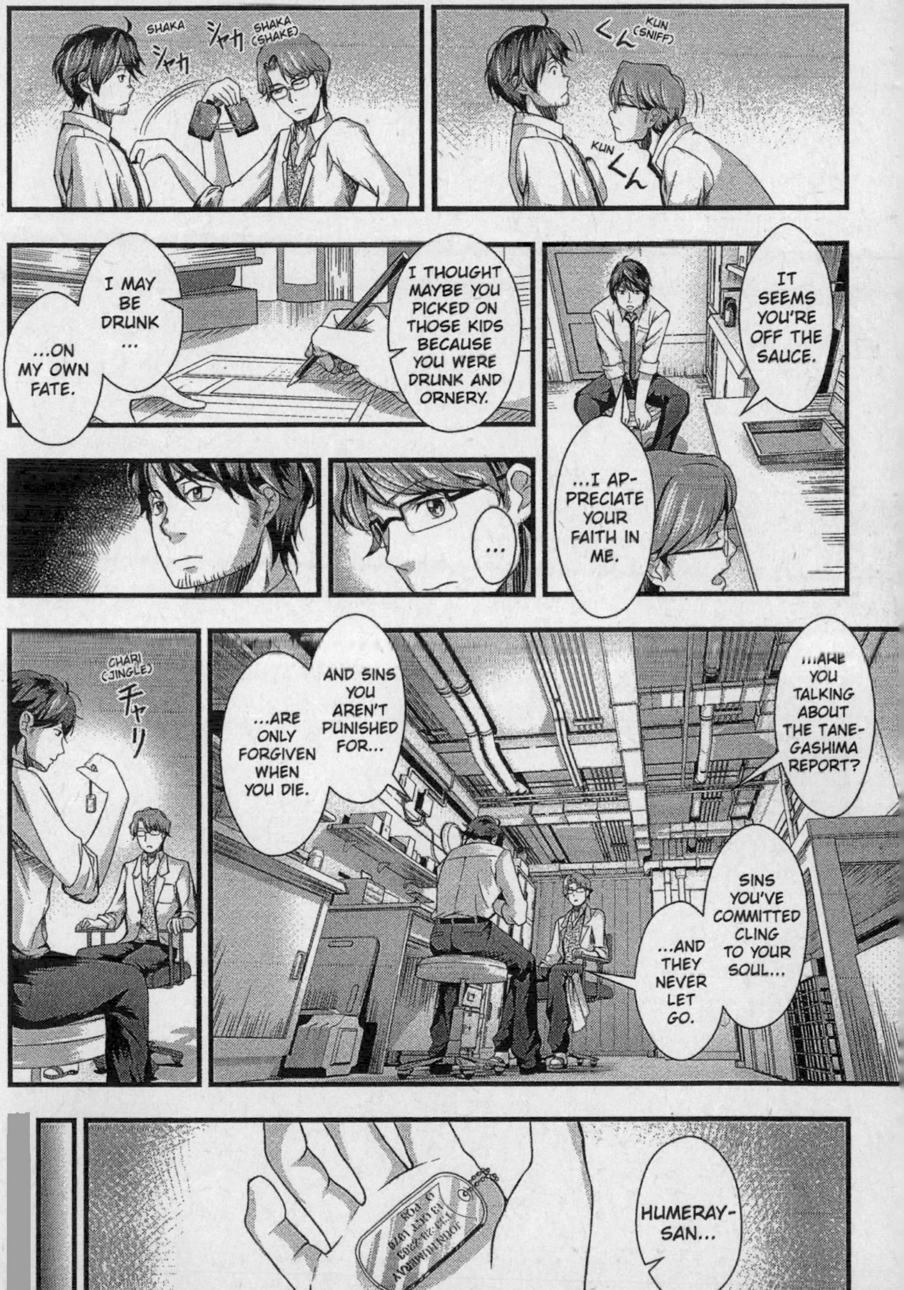
KUN (SNIFF)
くん
KUN
くん
SHAKA
シャカ
SHAKA (SHAKE)
シャカ
IT SEEMS YOU'RE OFF THE SAUCE.
...I APPRECIATE YOUR FAITH IN ME.
I THOUGHT MAYBE YOU PICKED ON THOSE KIDS BECAUSE YOU WERE DRUNK AND ORNERY.
I MAY BE DRUNK...
...ON MY OWN FATE.
...
...ARE YOU TALKING ABOUT THE TANEGASHIMA REPORT?
SINS YOU'VE COMMITTED CLING TO YOUR SOUL...
...AND THEY NEVER LET GO.
AND SINS YOU AREN'T PUNISHED FOR...
...ARE ONLY FORGIVEN WHEN YOU DIE.
CHARI (JINGLE)
チャリ
HUMERAY-SAN...

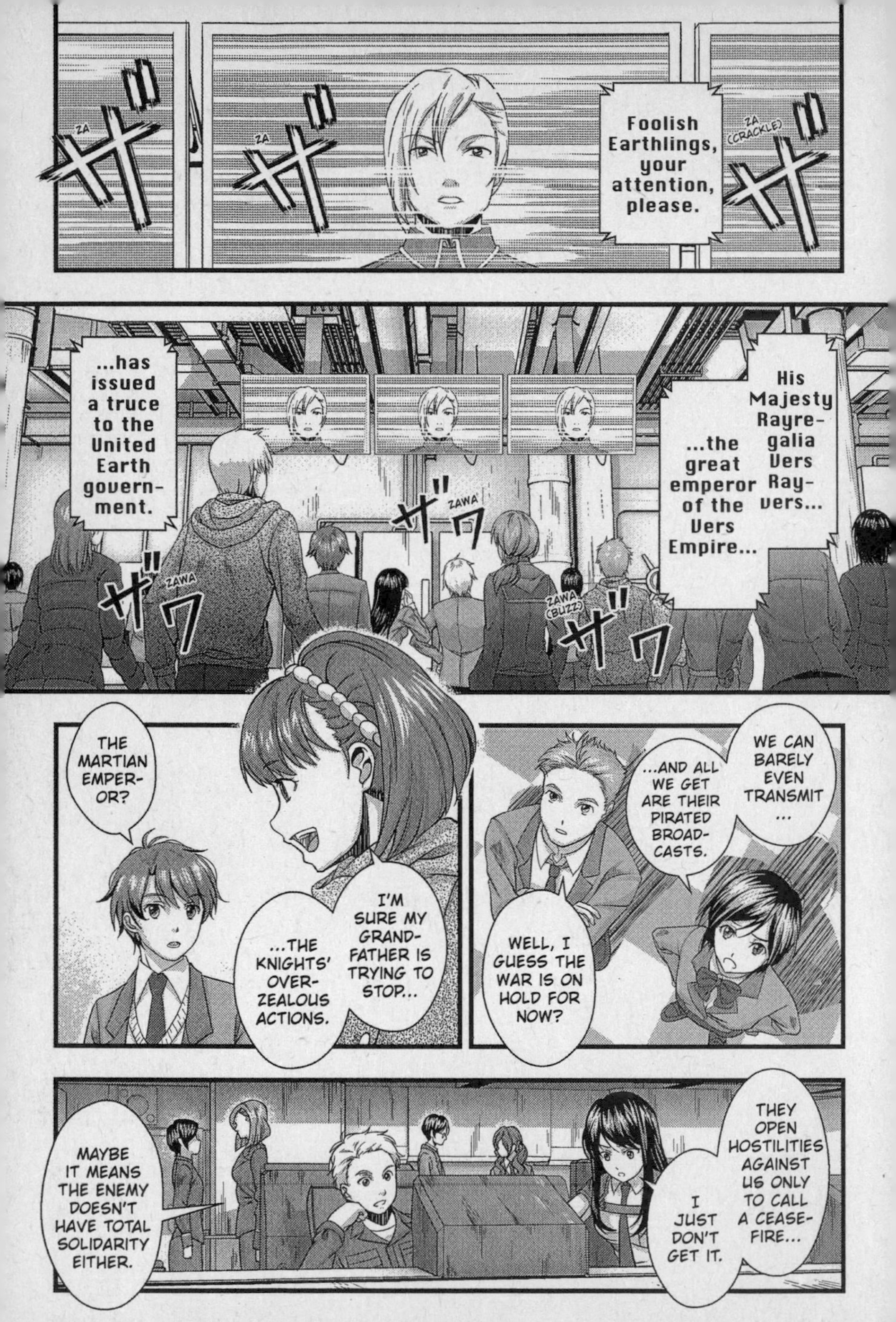
ZA (CRACKLE)
Foolish Earthlings, your attention, please.
ZA
ZA
His Majesty Rayregalia Vers Rayvers...
...the great emperor of the Vers Empire...
...has issued a truce to the United Earth government.
ZAWA (BUZZ)
ZAWA
ZAWA
WE CAN BARELY EVEN TRANSMIT...
...AND ALL WE GET ARE THEIR PIRATED BROADCASTS.
WELL, I GUESS THE WAR IS ON HOLD FOR NOW?
THE MARTIAN EMPEROR?
I'M SURE MY GRANDFATHER IS TRYING TO STOP...
...THE KNIGHTS' OVERZEALOUS ACTIONS.
THEY OPEN HOSTILITIES AGAINST US ONLY TO CALL A CEASEFIRE...
I JUST DON'T GET IT.
MAYBE IT MEANS THE ENEMY DOESN'T HAVE TOTAL SOLIDARITY EITHER.

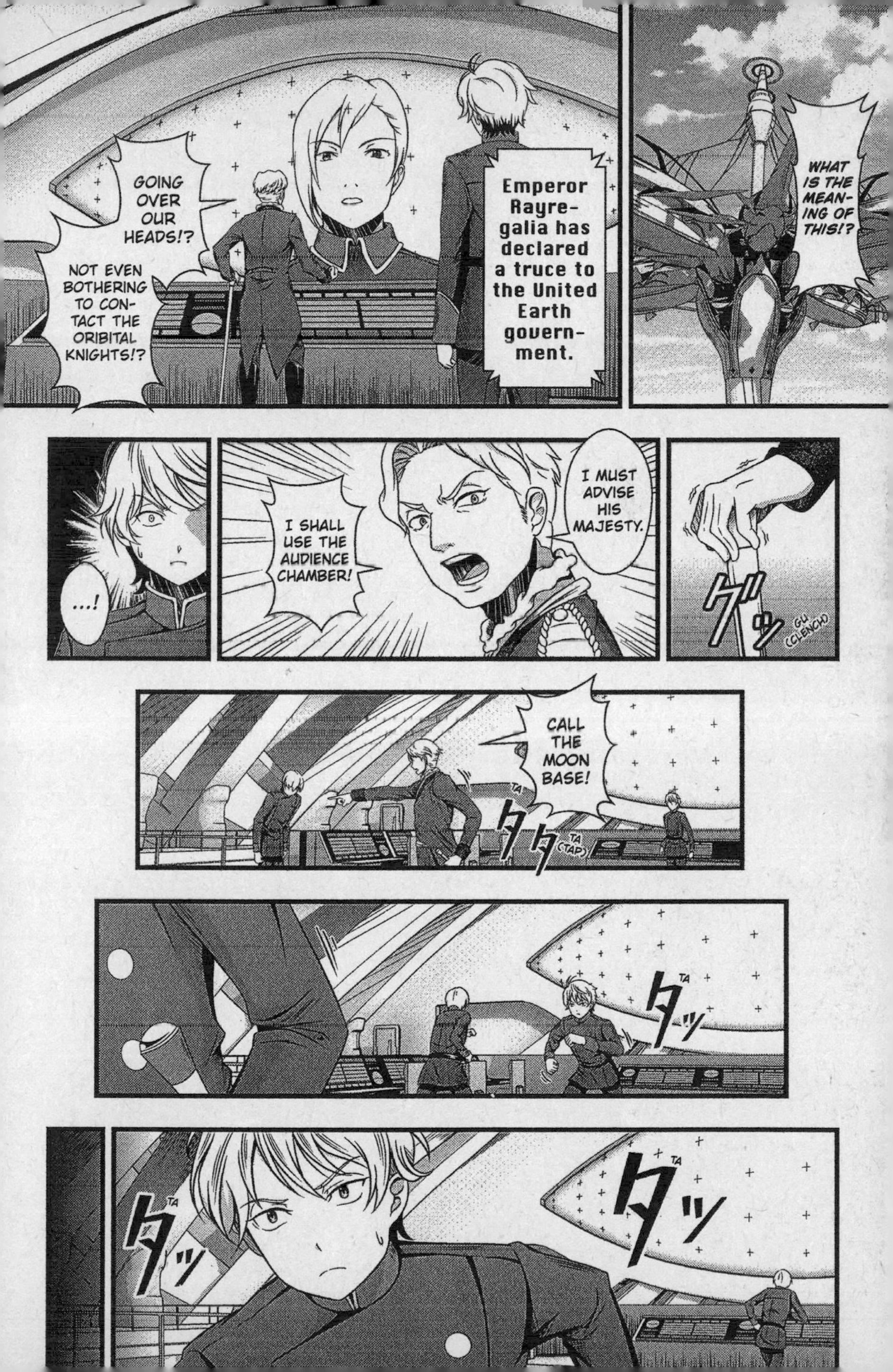
WHAT IS THE MEANING OF THIS!?
Emperor Rayregalia has declared a truce to the United Earth government.
GOING OVER OUR HEADS!?
NOT EVEN BOTHERING TO CONTACT THE ORIBITAL KNIGHTS!?
グッ
GU (CLENCH)
I MUST ADVISE HIS MAJESTY.
I SHALL USE THE AUDIENCE CHAMBER!
...!
CALL THE MOON BASE!
タタ
TA TA (TAP)
タッ
TA
タッ
TA
タッ
TA

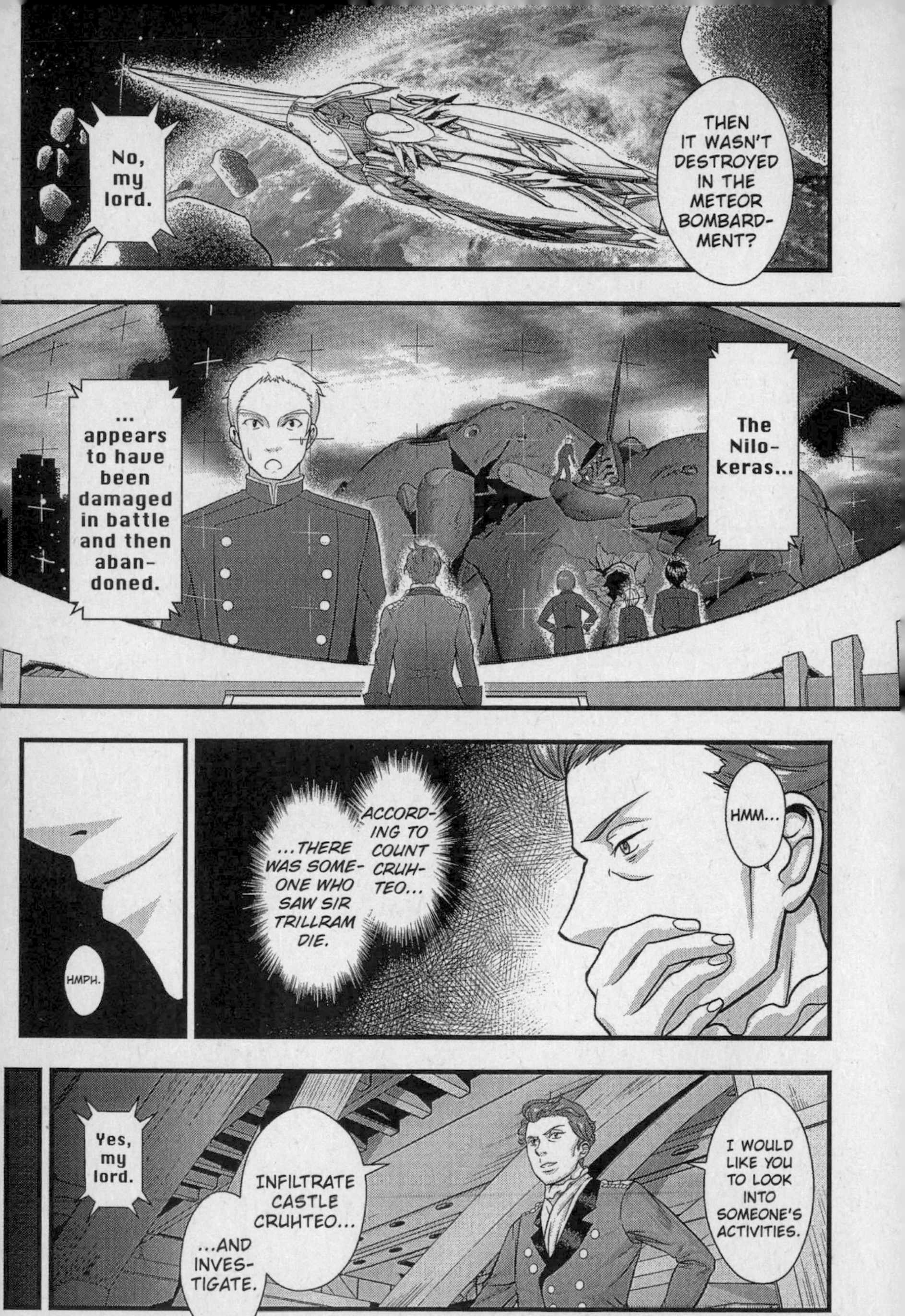
THEN IT WASN'T DESTROYED IN THE METEOR BOMBARD-MENT?
No, my lord.
The Nilo-keras...
... appears to have been damaged in battle and then aban-doned.
HMM...
ACCORD-ING TO COUNT CRUH-TEO...
...THERE WAS SOME-ONE WHO SAW SIR TRILLRAM DIE.
HMPH.
I WOULD LIKE YOU TO LOOK INTO SOMEONE'S ACTIVITIES.
INFILTRATE CASTLE CRUHTEO...
...AND INVES-TIGATE.
Yes, my lord.

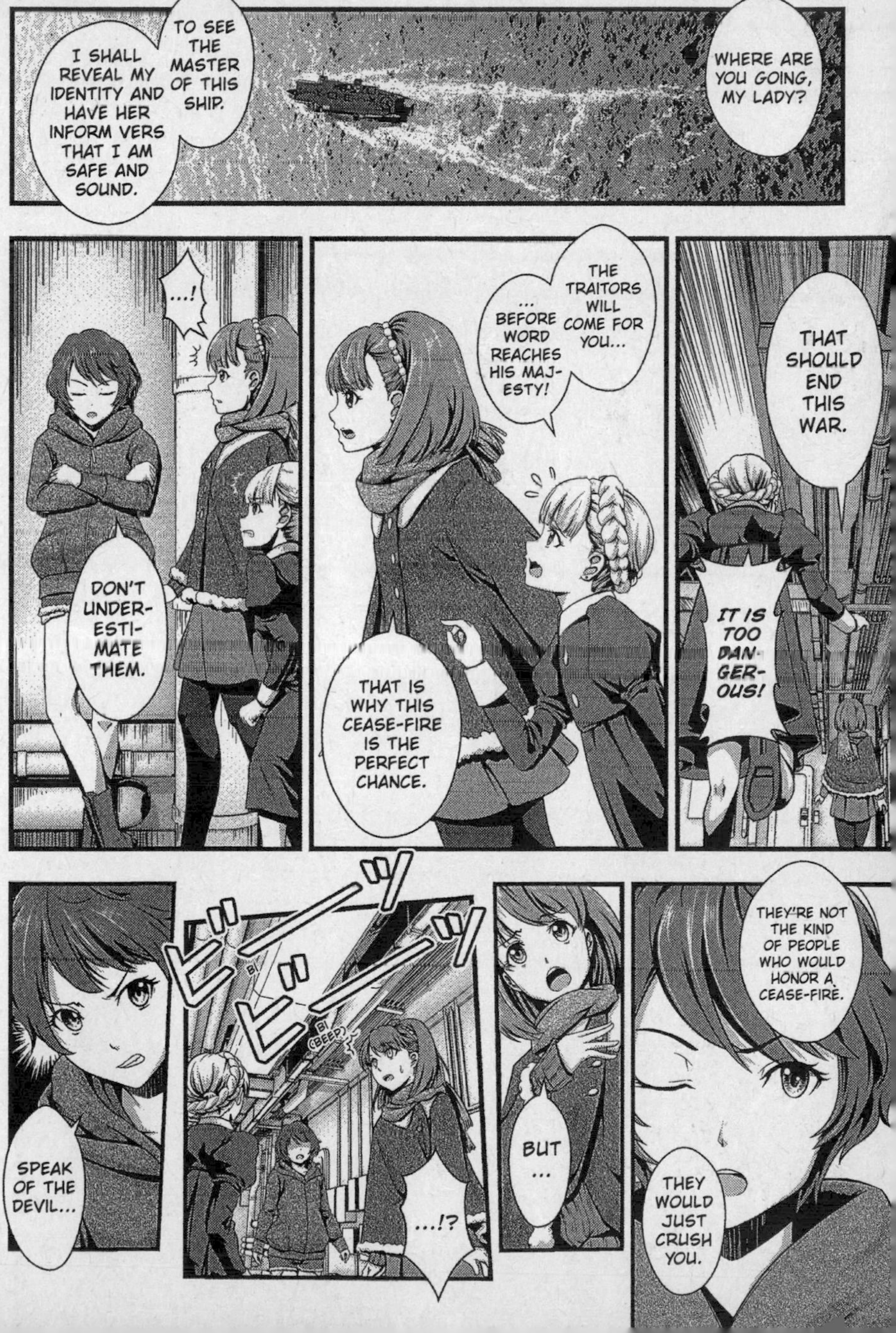
WHERE ARE YOU GOING, MY LADY?
TO SEE THE MASTER OF THIS SHIP.
I SHALL REVEAL MY IDENTITY AND HAVE HER INFORM VERS THAT I AM SAFE AND SOUND.
THAT SHOULD END THIS WAR.
IT IS TOO DANGEROUS!
THE TRAITORS WILL COME FOR YOU...
... BEFORE WORD REACHES HIS MAJESTY!
THAT IS WHY THIS CEASE-FIRE IS THE PERFECT CHANCE.
...!
DON'T UNDERESTIMATE THEM.
THEY'RE NOT THE KIND OF PEOPLE WHO WOULD HONOR A CEASE-FIRE.
THEY WOULD JUST CRUSH YOU.
BUT ...
BI
BI (BEEP)
...!?
SPEAK OF THE DEVIL...

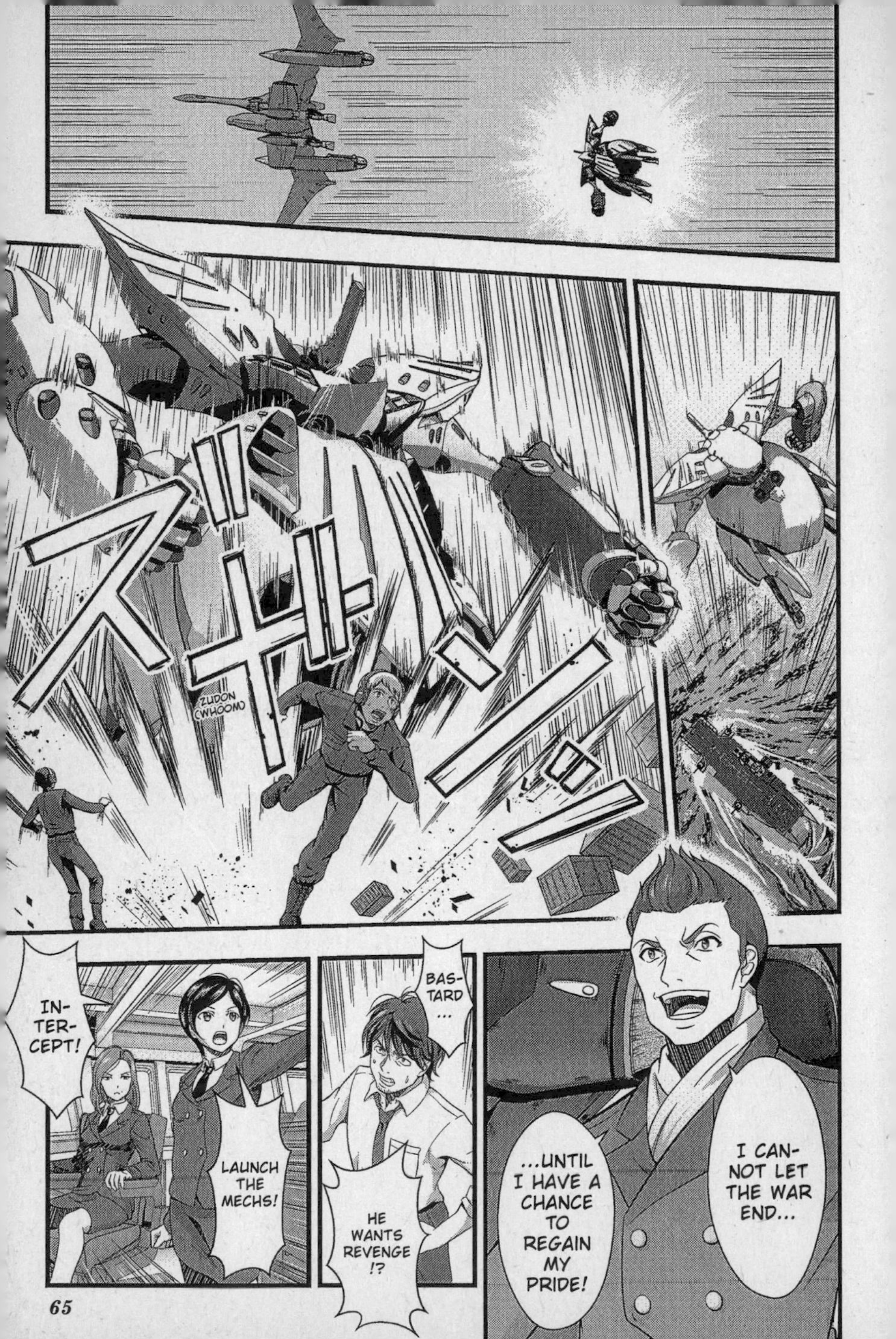
ZUDON (WHOOM)
I CANNOT LET THE WAR END...
...UNTIL I HAVE A CHANCE TO REGAIN MY PRIDE!
BASTARD...
HE WANTS REVENGE!?
INTERCEPT!
LAUNCH THE MECHS!

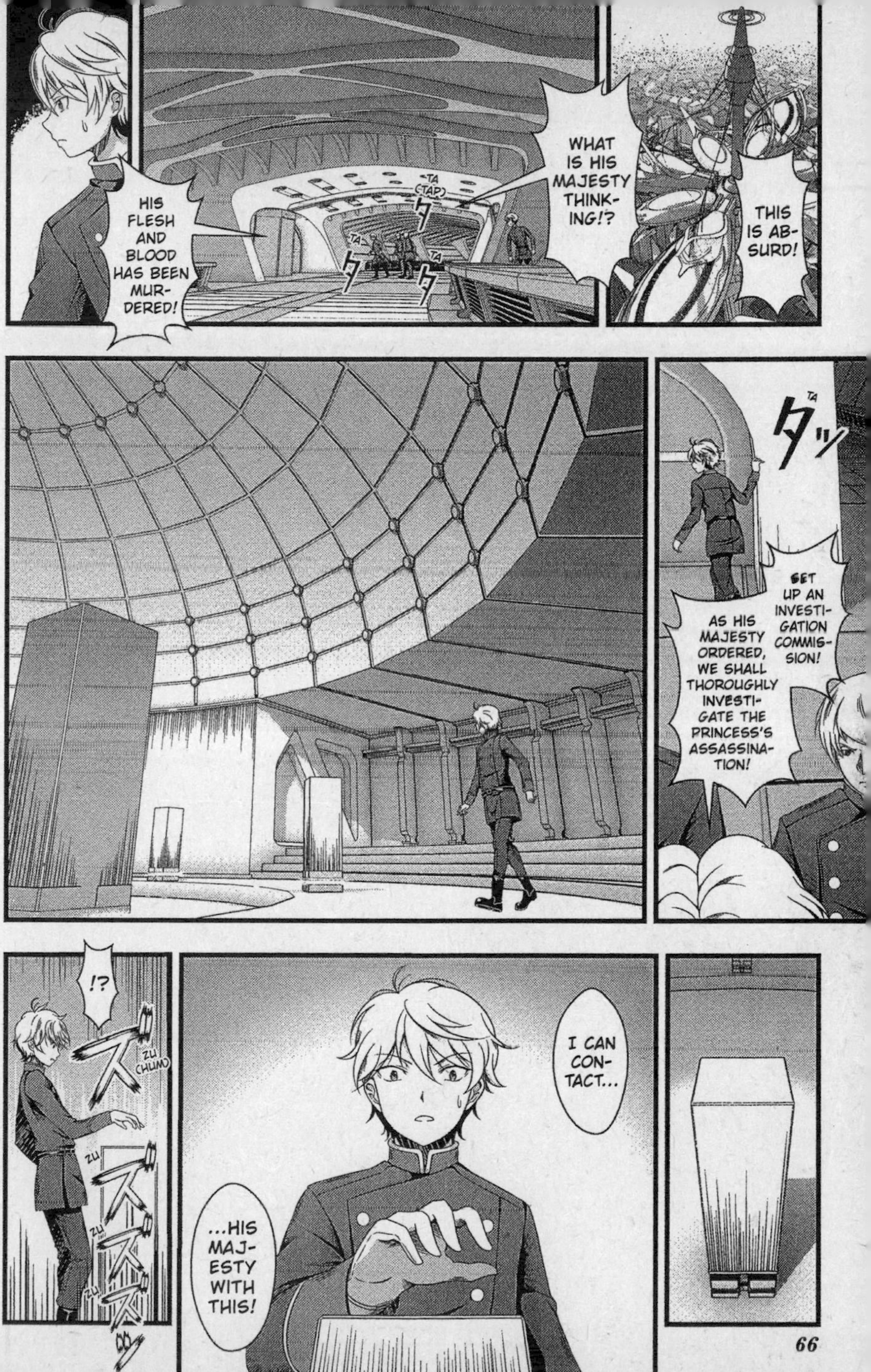
THIS IS ABSURD!
WHAT IS HIS MAJESTY THINKING!?
TA (TAP)
TA
TA
HIS FLESH AND BLOOD HAS BEEN MURDERED!
TA
SET UP AN INVESTIGATION COMMISSION!
AS HIS MAJESTY ORDERED, WE SHALL THOROUGHLY INVESTIGATE THE PRINCESS'S ASSASSINATION!
I CAN CONTACT...
...HIS MAJESTY WITH THIS!
!?
ZU (CHUM)
ZU
ZU
ZU

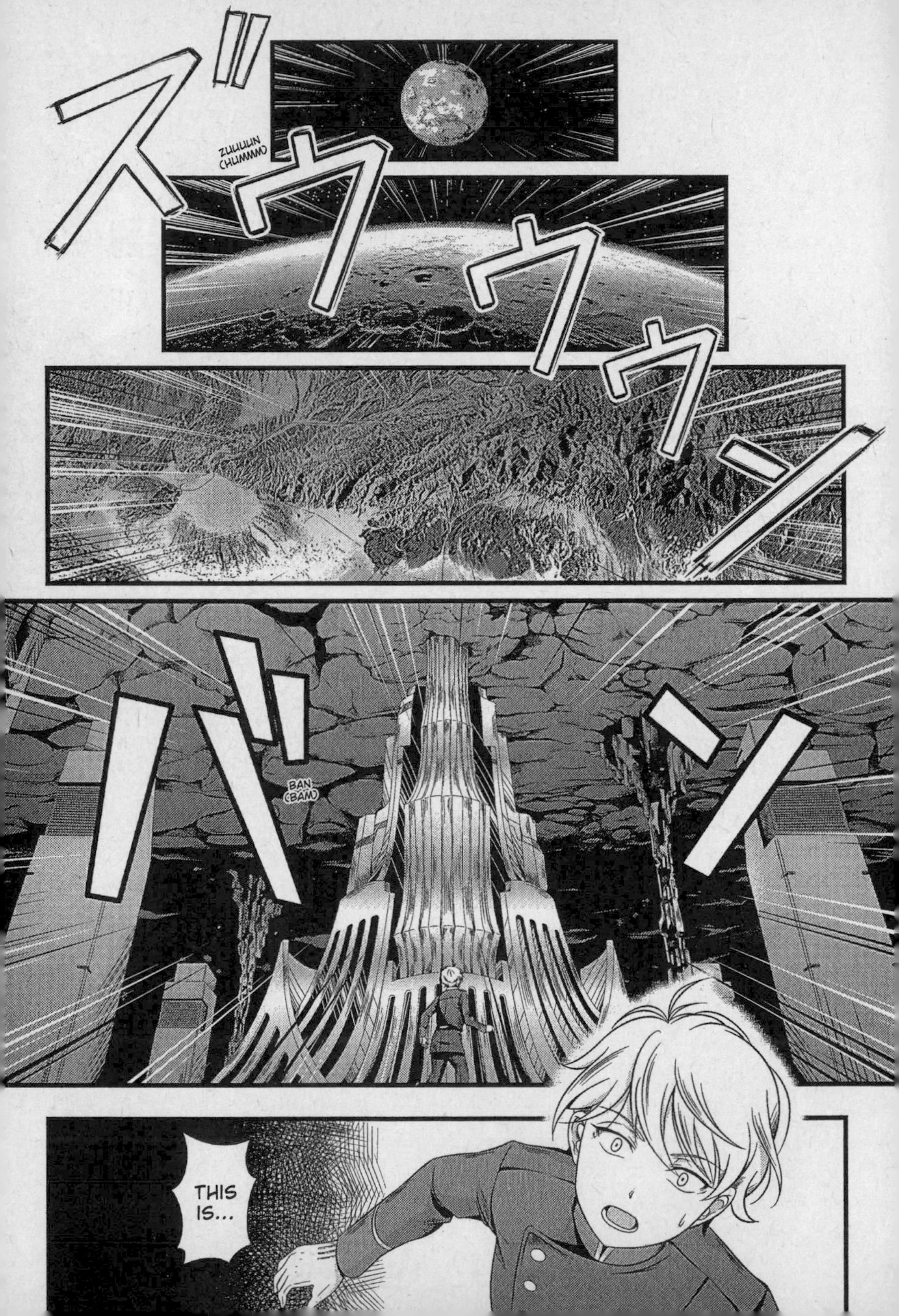
ズウウウウン
ZUUUUUN (CHUMMM)
バン
BAN (BAM)
THIS IS...

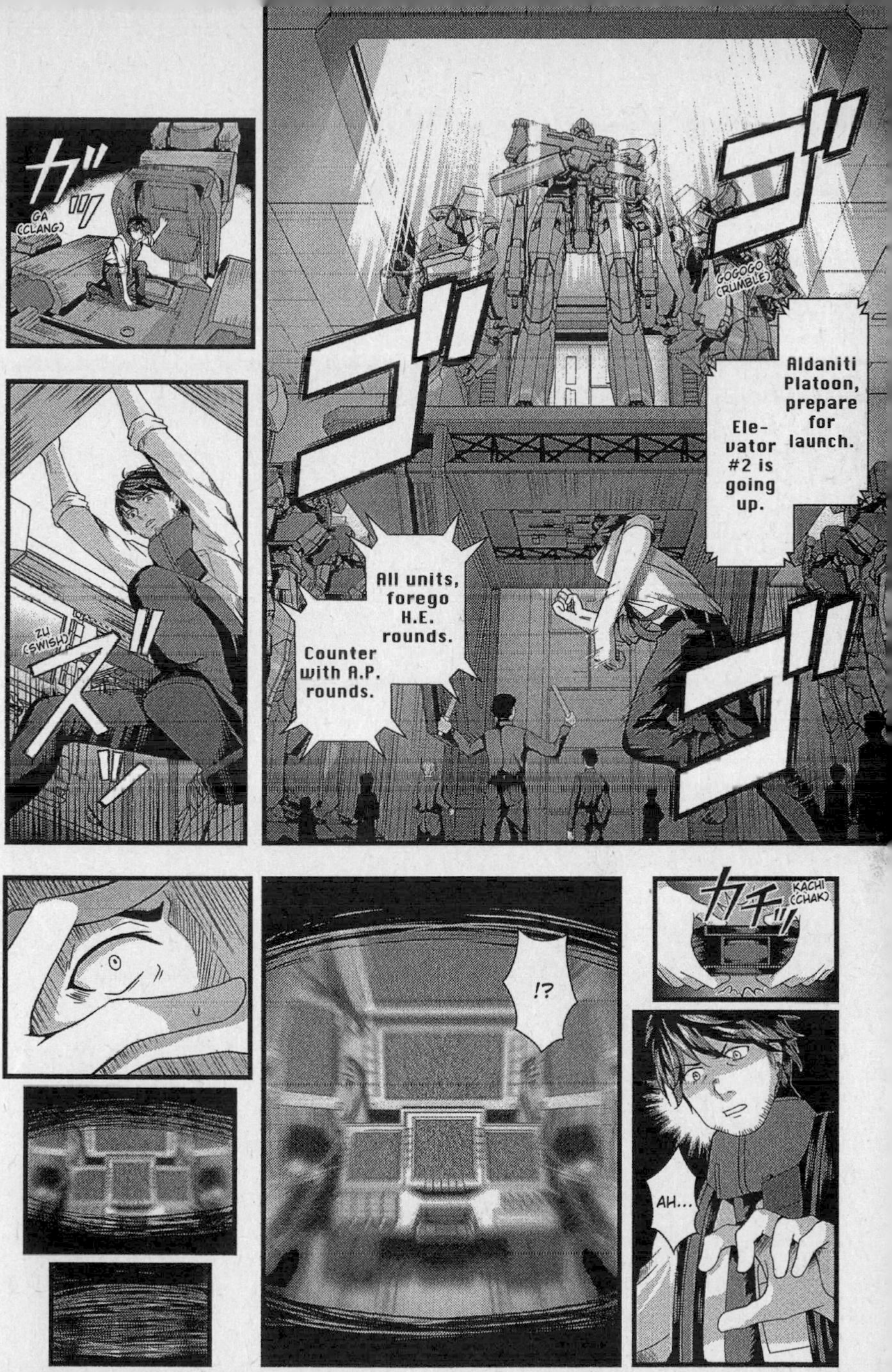

GOGOGO (RUMBLE)
Aldaniti Platoon, prepare for launch.
Ele-vator #2 is going up.
All units, forego H.E. rounds.
Counter with A.P. rounds.
GA (CLANG)
ZU (SWISH)
KACHI (CHAK)
AH...
!?

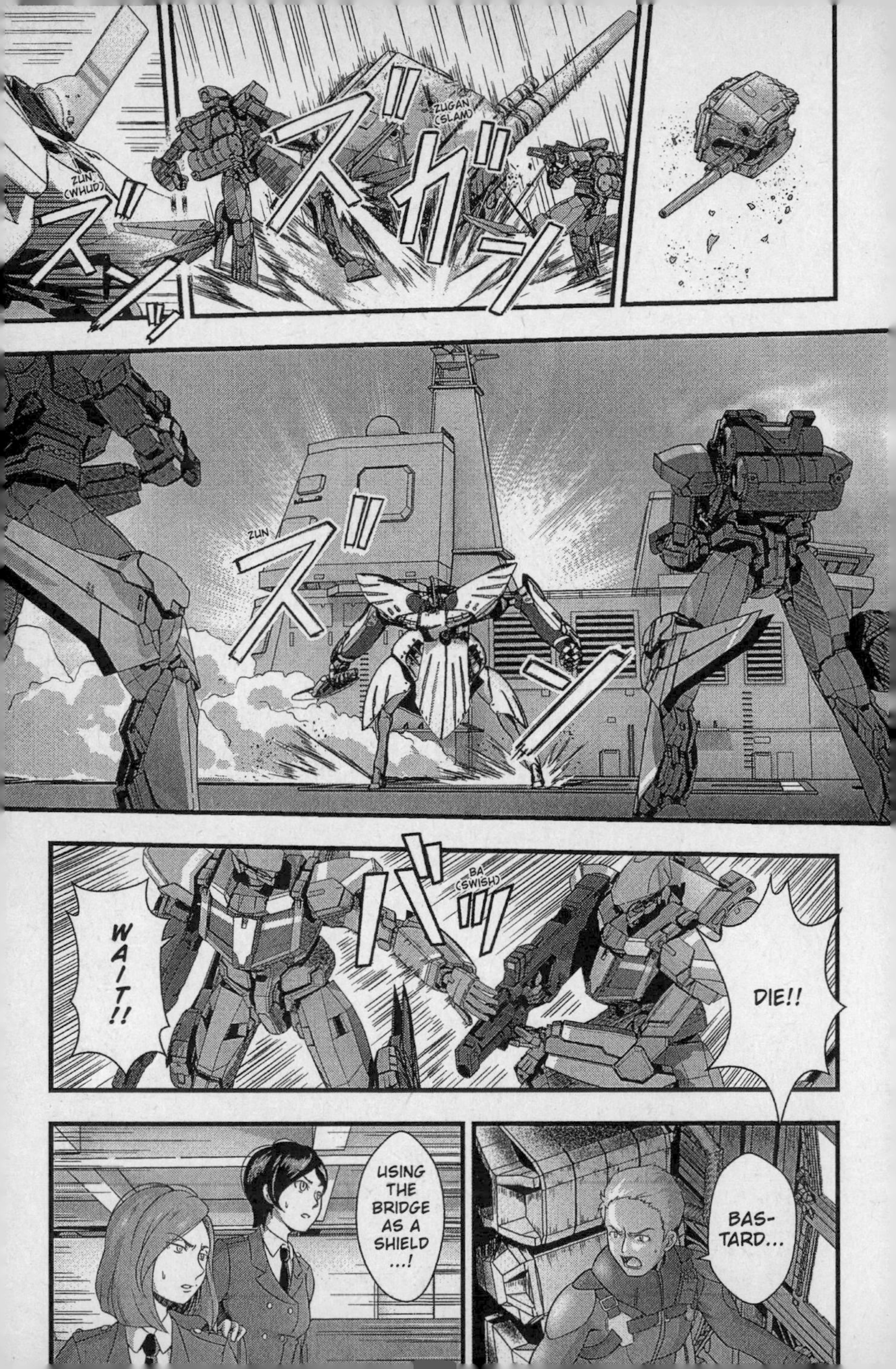
ZUGAN (SLAM)
ZUN (WHUD)
ZUN
BA (SWISH)
DIE!!
WAIT!!
BAS-TARD...
USING THE BRIDGE AS A SHIELD ...!

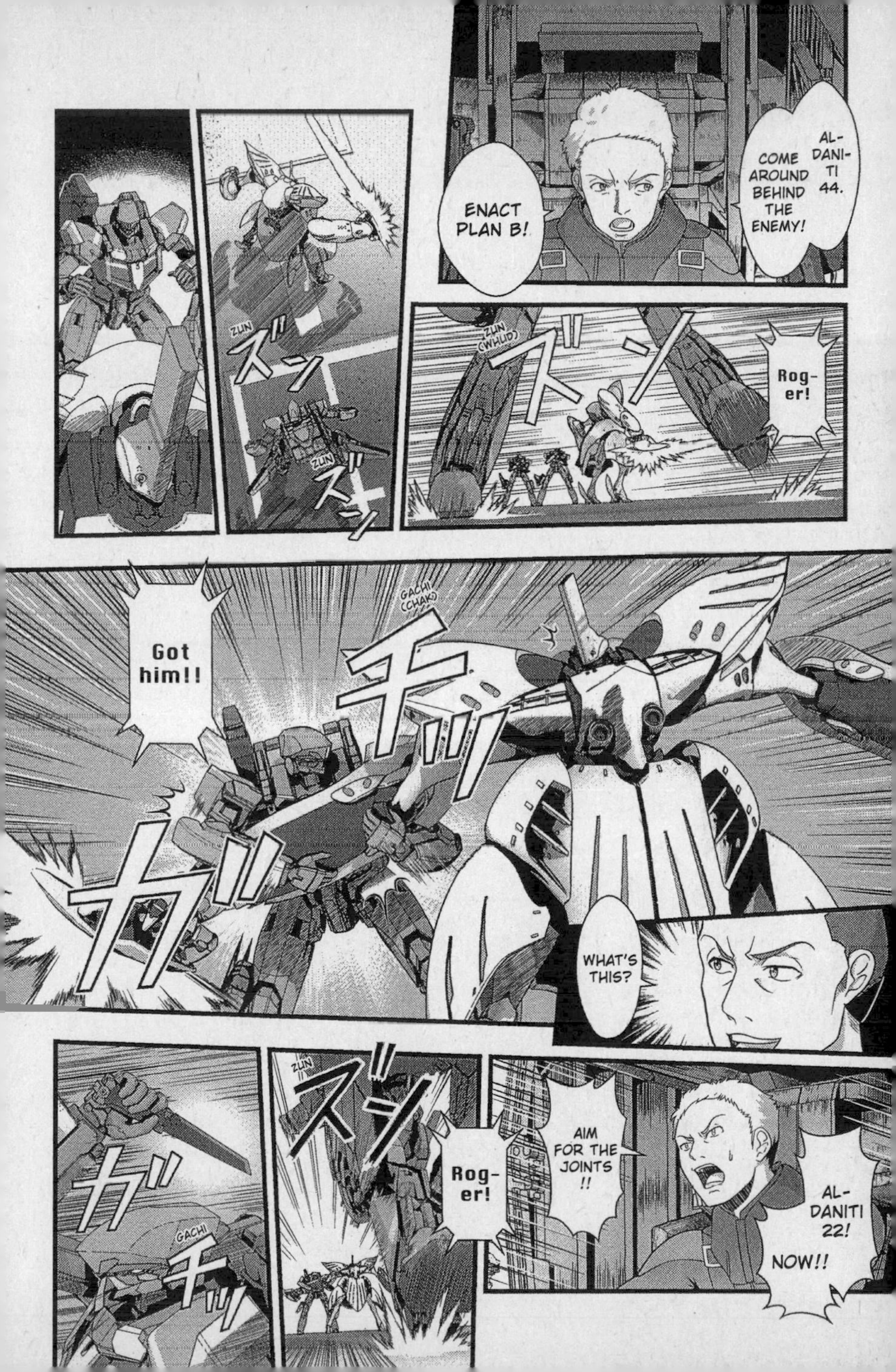
AL-DANI-TI 44.
COME AROUND BEHIND THE ENEMY!
ENACT PLAN B!
ZUN (WHUD)
Rog-er!
ZUN
ZUN
GACHI (CHAK)
Got him!!
WHAT'S THIS?
AL-DANITI 22!
NOW!!
AIM FOR THE JOINTS!!
ZUN
Rog-er!
GACHI

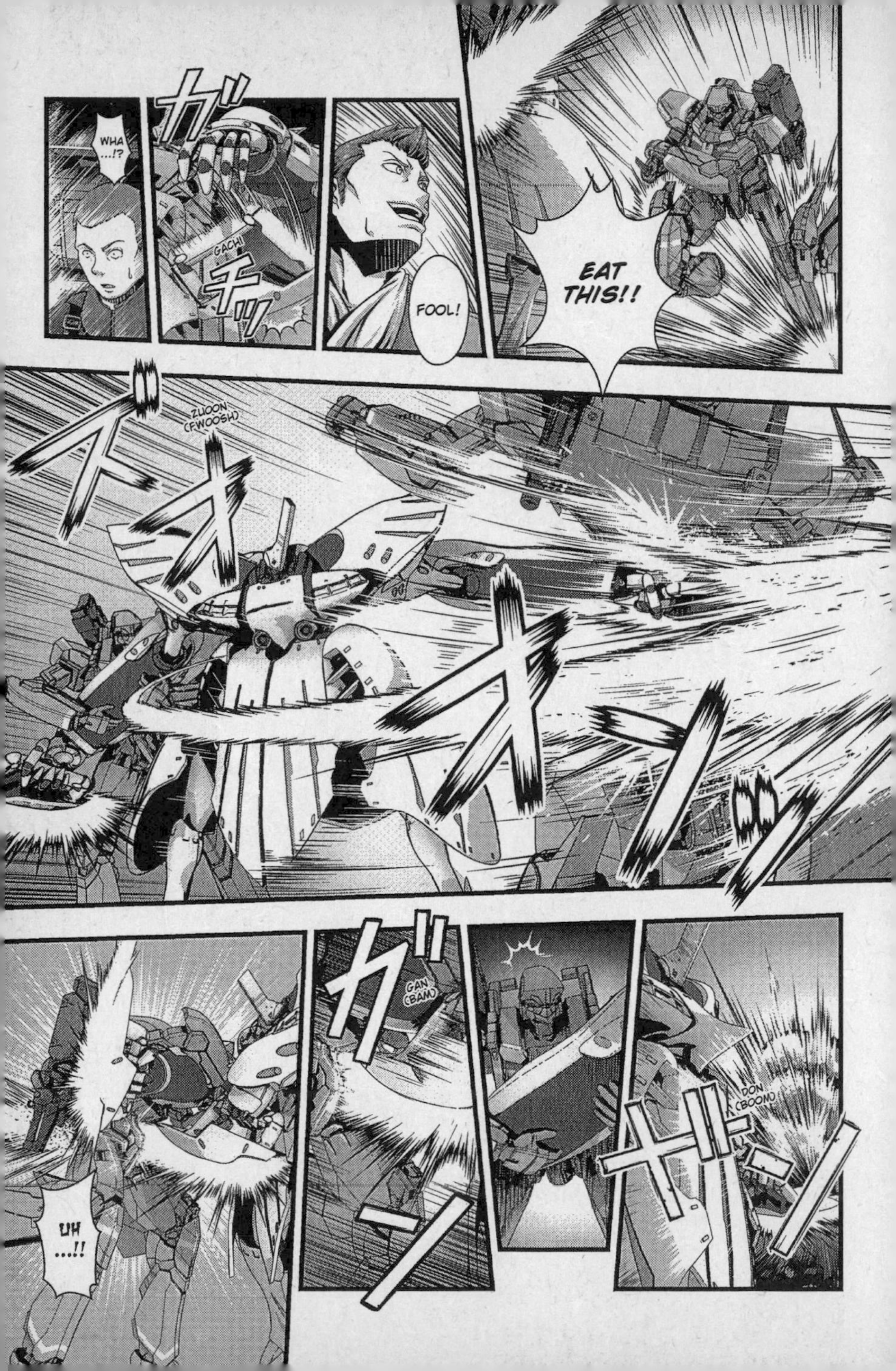
EAT THIS!!
FOOL!
GACHI
WHA ...!?
ZUOON (FWOOSH)
DON (BOOM)
GAN (BAM)
UH ...!!

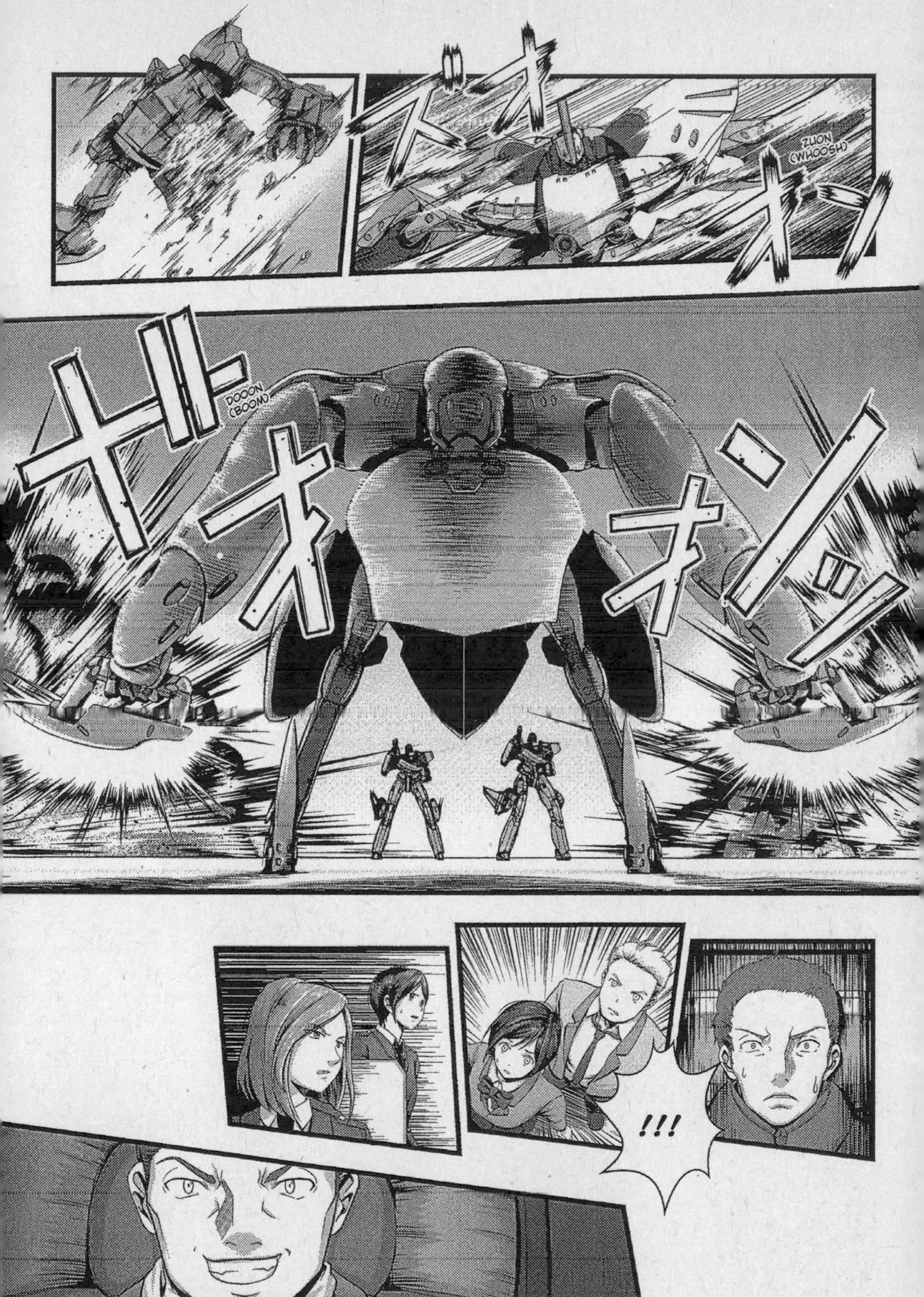
ZUON (WHOOSH)
DOOON (BOOM)
!!!

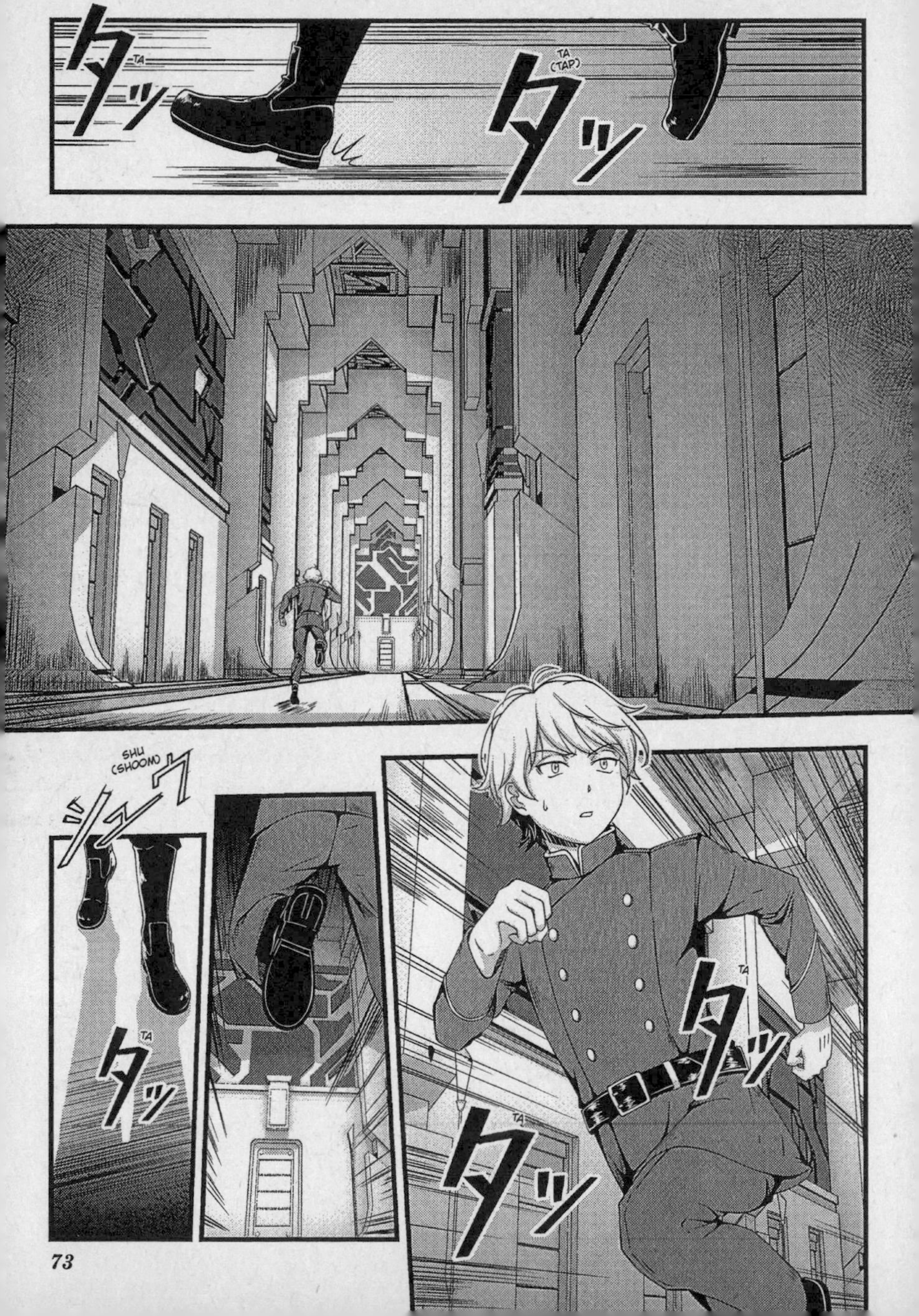
タッ
TA (TAP)
タッ
TA
タッ
TA
タッ
TA
シュウ
SHU (SHOOM)
タッ
TA

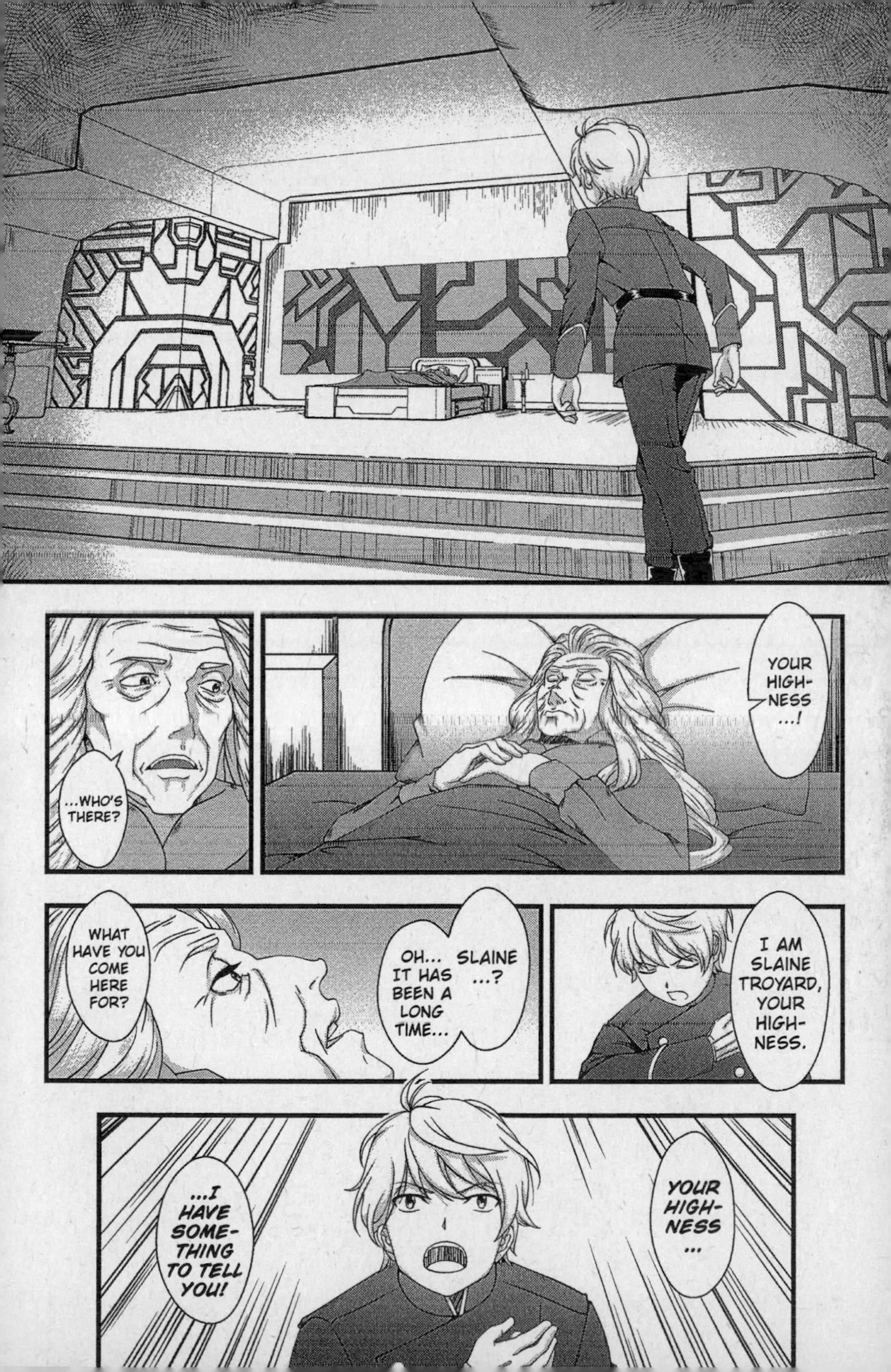
YOUR HIGHNESS...!
...WHO'S THERE?
I AM SLAINE TROYARD, YOUR HIGHNESS.
SLAINE...?
OH... IT HAS BEEN A LONG TIME...
WHAT HAVE YOU COME HERE FOR?
YOUR HIGHNESS...
...I HAVE SOMETHING TO TELL YOU!

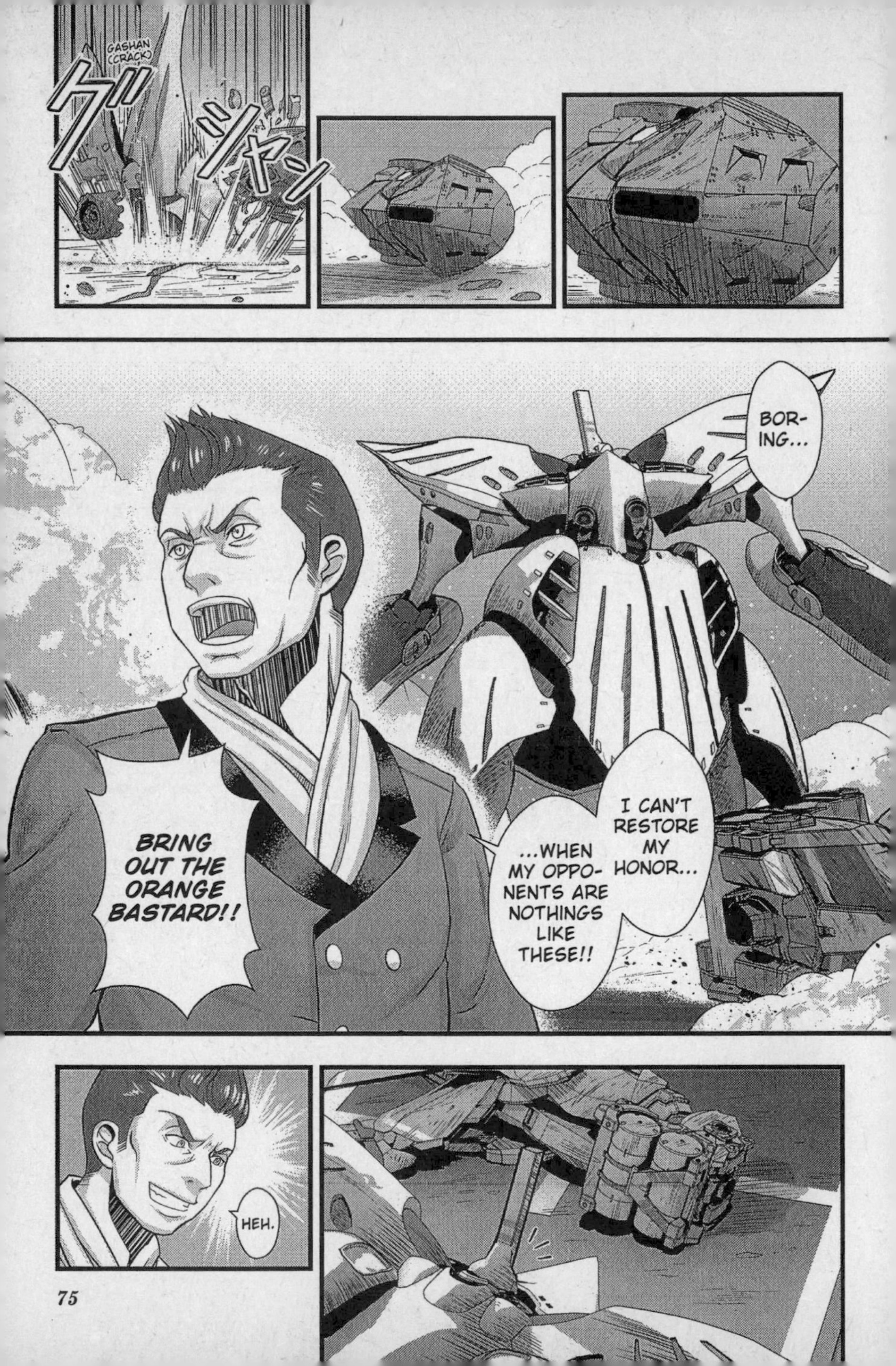
GASHAN (CRACK)
グシャーン
BOR-ING...
I CAN'T RESTORE MY HONOR...
...WHEN MY OPPONENTS ARE NOTHINGS LIKE THESE!!
BRING OUT THE ORANGE BASTARD!!
HEH.

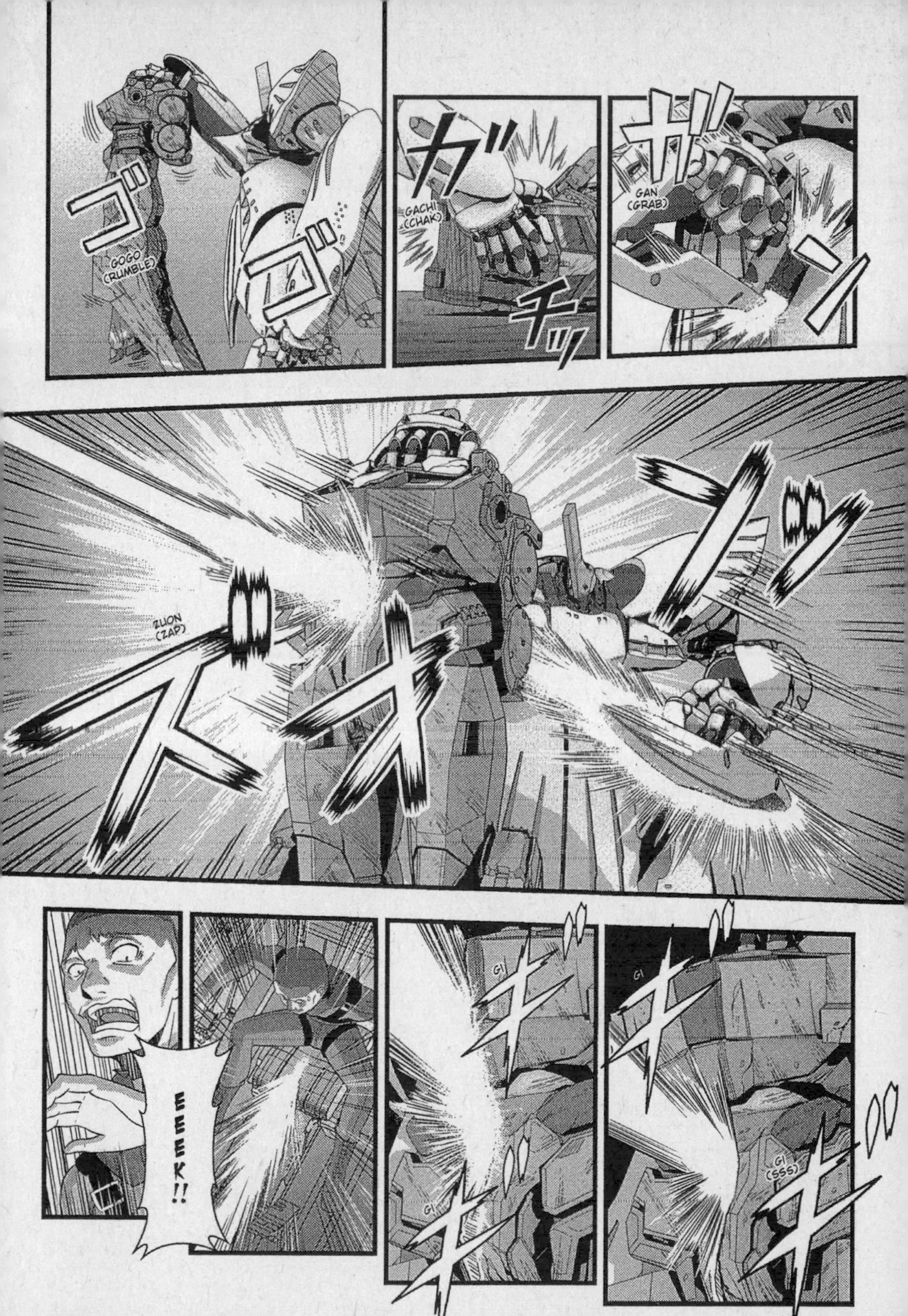
GAN (GRAB)
GACHI (CHAK)
GOGO (RUMBLE)
ZUON (ZAP)
GI
GI (SSS)
GI
GI
EEEK!!

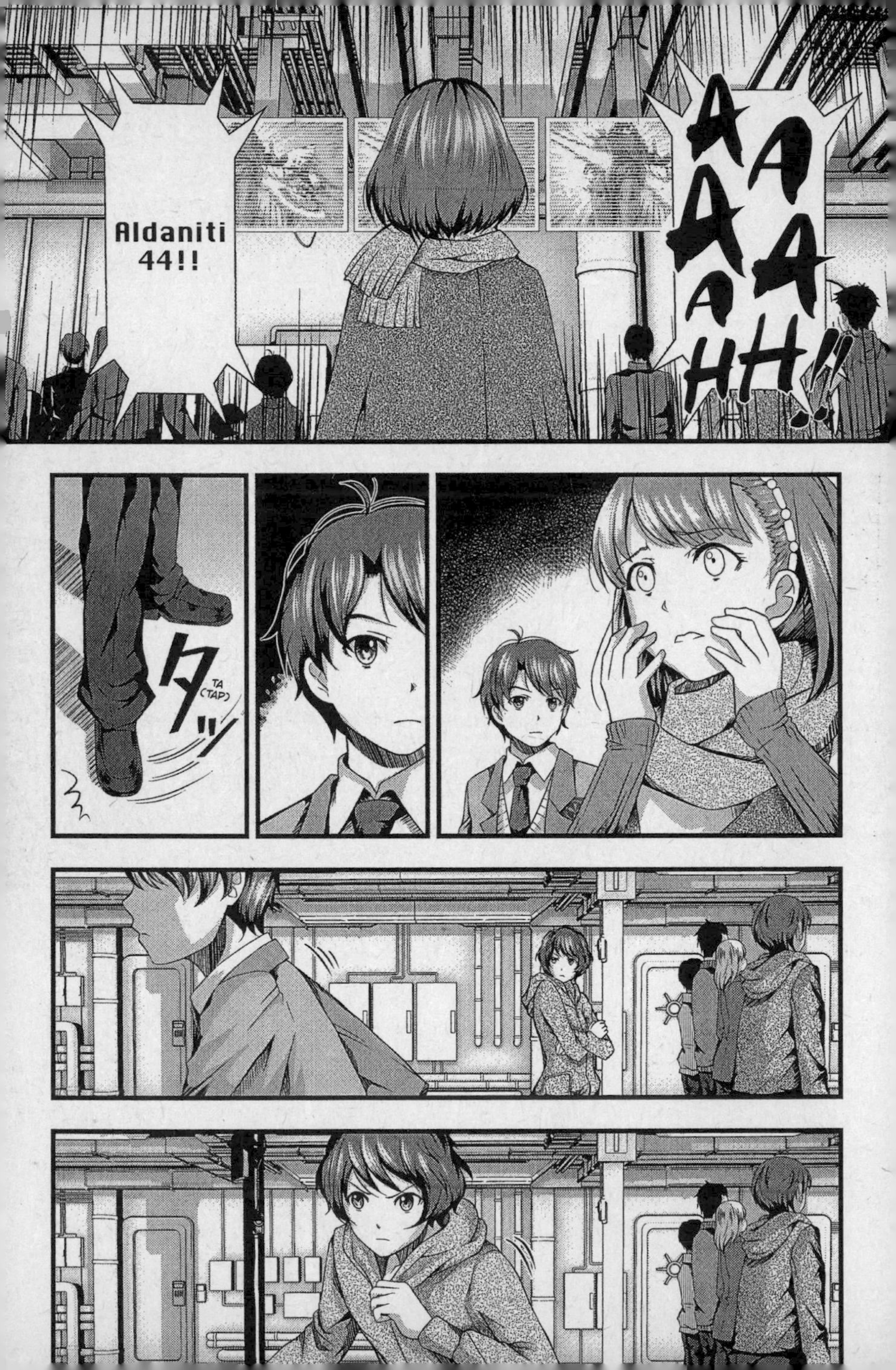
AAAAAHH!!
Aldaniti 44!!
タッ
TA (TAP)

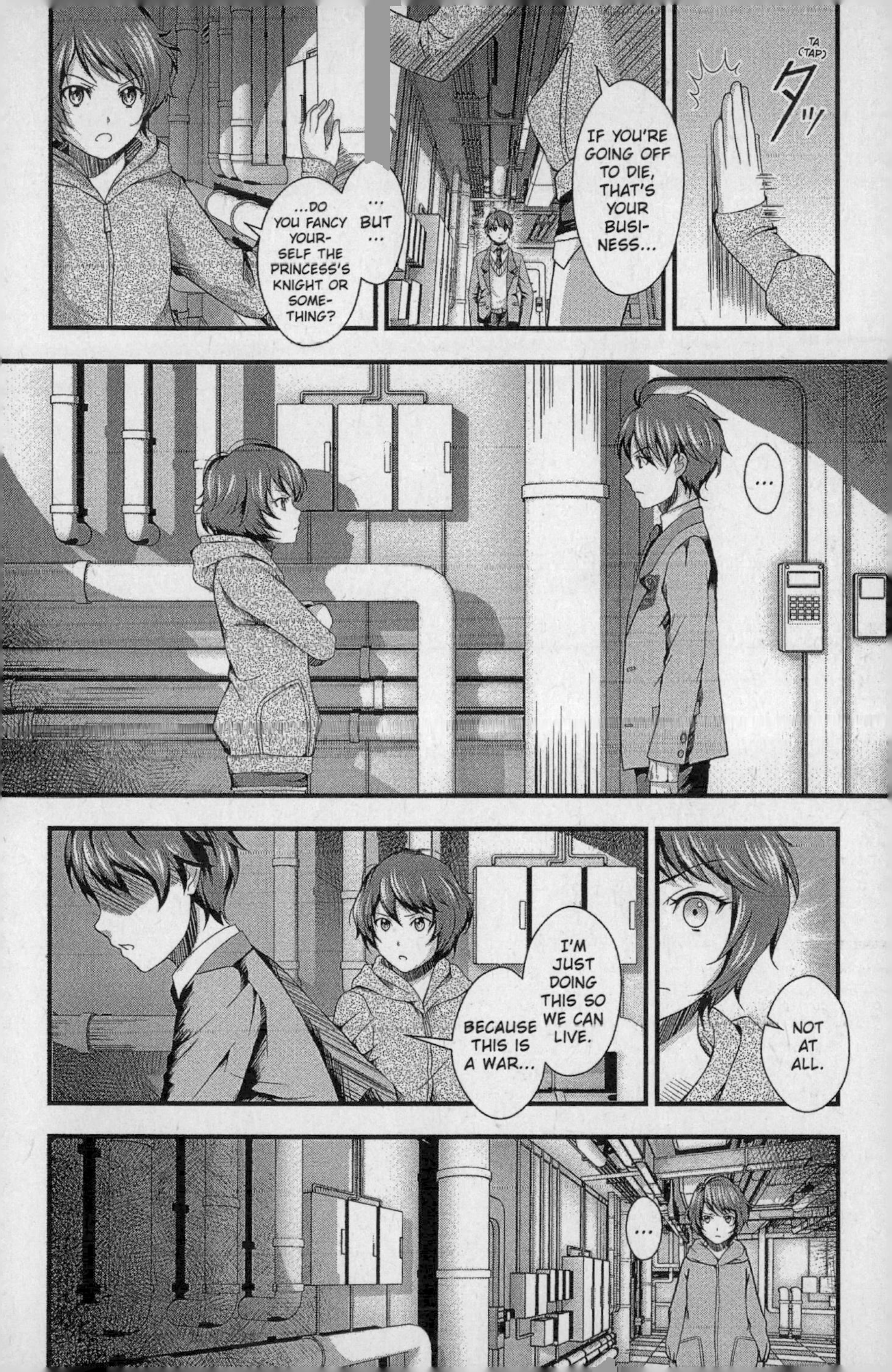

TA (TAP)
タッ
IF YOU'RE GOING OFF TO DIE, THAT'S YOUR BUSINESS...
... BUT ...
...DO YOU FANCY YOURSELF THE PRINCESS'S KNIGHT OR SOMETHING?
...
NOT AT ALL.
I'M JUST DOING THIS SO WE CAN LIVE.
BECAUSE THIS IS A WAR...
...

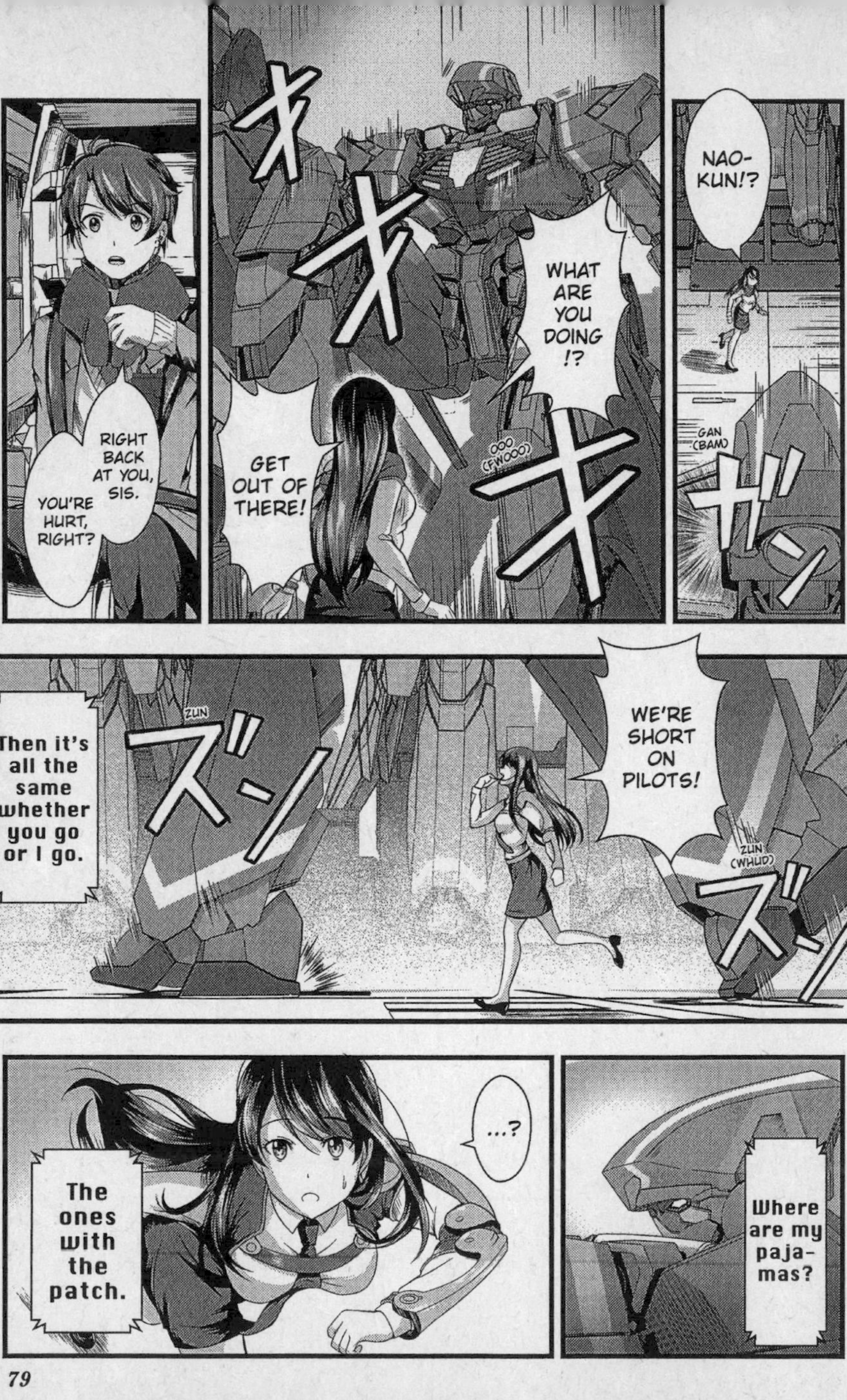
NAO-KUN!?
GAN (BAM)
WHAT ARE YOU DOING!?
GET OUT OF THERE!
OOO (FWOOO)
RIGHT BACK AT YOU, SIS.
YOU'RE HURT, RIGHT?
WE'RE SHORT ON PILOTS!
ZUN (WHUD)
ZUN
Then it's all the same whether you go or I go.
Where are my paja-mas?
...?
The ones with the patch.

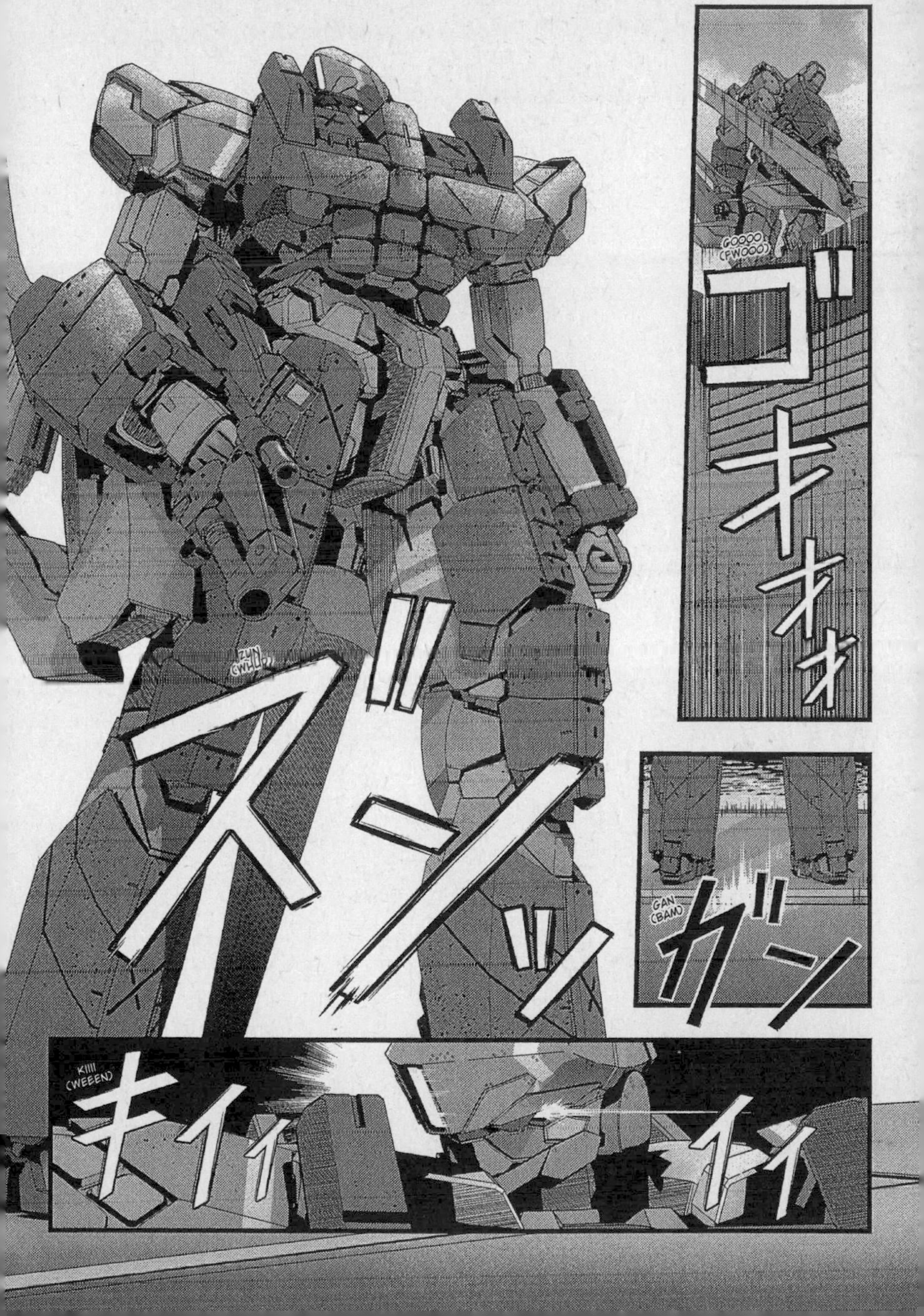
GOOOO (FWOOO)
ゴォォォ
GAN (BAM)
ガンッ
ZUN (WHUD)
ズーンッ
KIIII (WEEEN)
キイイーイイ

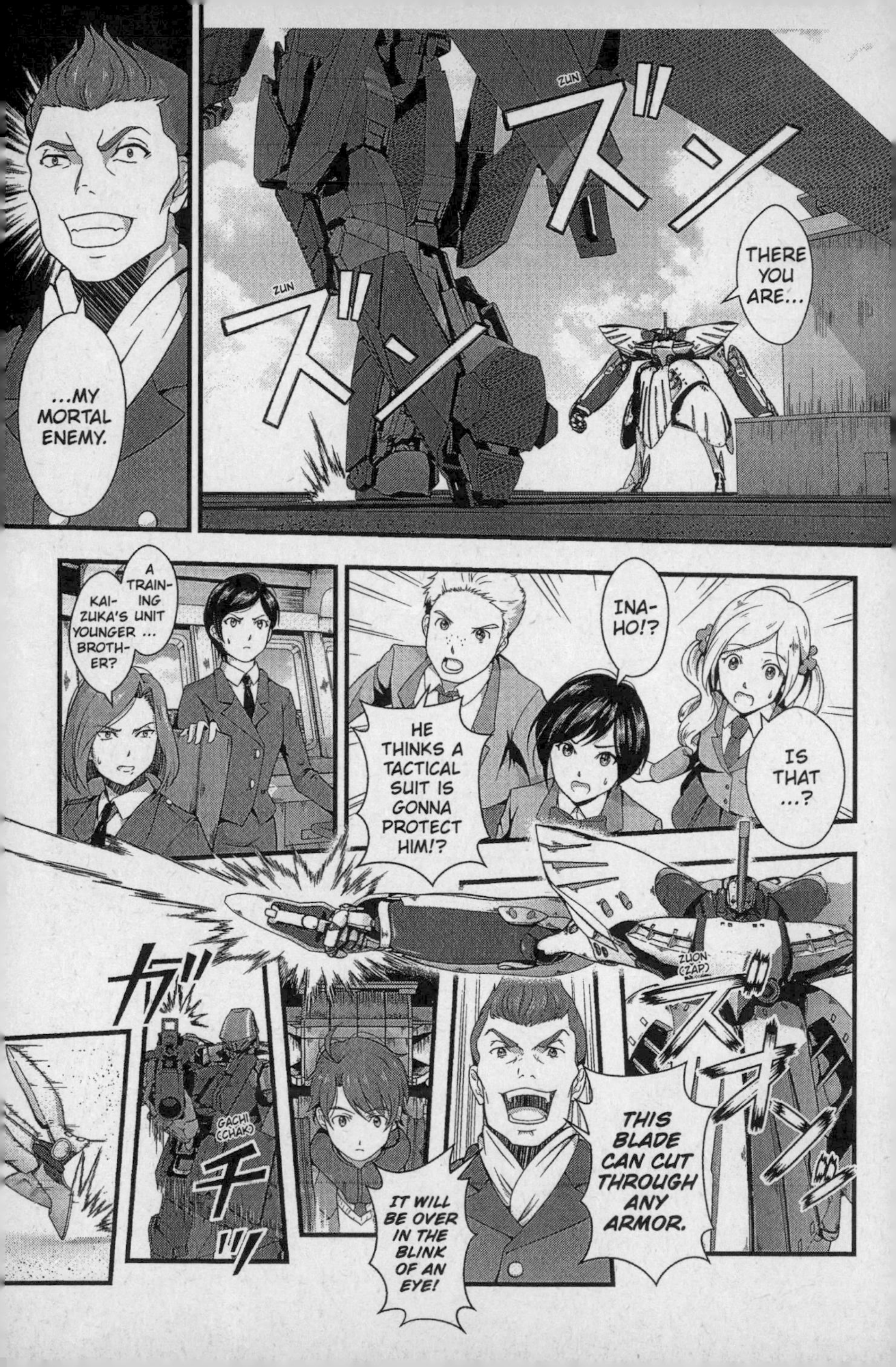
ZUN
ZUN
THERE YOU ARE...
...MY MORTAL ENEMY.
INA-HO!?
IS THAT ...?
HE THINKS A TACTICAL SUIT IS GONNA PROTECT HIM!?
A TRAINING UNIT ...
KAIZUKA'S YOUNGER BROTHER?
ZUON (ZAP)
THIS BLADE CAN CUT THROUGH ANY ARMOR.
IT WILL BE OVER IN THE BLINK OF AN EYE!
GACHI (CHAK)

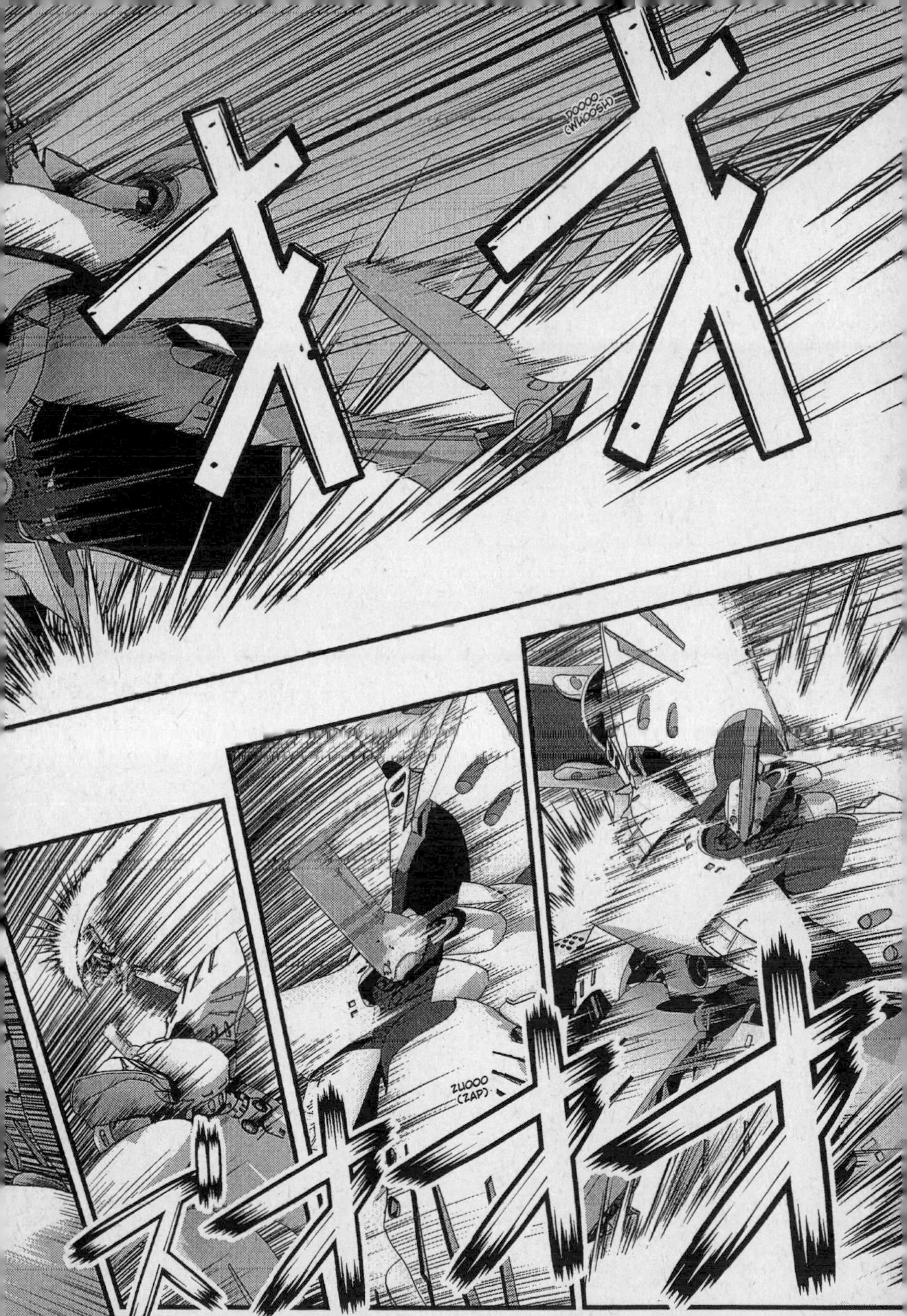
DOOOO (WHOOSH)
ZUOOO (ZAP)

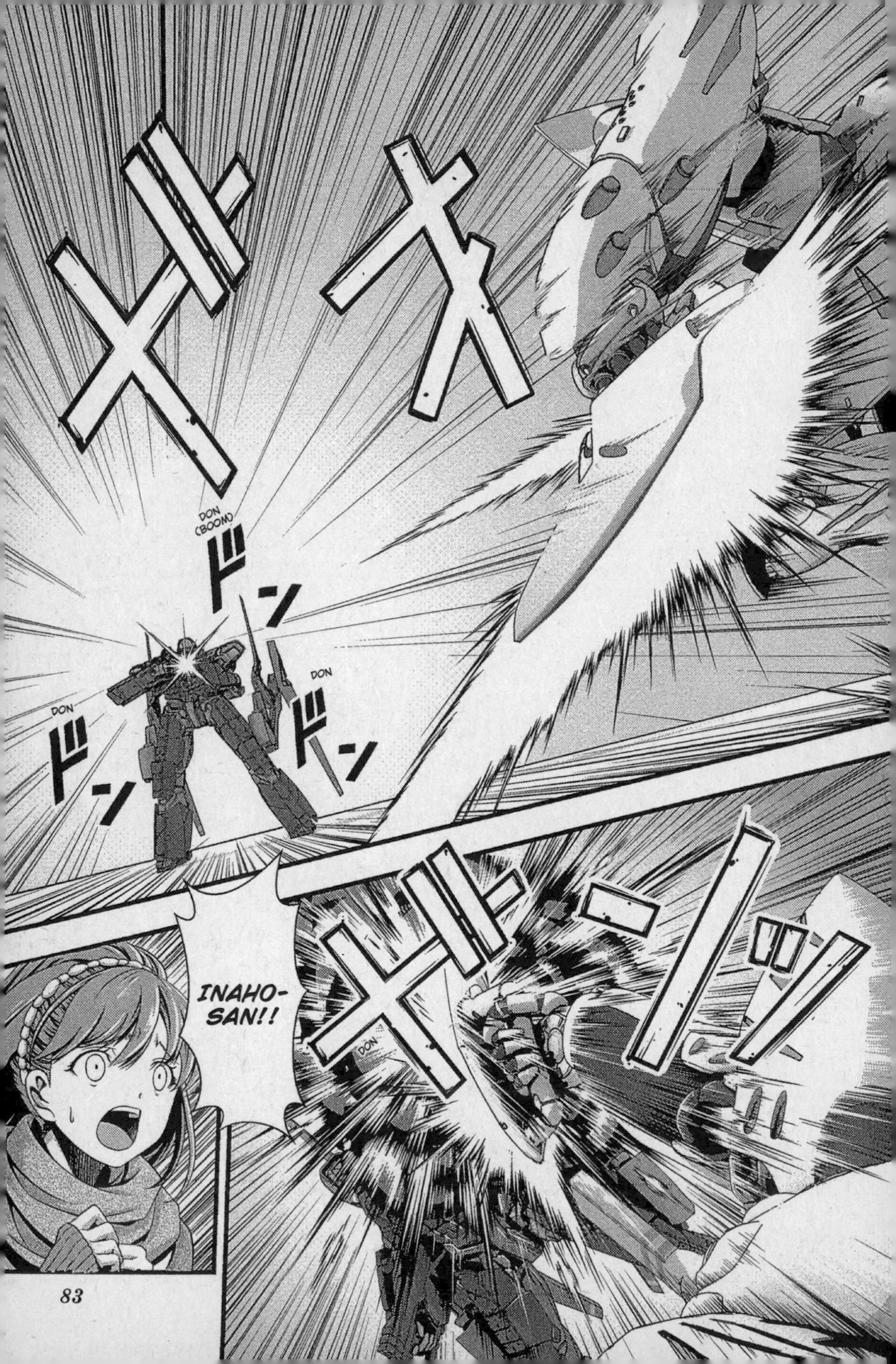
ズドオ
DON (BOOM)
ドン
DON
ドン
DON
ドン
DON
ズドーンッ
INAHO-SAN!!

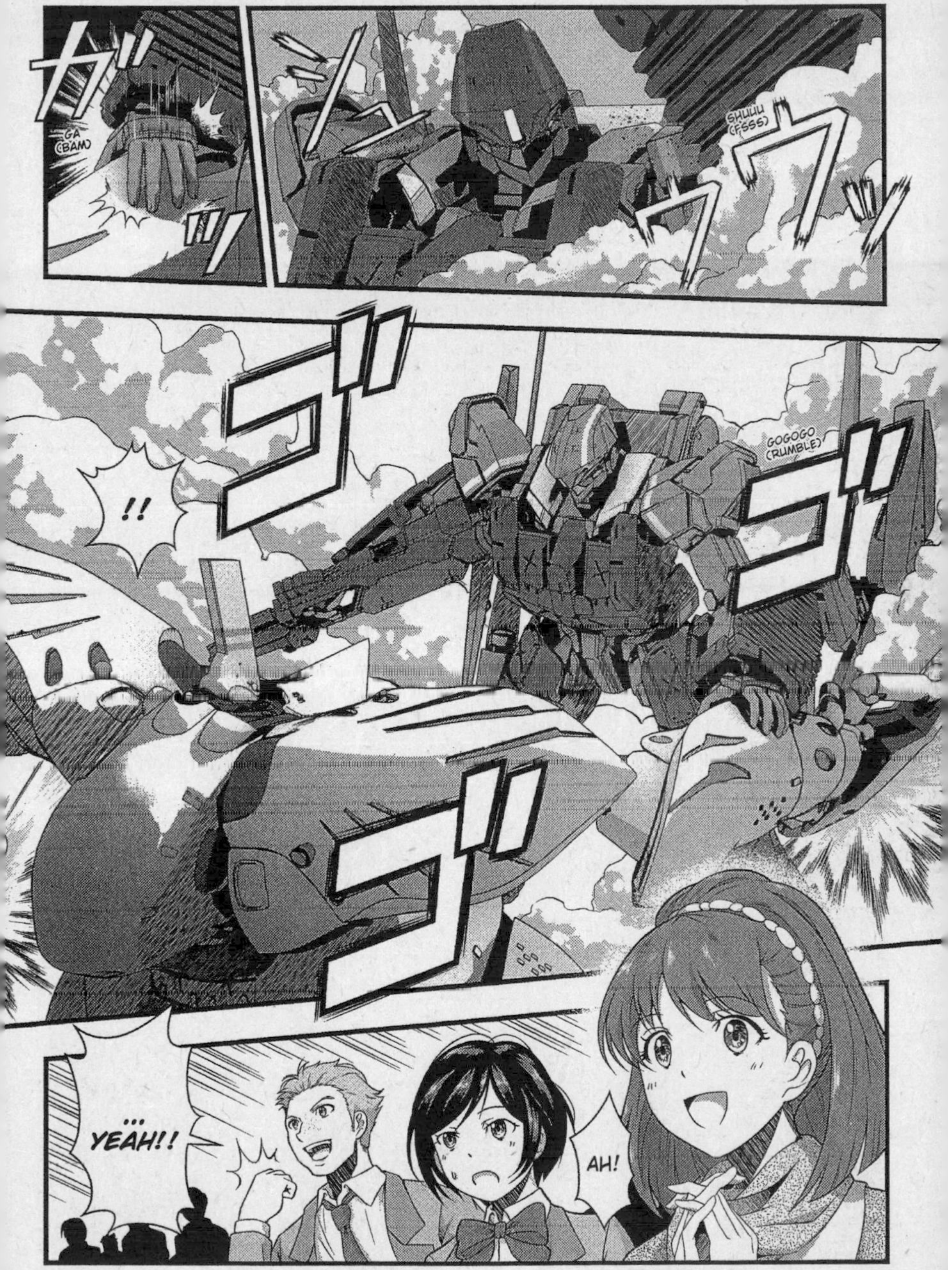
シュウウッ
SHUUU (FSSS)
ガッ
GA (BAM)
ゴゴゴ
GOGOGO (RUMBLE)
!!
AH!
... YEAH!!

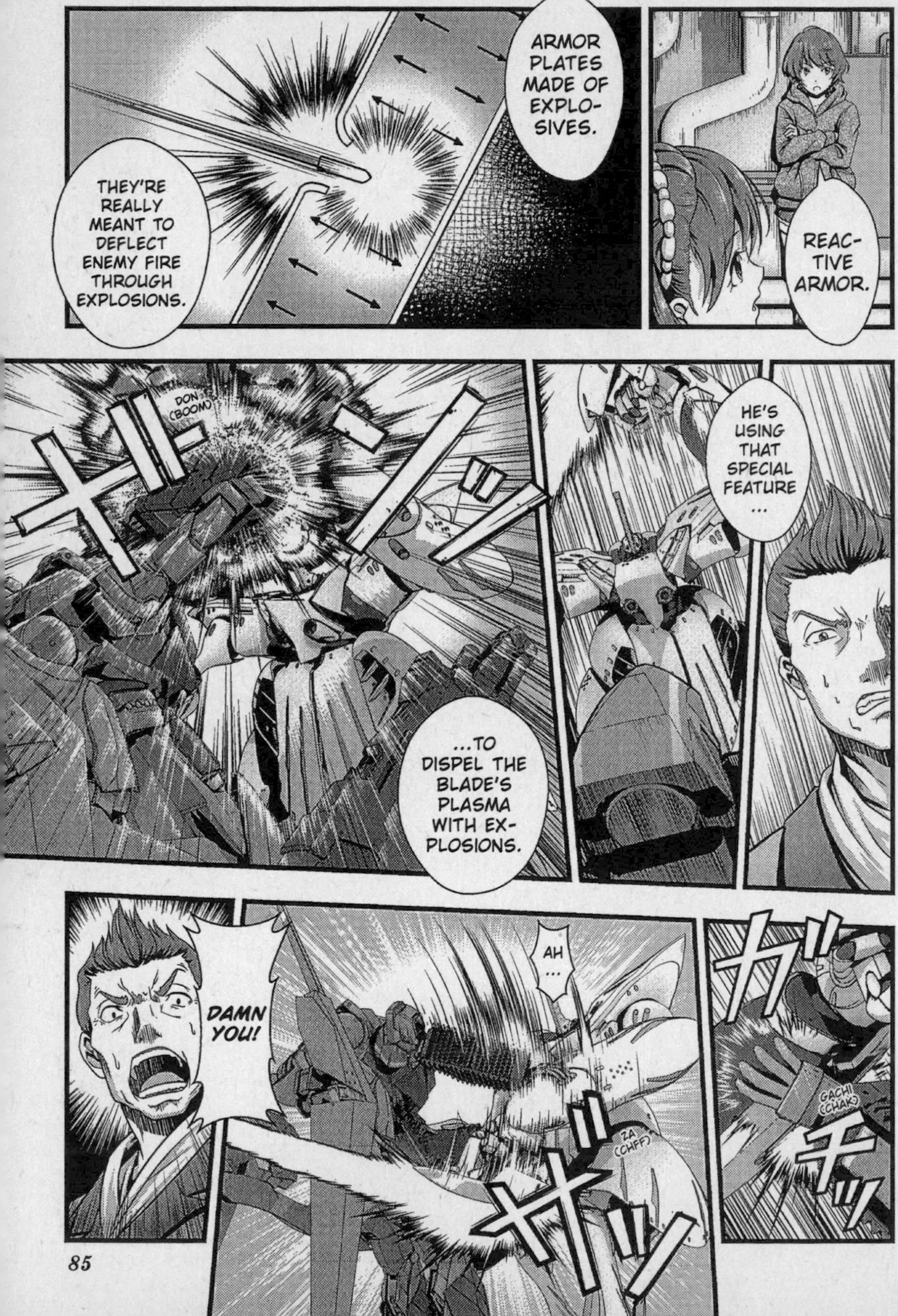

REAC-TIVE ARMOR.
ARMOR PLATES MADE OF EXPLO-SIVES.
THEY'RE REALLY MEANT TO DEFLECT ENEMY FIRE THROUGH EXPLOSIONS.
HE'S USING THAT SPECIAL FEATURE ...
...TO DISPEL THE BLADE'S PLASMA WITH EX-PLOSIONS.
DON (BOOM)
GACHI (CHAK)
AH ...
ZA (CHFF)
DAMN YOU!

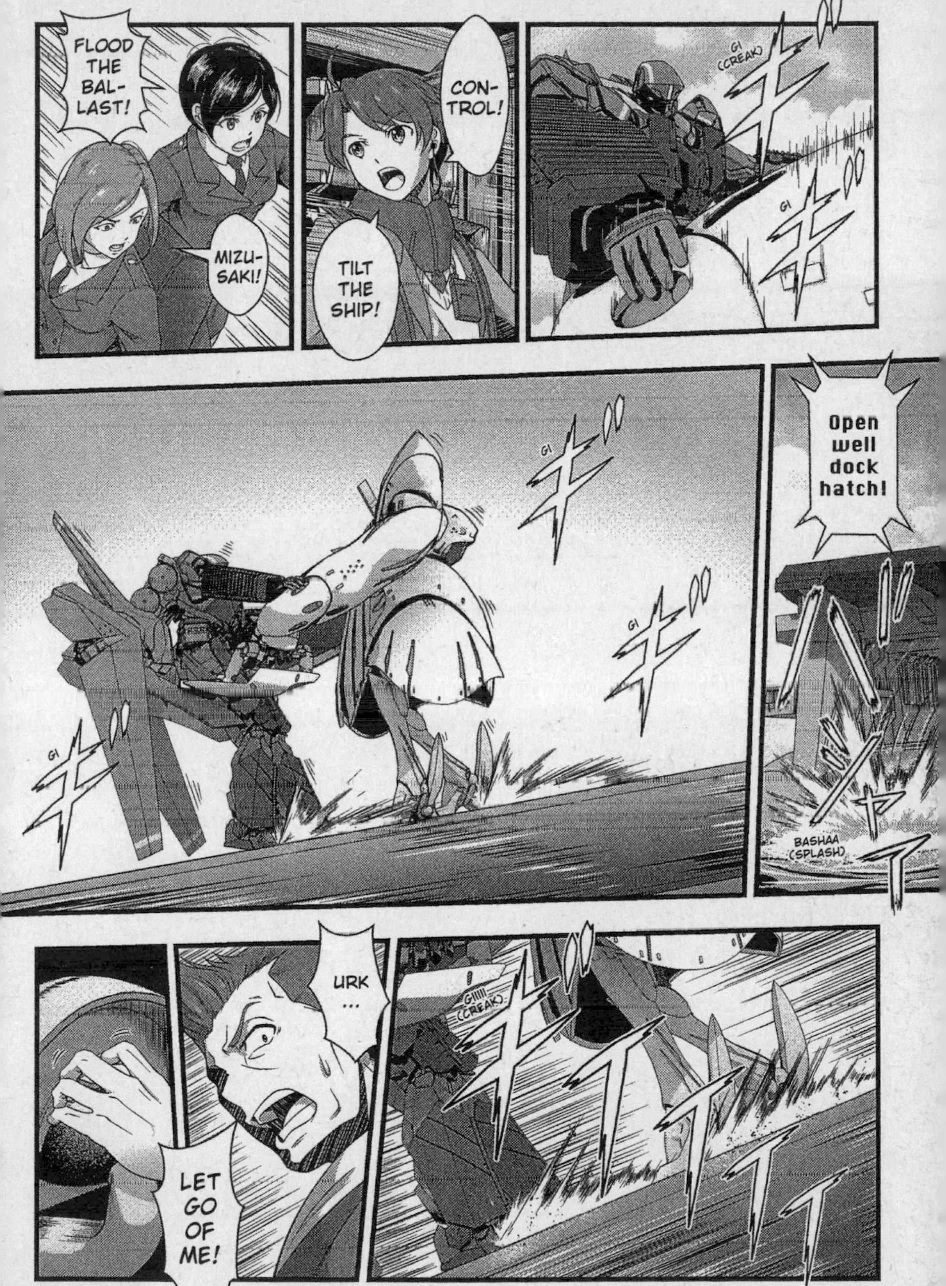
GI (CREAK)
GI
CON-TROL!
TILT THE SHIP!
FLOOD THE BAL-LAST!
MIZU-SAKI!
Open well dock hatch!
BASHAA (SPLASH)
GI
GI
GI
GIIII (CREAK)
URK ...
LET GO OF ME!

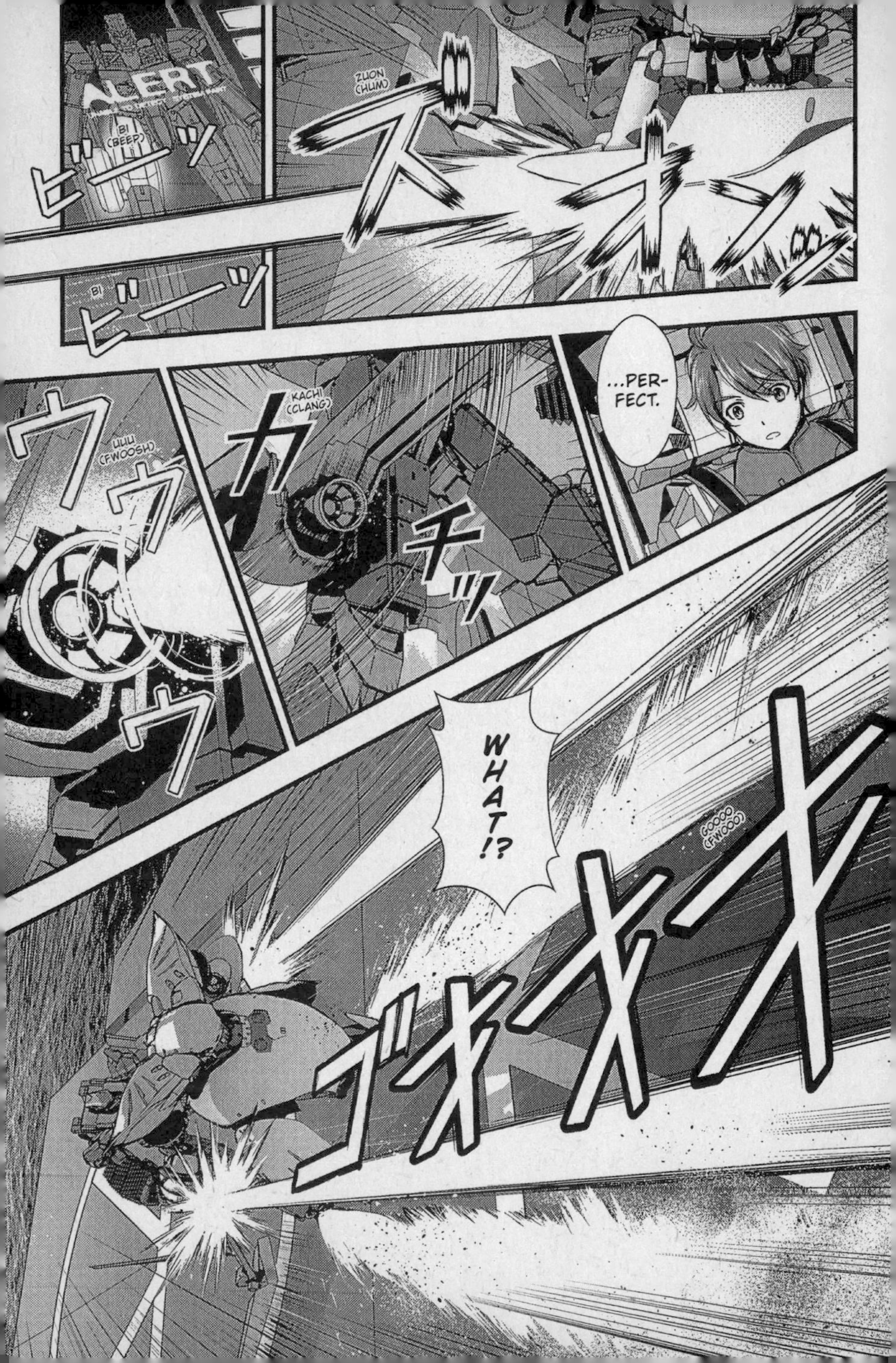
ZUON (HUM)
ALERT
BI (BEEP)
BI
...PER-FECT.
KACHI (CLANG)
UUU (FWOOSH)
WHAT!?
GOOOO (FWOOO)

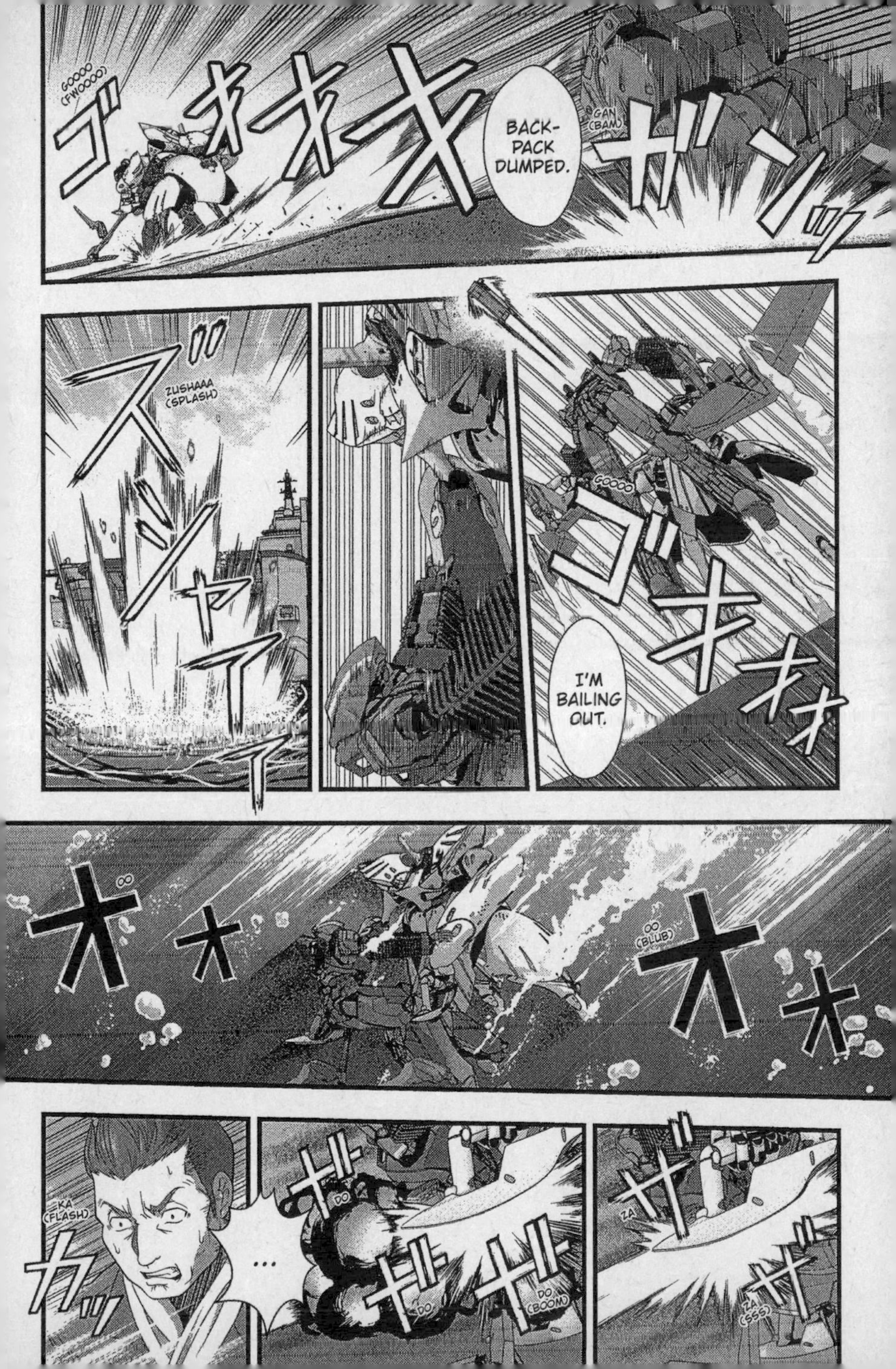
GAN (BAM)
BACK-PACK DUMPED.
GOOOO (FWOOOO)
GOOOO
I'M BAILING OUT.
ZUSHAAA (SPLASH)
OO (BLUB)
ZA
ZA (SSS)
DO
DO
DO (BOOM)
...
KA (FLASH)

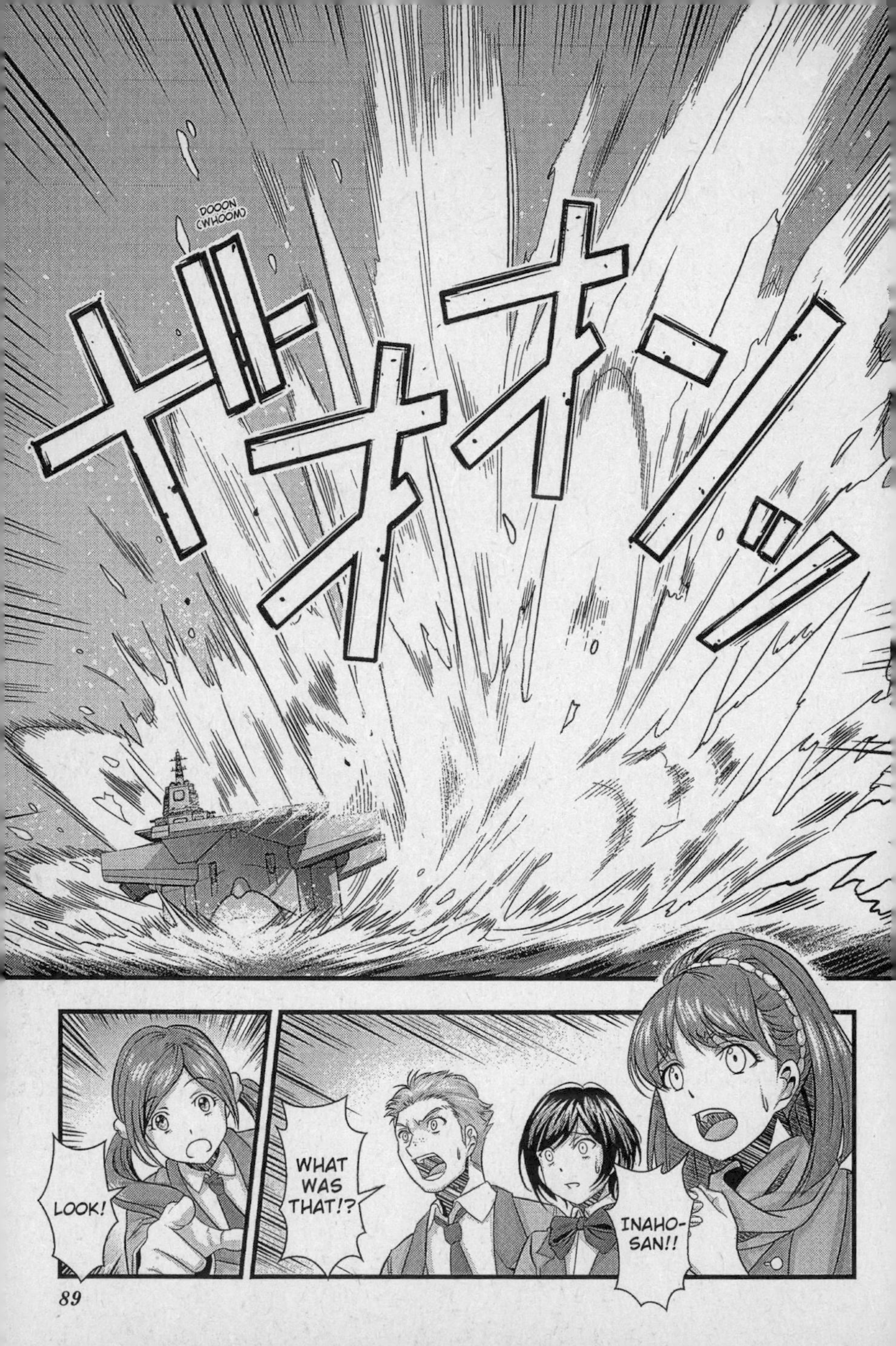
DOOON (WHOOM)
ザオーンッ
INAHO-SAN!!
WHAT WAS THAT!?
LOOK!

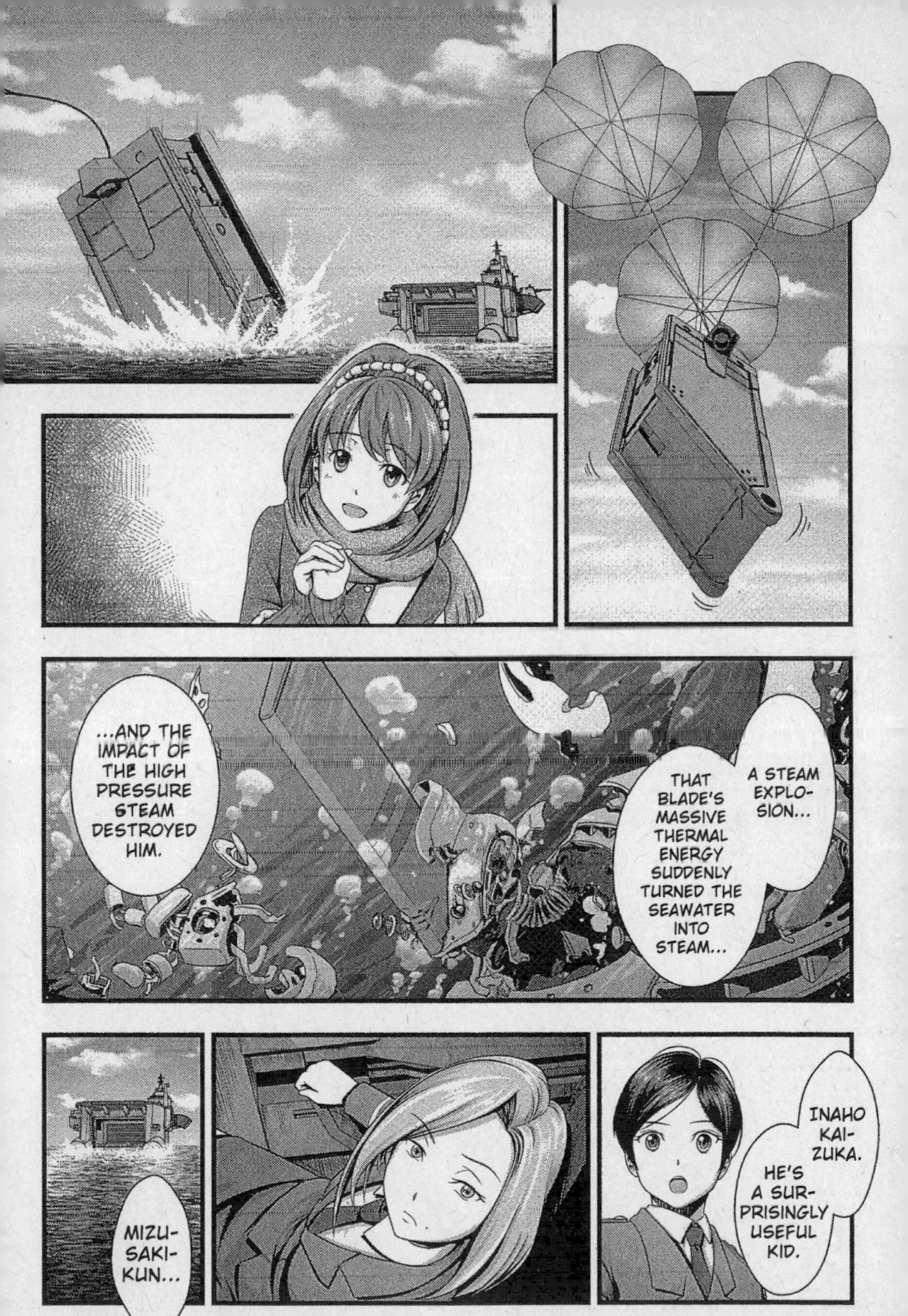
A STEAM EXPLO-SION...
THAT BLADE'S MASSIVE THERMAL ENERGY SUDDENLY TURNED THE SEAWATER INTO STEAM...
...AND THE IMPACT OF THE HIGH PRESSURE STEAM DESTROYED HIM.
INAHO KAI-ZUKA.
HE'S A SUR-PRISINGLY USEFUL KID.
MIZU-SAKI-KUN...

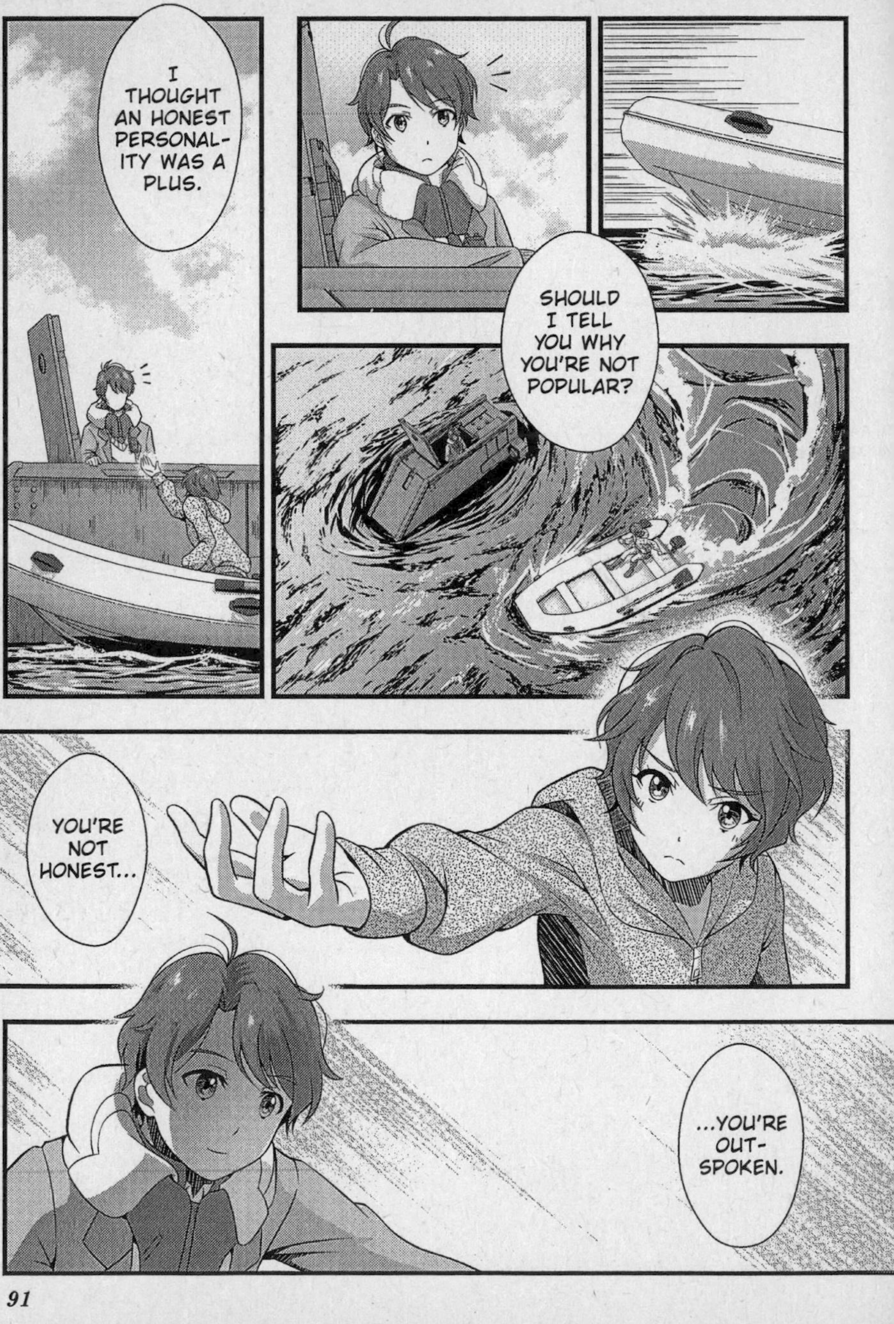
SHOULD I TELL YOU WHY YOU'RE NOT POPULAR?
I THOUGHT AN HONEST PERSONAL-ITY WAS A PLUS.
YOU'RE NOT HONEST...
...YOU'RE OUT-SPOKEN.

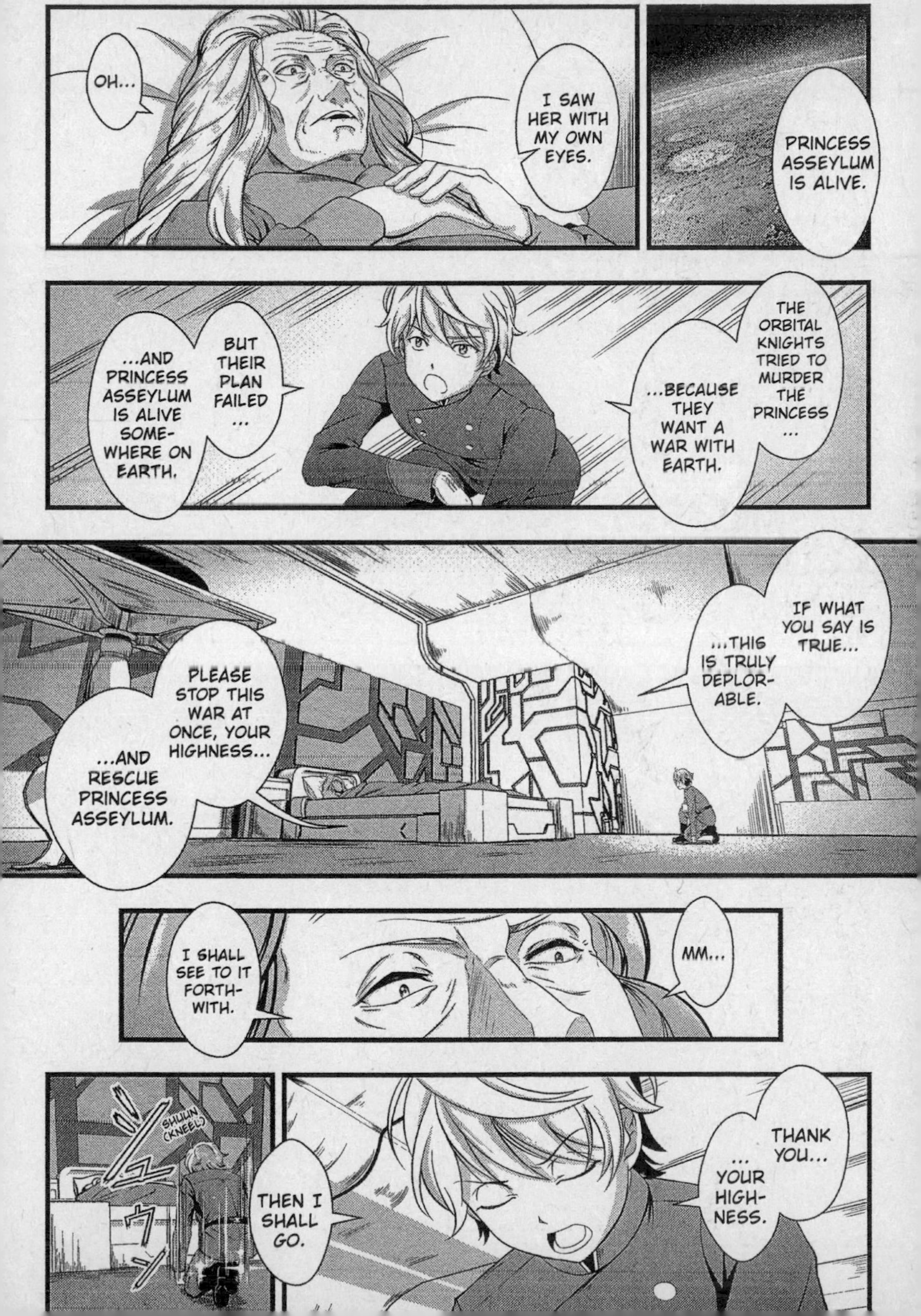
PRINCESS ASSEYLUM IS ALIVE.
I SAW HER WITH MY OWN EYES.
OH...
THE ORBITAL KNIGHTS TRIED TO MURDER THE PRINCESS...
...BECAUSE THEY WANT A WAR WITH EARTH.
BUT THEIR PLAN FAILED...
...AND PRINCESS ASSEYLUM IS ALIVE SOME-WHERE ON EARTH.
IF WHAT YOU SAY IS TRUE...
...THIS IS TRULY DEPLOR-ABLE.
PLEASE STOP THIS WAR AT ONCE, YOUR HIGHNESS...
...AND RESCUE PRINCESS ASSEYLUM.
MM...
I SHALL SEE TO IT FORTH-WITH.
THANK YOU...
...YOUR HIGH-NESS.
THEN I SHALL GO.
SHUUN (KNEEL)

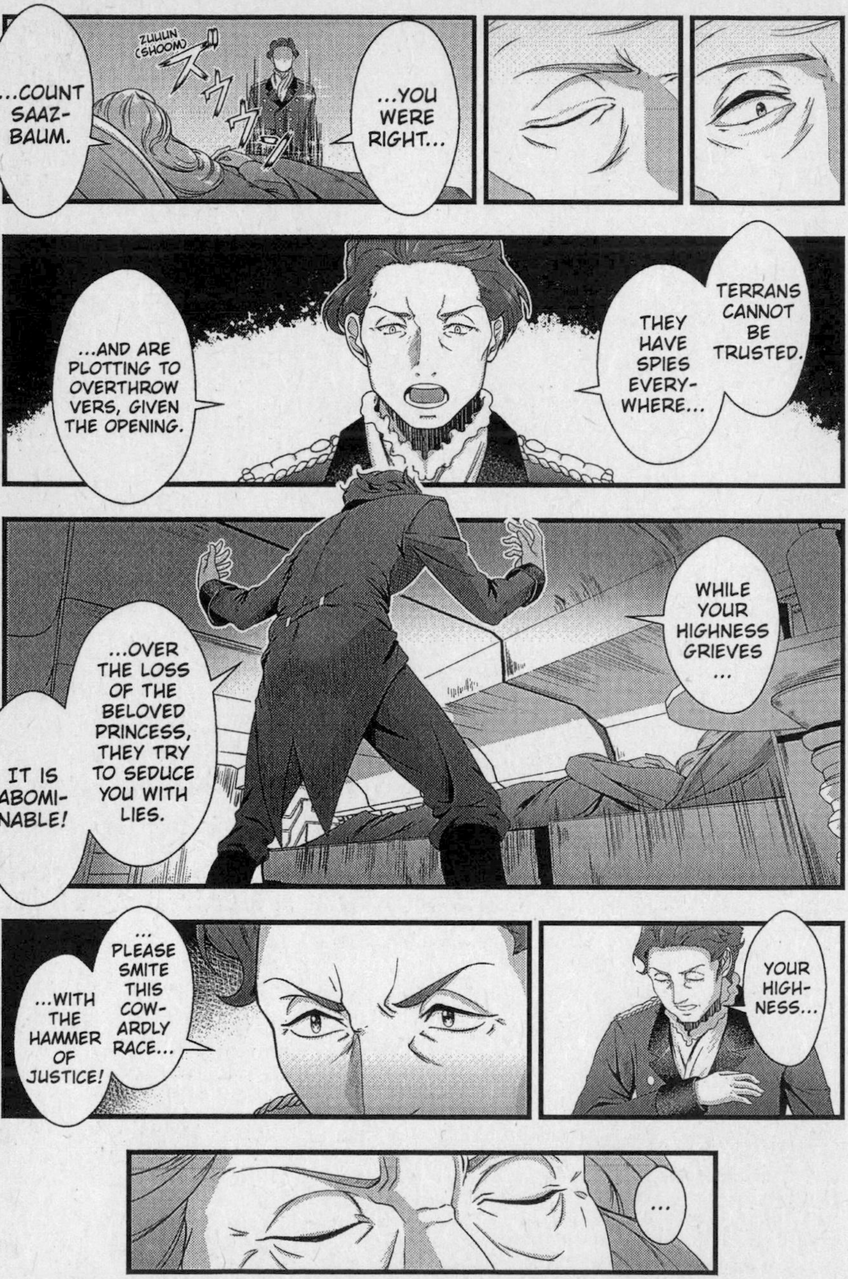
...YOU WERE RIGHT...
ZUUUN (SHOOM)
...COUNT SAAZBAUM.
TERRANS CANNOT BE TRUSTED.
THEY HAVE SPIES EVERYWHERE...
...AND ARE PLOTTING TO OVERTHROW VERS, GIVEN THE OPENING.
WHILE YOUR HIGHNESS GRIEVES...
...OVER THE LOSS OF THE BELOVED PRINCESS, THEY TRY TO SEDUCE YOU WITH LIES.
IT IS ABOMINABLE!
YOUR HIGHNESS...
...PLEASE SMITE THIS COWARDLY RACE...
...WITH THE HAMMER OF JUSTICE!
...

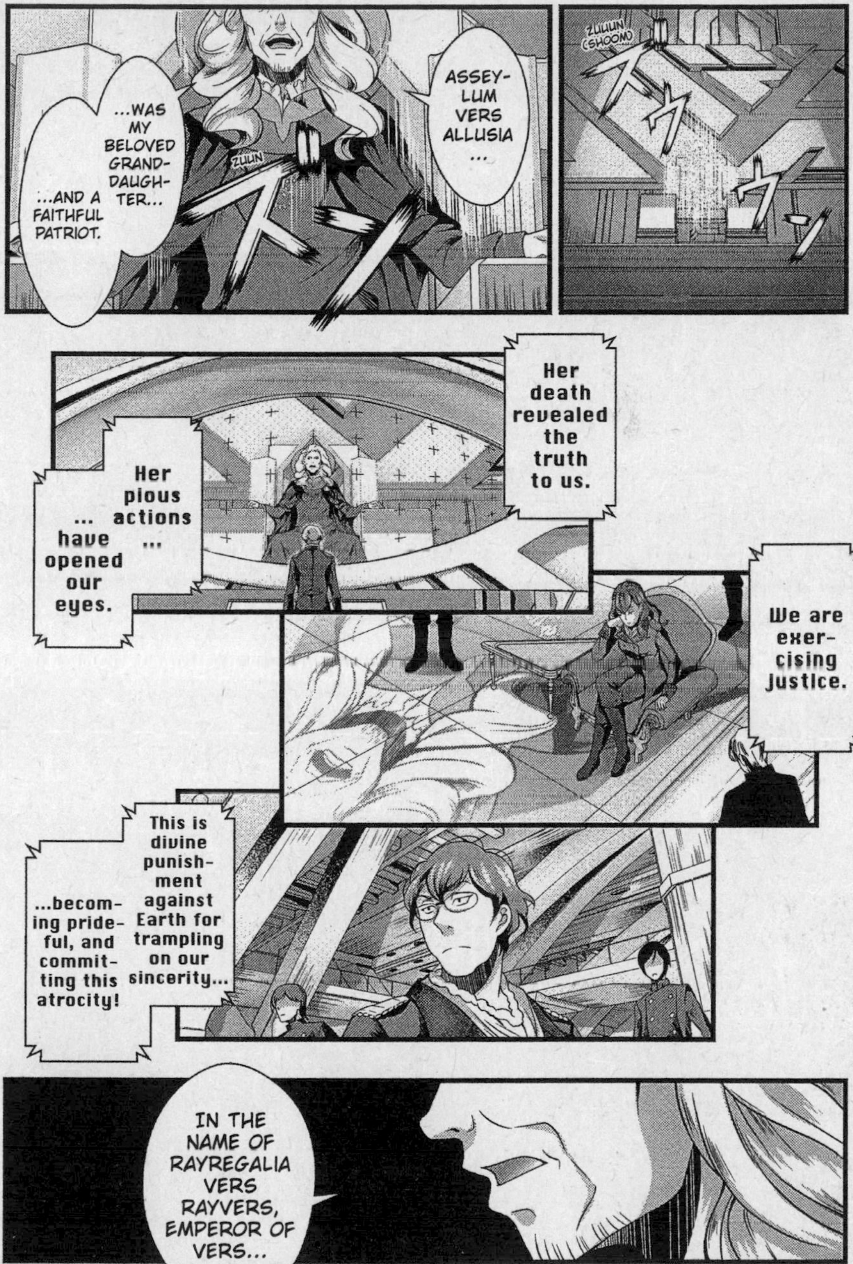
ZUUUN (SHOOM)
ASSEYLUM VERS ALLUSIA ...
ZUUN
...WAS MY BELOVED GRANDDAUGHTER...
...AND A FAITHFUL PATRIOT.
Her death revealed the truth to us.
Her pious actions ...
... have opened our eyes.
We are exercising justice.
This is divine punishment against Earth for trampling on our sincerity...
...becoming prideful, and committing this atrocity!
IN THE NAME OF RAYREGALIA VERS RAYVERS, EMPEROR OF VERS...

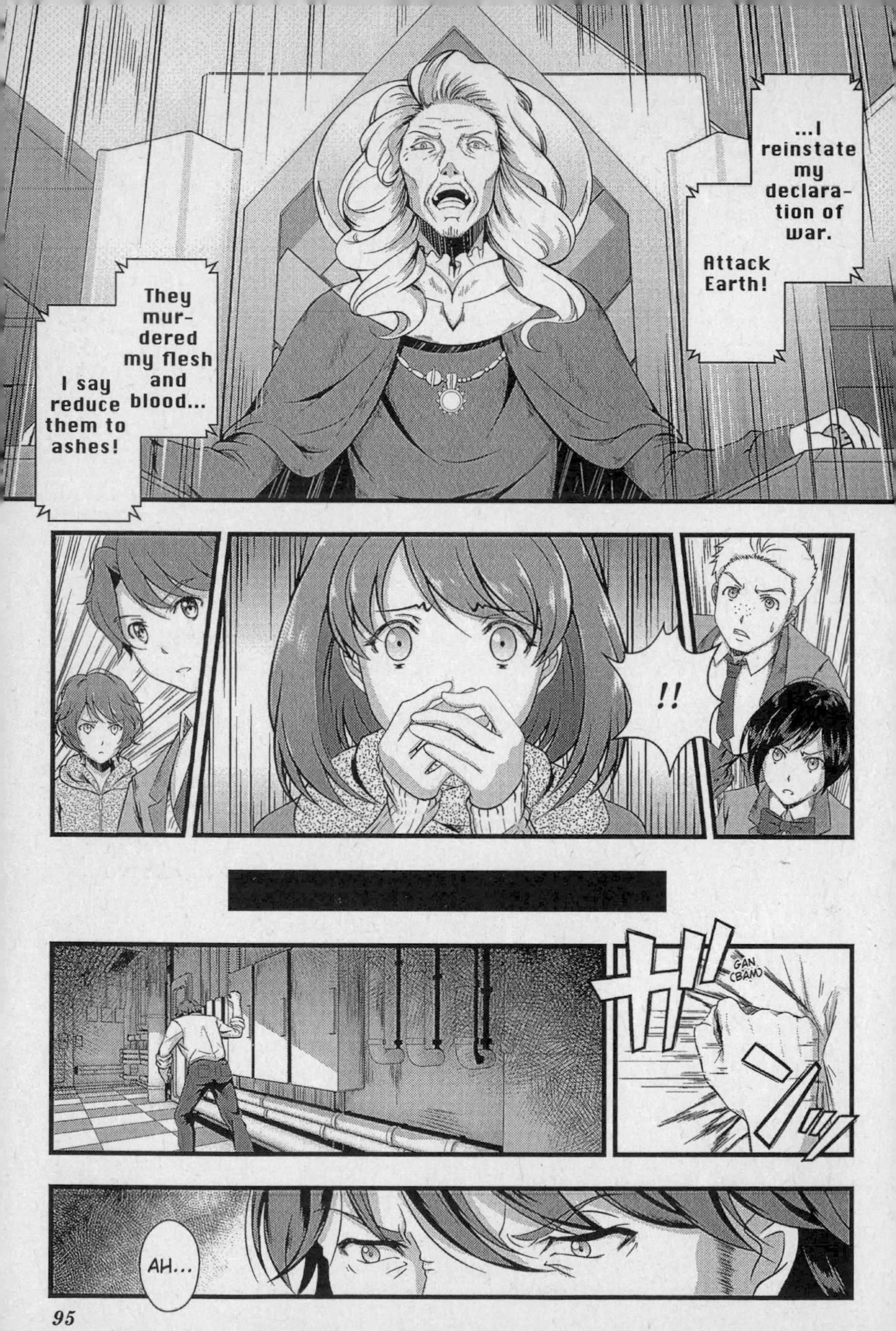
...I reinstate my declaration of war.
Attack Earth!
They murdered my flesh and blood...
I say reduce them to ashes!
!!
[redacted]
GAN (BAM)
AH...

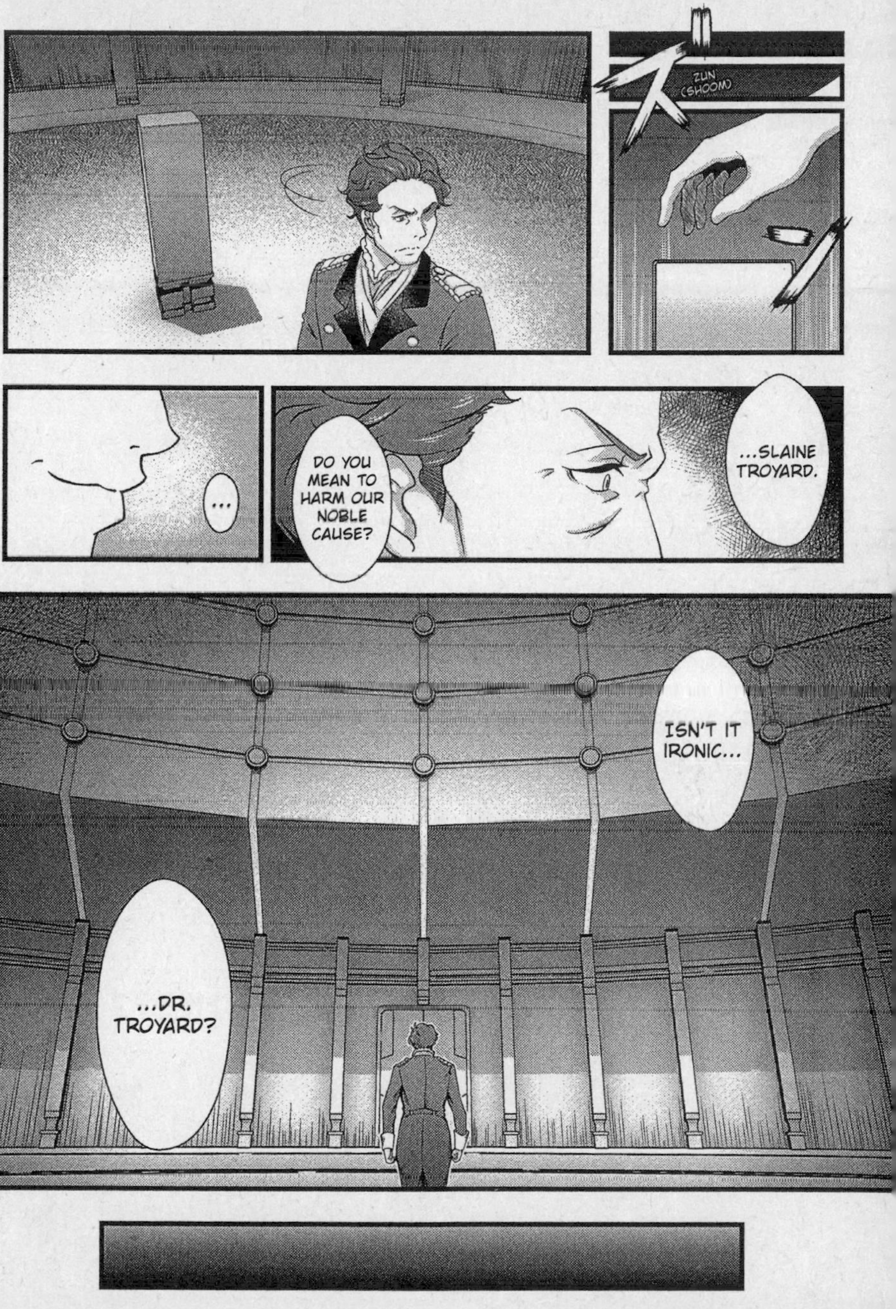
ZUN (SHOOM)
...SLAINE TROYARD.
DO YOU MEAN TO HARM OUR NOBLE CAUSE?
...
ISN'T IT IRONIC...
...DR. TROYARD?

EP06 Island of Memory — Steel Step Suite —

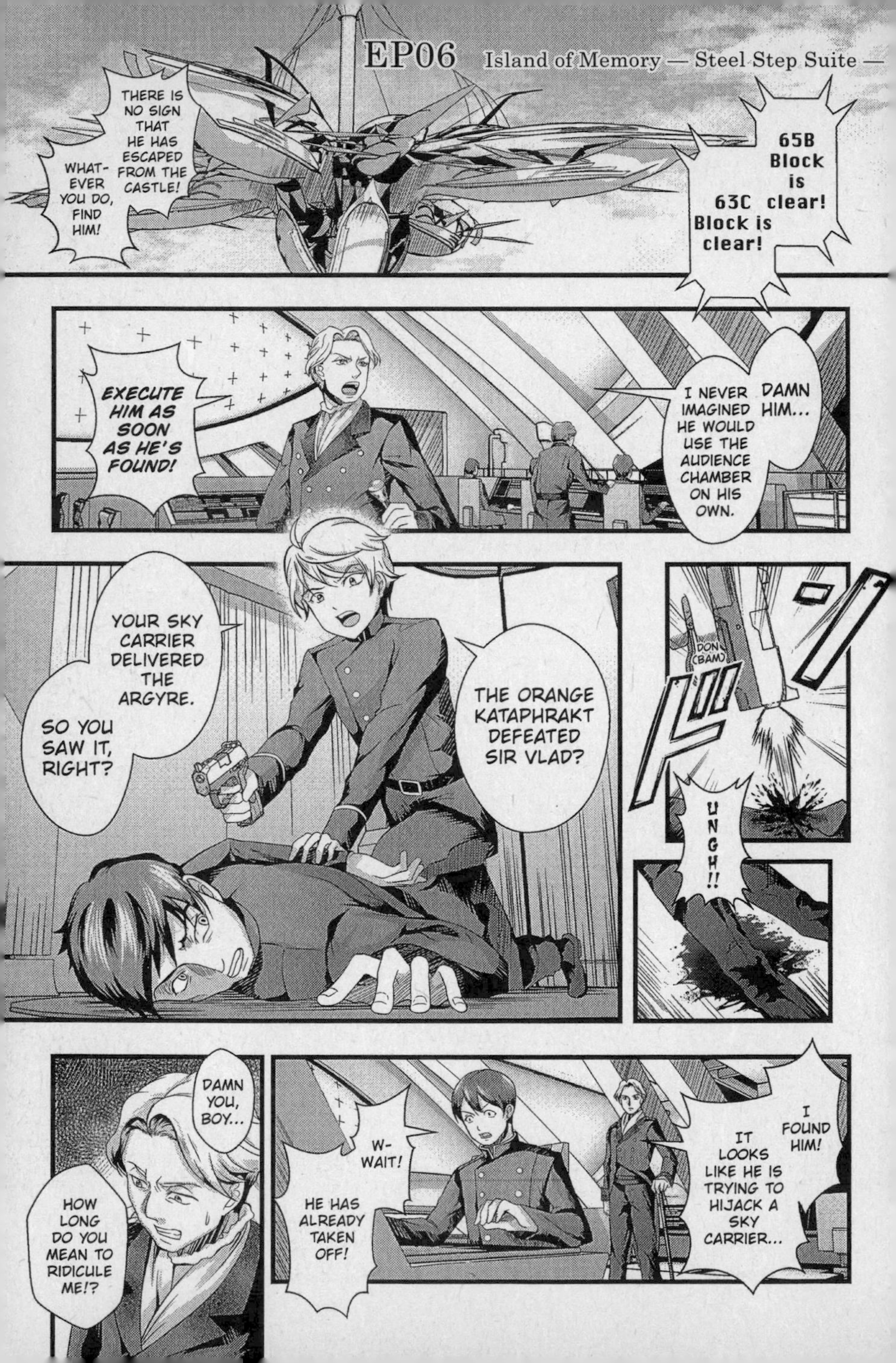
65B Block is clear!
63C Block is clear!
THERE IS NO SIGN THAT HE HAS ESCAPED FROM THE CASTLE!
WHATEVER YOU DO, FIND HIM!
DAMN HIM...
I NEVER IMAGINED HE WOULD USE THE AUDIENCE CHAMBER ON HIS OWN.
EXECUTE HIM AS SOON AS HE'S FOUND!
DON (BAM)
UNGH!!
THE ORANGE KATAPHRAKT DEFEATED SIR VLAD?
YOUR SKY CARRIER DELIVERED THE ARGYRE.
SO YOU SAW IT, RIGHT?
I FOUND HIM!
IT LOOKS LIKE HE IS TRYING TO HIJACK A SKY CARRIER...
W-WAIT!
HE HAS ALREADY TAKEN OFF!
DAMN YOU, BOY...
HOW LONG DO YOU MEAN TO RIDICULE ME!?

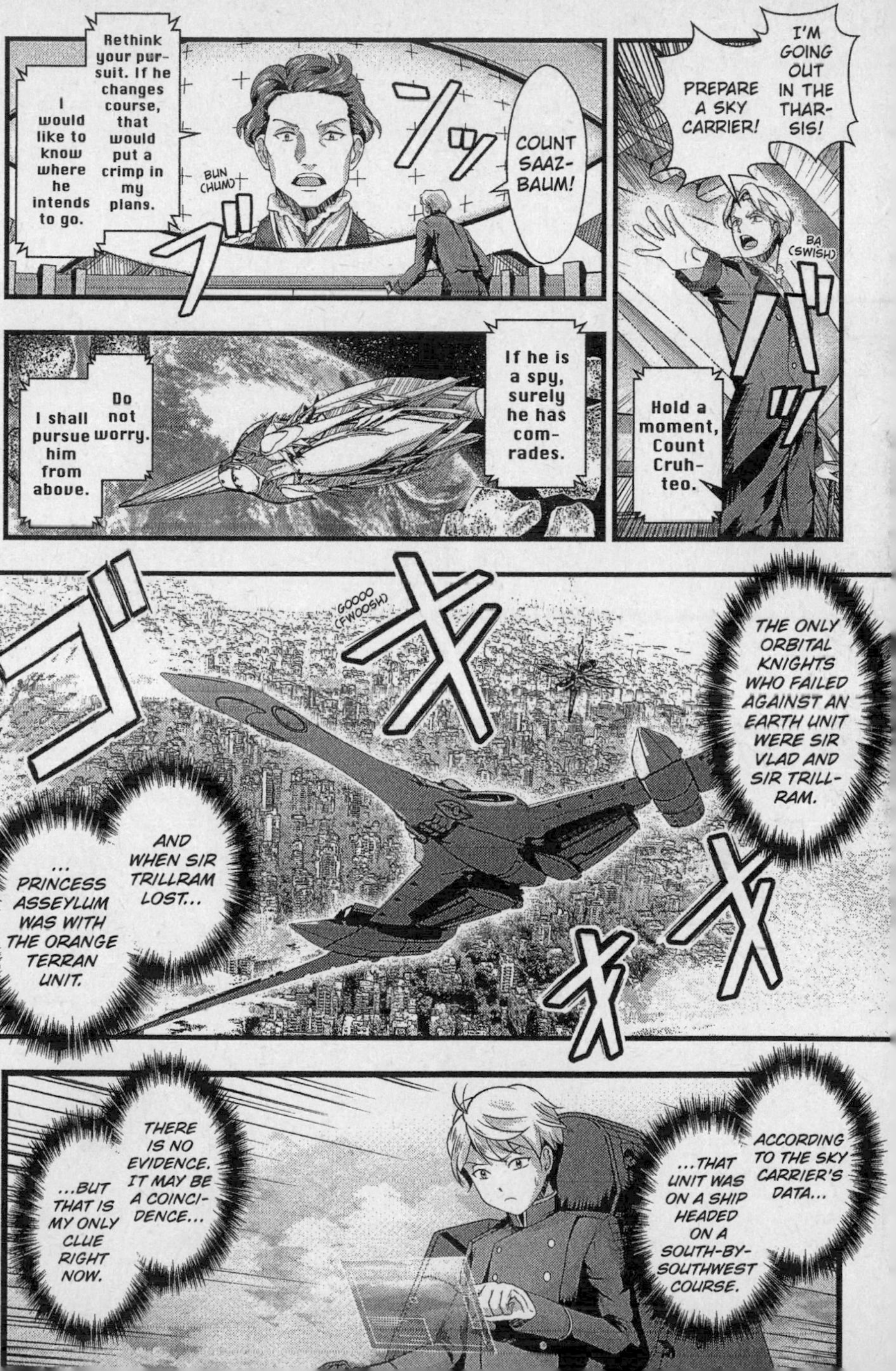
I'M GOING OUT IN THE THARSIS!
PREPARE A SKY CARRIER!
BA (SWISH)
Hold a moment, Count Cruhteo.
COUNT SAAZBAUM!
Rethink your pursuit. If he changes course, that would put a crimp in my plans.
BUN (HUM)
I would like to know where he intends to go.
If he is a spy, surely he has comrades.
Do not worry.
I shall pursue him from above.
GOOOO (FWOOSH)
THE ONLY ORBITAL KNIGHTS WHO FAILED AGAINST AN EARTH UNIT WERE SIR VLAD AND SIR TRILLRAM.
AND WHEN SIR TRILLRAM LOST...
...PRINCESS ASSEYLUM WAS WITH THE ORANGE TERRAN UNIT.
ACCORDING TO THE SKY CARRIER'S DATA...
...THAT UNIT WAS ON A SHIP HEADED ON A SOUTH-BY-SOUTHWEST COURSE.
THERE IS NO EVIDENCE. IT MAY BE A COINCIDENCE...
...BUT THAT IS MY ONLY CLUE RIGHT NOW.

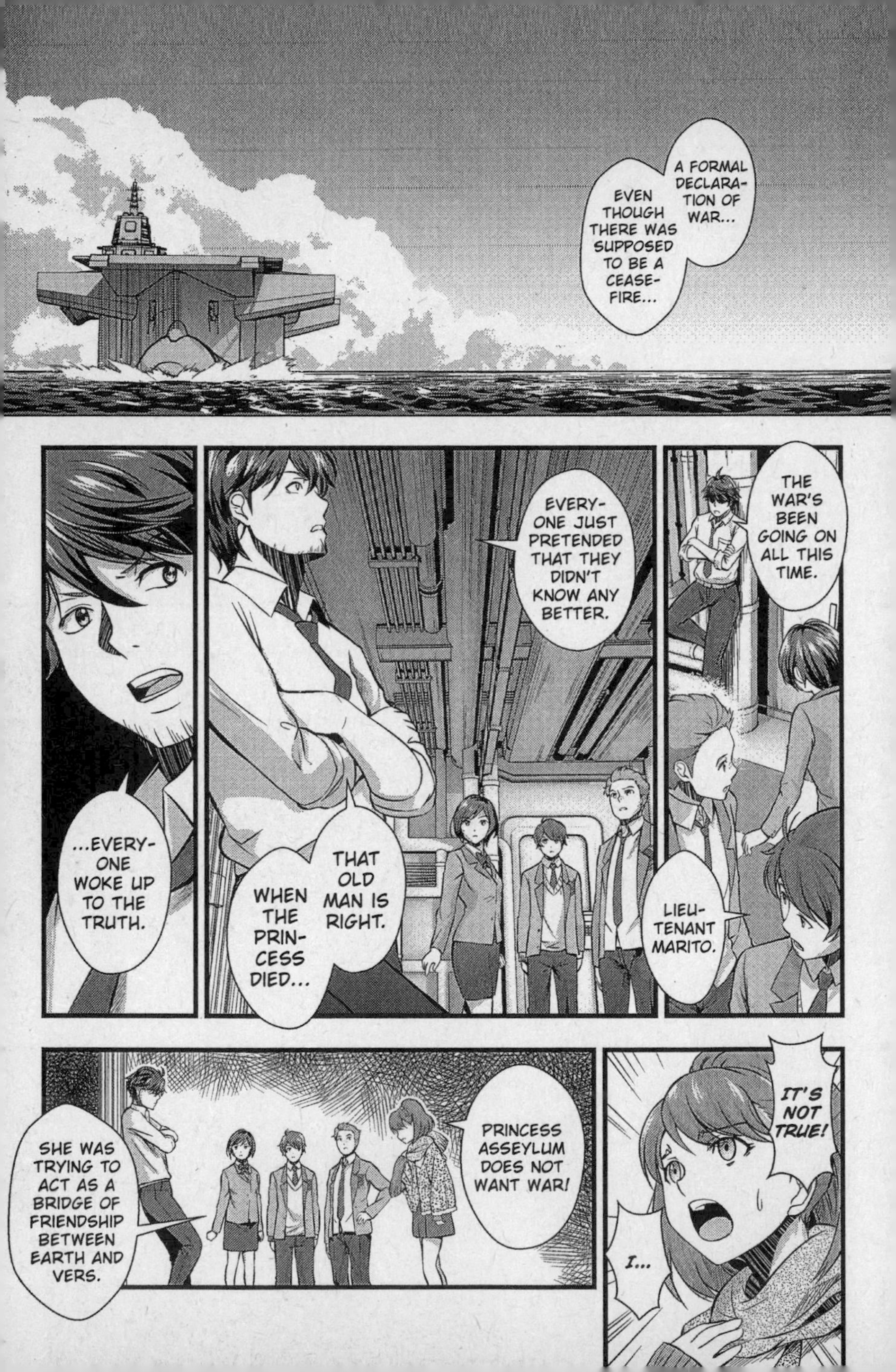
A FORMAL DECLARATION OF WAR...
EVEN THOUGH THERE WAS SUPPOSED TO BE A CEASE-FIRE...
THE WAR'S BEEN GOING ON ALL THIS TIME.
LIEUTENANT MARITO.
EVERYONE JUST PRETENDED THAT THEY DIDN'T KNOW ANY BETTER.
THAT OLD MAN IS RIGHT.
WHEN THE PRINCESS DIED...
...EVERYONE WOKE UP TO THE TRUTH.
IT'S NOT TRUE!
I...
PRINCESS ASSEYLUM DOES NOT WANT WAR!
SHE WAS TRYING TO ACT AS A BRIDGE OF FRIENDSHIP BETWEEN EARTH AND VERS.

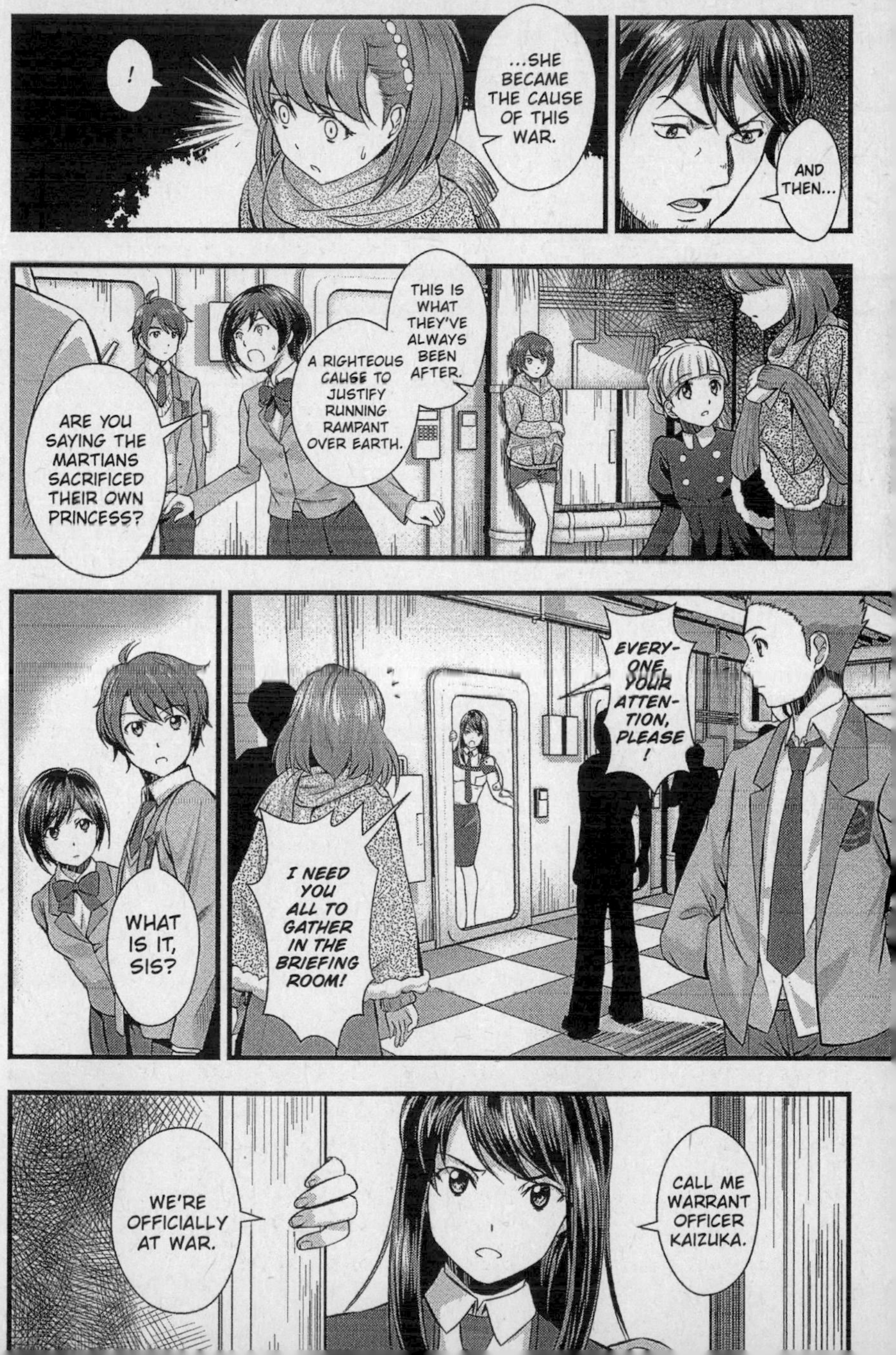
AND THEN...
...SHE BECAME THE CAUSE OF THIS WAR.
!
THIS IS WHAT THEY'VE ALWAYS BEEN AFTER.
A RIGHTEOUS CAUSE TO JUSTIFY RUNNING RAMPANT OVER EARTH.
ARE YOU SAYING THE MARTIANS SACRIFICED THEIR OWN PRINCESS?
EVERYONE, YOUR ATTENTION, PLEASE!
I NEED YOU ALL TO GATHER IN THE BRIEFING ROOM!
WHAT IS IT, SIS?
CALL ME WARRANT OFFICER KAIZUKA.
WE'RE OFFICIALLY AT WAR.

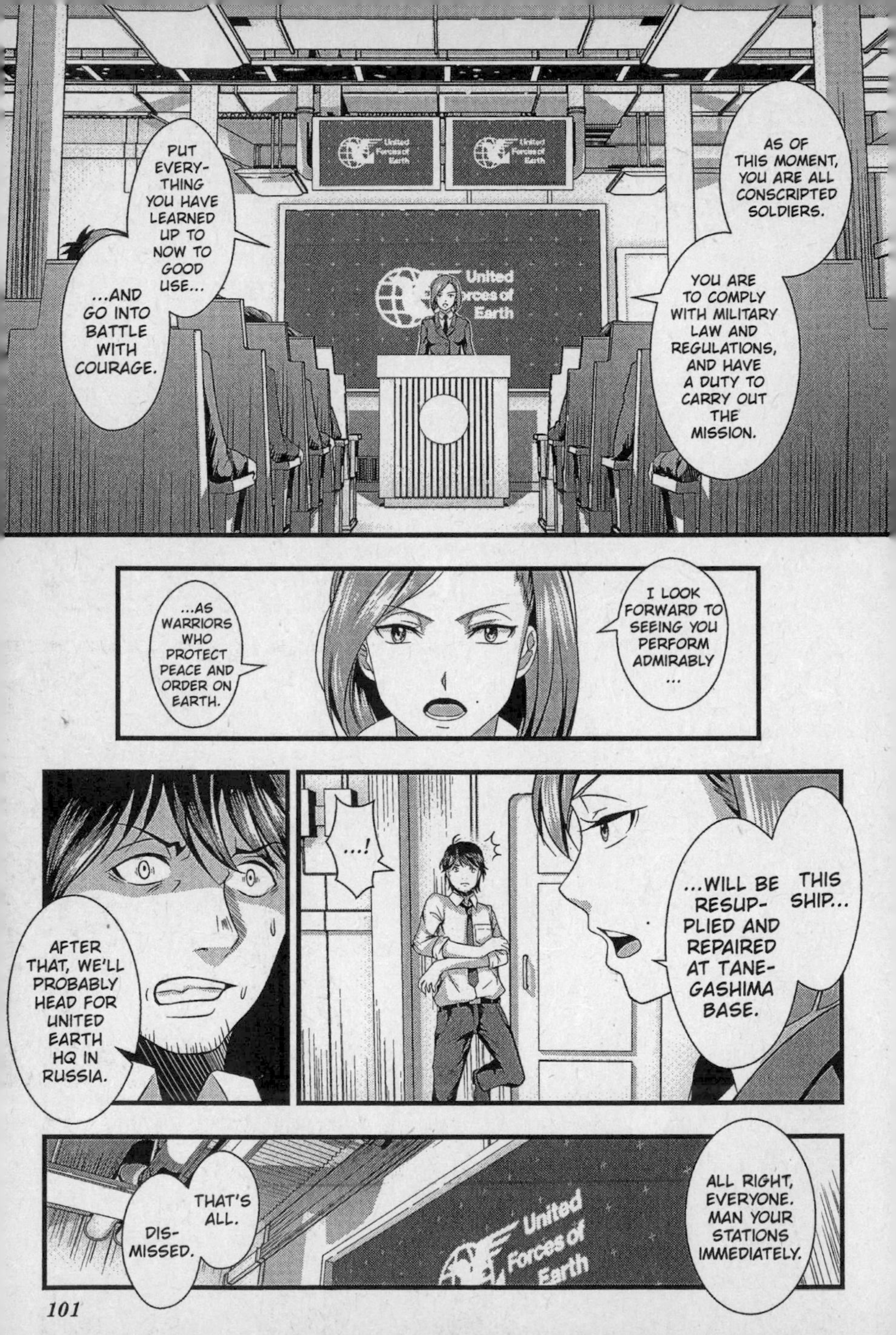
AS OF THIS MOMENT, YOU ARE ALL CONSCRIPTED SOLDIERS.
YOU ARE TO COMPLY WITH MILITARY LAW AND REGULATIONS, AND HAVE A DUTY TO CARRY OUT THE MISSION.
United Forces of Earth
PUT EVERY-THING YOU HAVE LEARNED UP TO NOW TO GOOD USE...
...AND GO INTO BATTLE WITH COURAGE.
I LOOK FORWARD TO SEEING YOU PERFORM ADMIRABLY ...
...AS WARRIORS WHO PROTECT PEACE AND ORDER ON EARTH.
THIS SHIP...
...WILL BE RESUP-PLIED AND REPAIRED AT TANE-GASHIMA BASE.
...!
AFTER THAT, WE'LL PROBABLY HEAD FOR UNITED EARTH HQ IN RUSSIA.
ALL RIGHT, EVERYONE. MAN YOUR STATIONS IMMEDIATELY.
THAT'S ALL.
DIS-MISSED.
United Forces of Earth

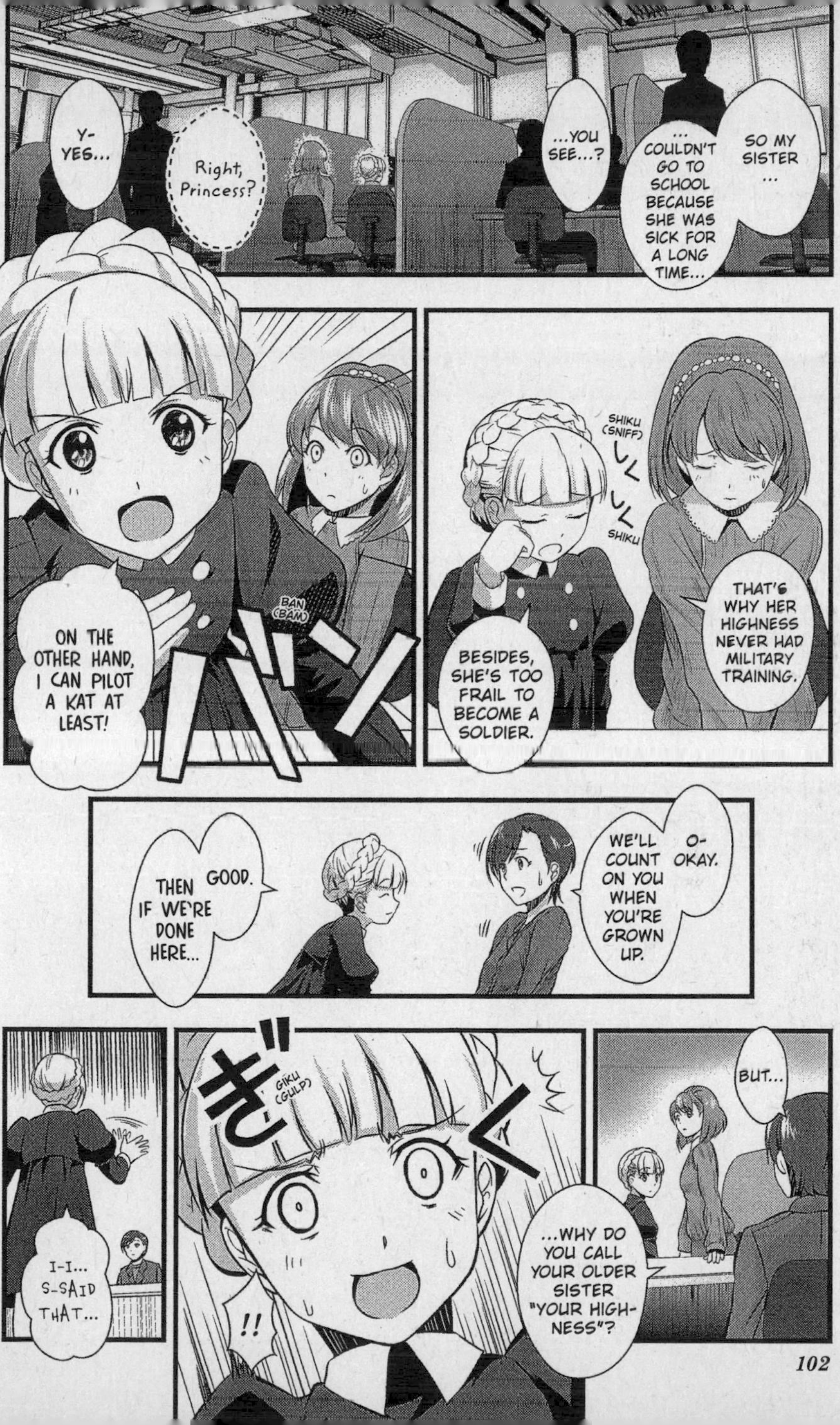
SO MY SISTER ...
... COULDN'T GO TO SCHOOL BECAUSE SHE WAS SICK FOR A LONG TIME...
...YOU SEE...?
Right, Princess?
Y-YES...
THAT'S WHY HER HIGHNESS NEVER HAD MILITARY TRAINING.
SHIKU (SNIFF)
SHIKU
BESIDES, SHE'S TOO FRAIL TO BECOME A SOLDIER.
BAN (BAM)
ON THE OTHER HAND, I CAN PILOT A KAT AT LEAST!
O-OKAY.
WE'LL COUNT ON YOU WHEN YOU'RE GROWN UP.
GOOD.
THEN IF WE'RE DONE HERE...
BUT...
...WHY DO YOU CALL YOUR OLDER SISTER "YOUR HIGH-NESS"?
GIKU (GULP)
!!
I-I... S-SAID THAT...

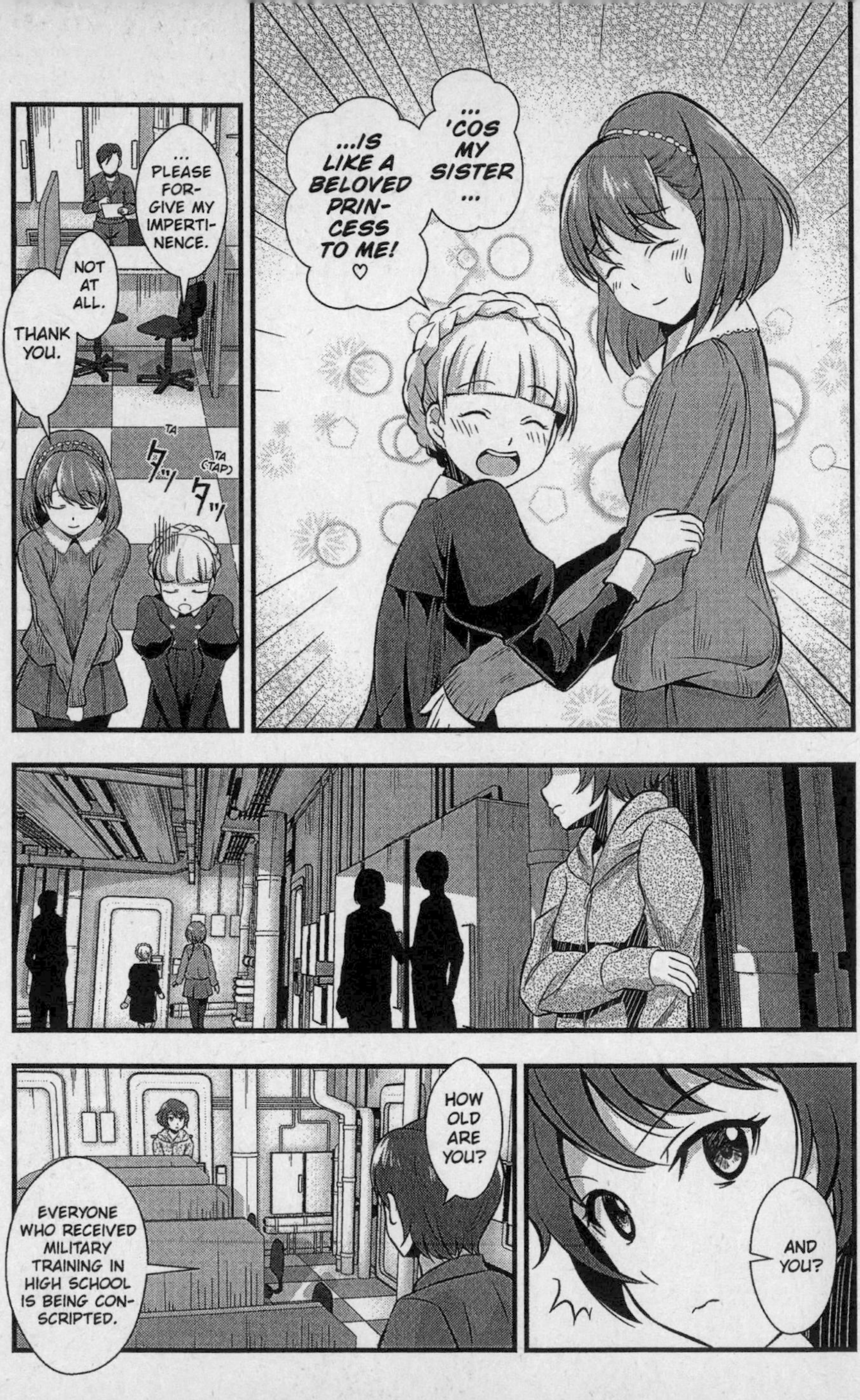
...'COS MY SISTER ...
...IS LIKE A BELOVED PRIN-CESS TO ME! ♡
... PLEASE FOR-GIVE MY IMPERTI-NENCE.
NOT AT ALL.
THANK YOU.
TA
TA (TAP)
AND YOU?
HOW OLD ARE YOU?
EVERYONE WHO RECEIVED MILITARY TRAINING IN HIGH SCHOOL IS BEING CON-SCRIPTED.

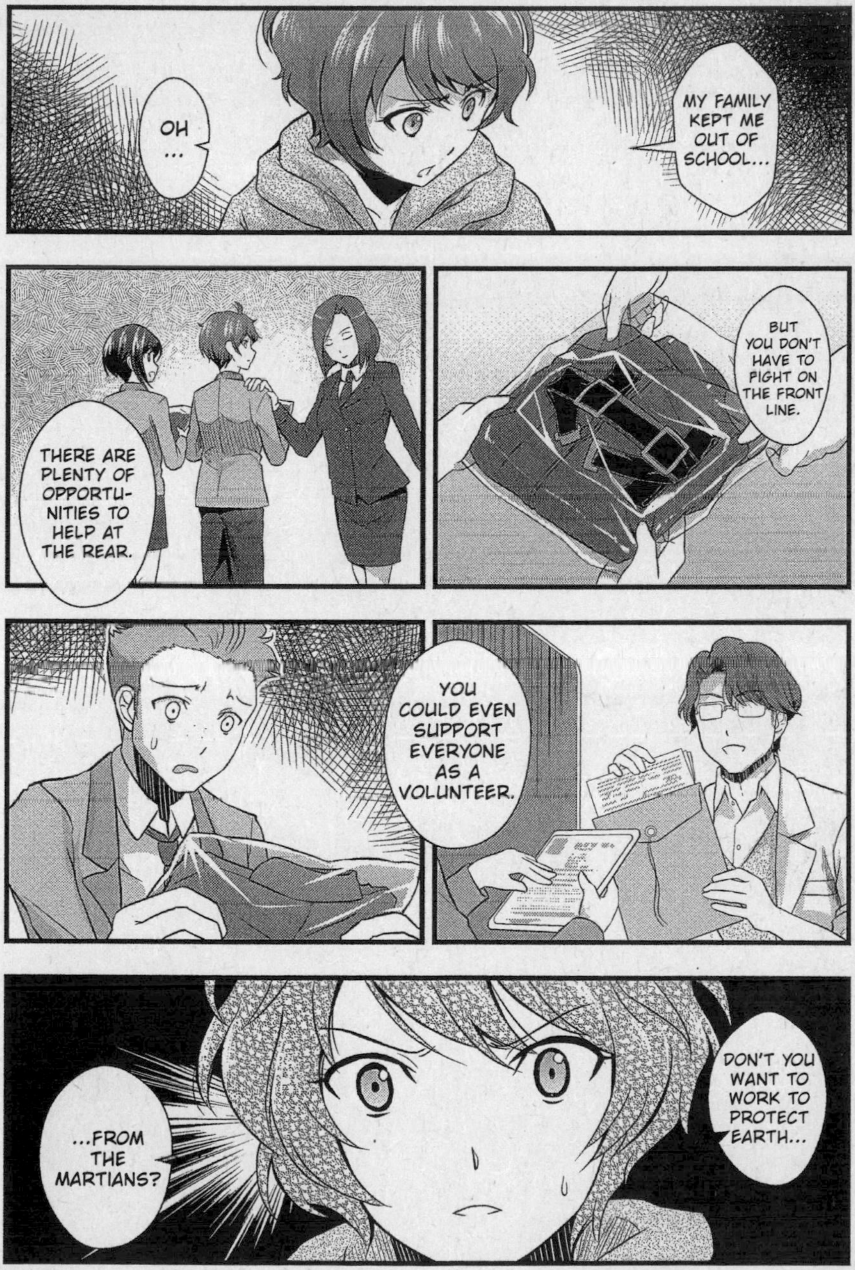
MY FAMILY KEPT ME OUT OF SCHOOL...
OH ...
BUT YOU DON'T HAVE TO FIGHT ON THE FRONT LINE.
THERE ARE PLENTY OF OPPORTU-NITIES TO HELP AT THE REAR.
YOU COULD EVEN SUPPORT EVERYONE AS A VOLUNTEER.
DON'T YOU WANT TO WORK TO PROTECT EARTH...
...FROM THE MARTIANS?

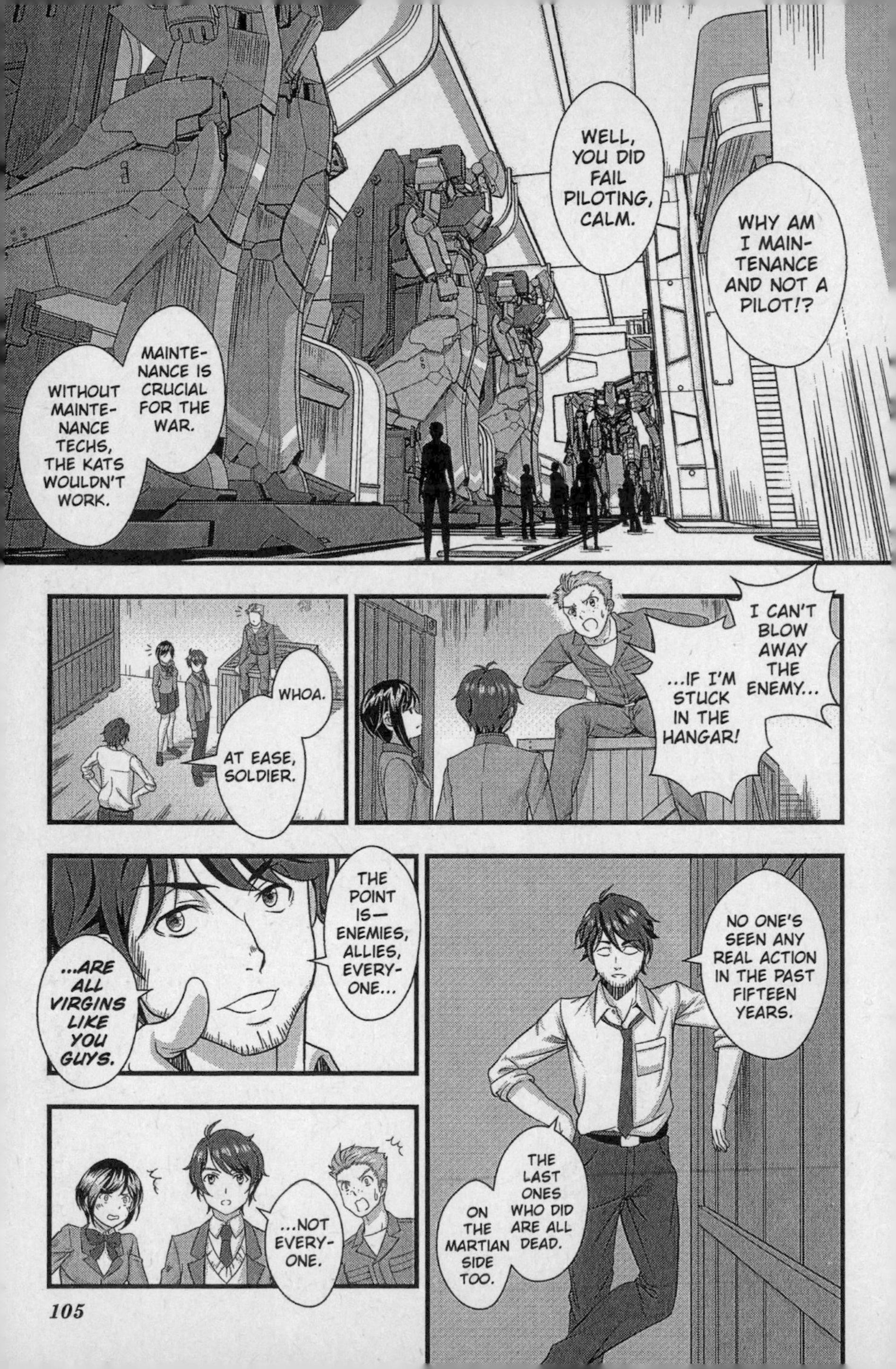
WHY AM I MAINTENANCE AND NOT A PILOT!?
WELL, YOU DID FAIL PILOTING, CALM.
MAINTENANCE IS CRUCIAL FOR THE WAR.
WITHOUT MAINTENANCE TECHS, THE KATS WOULDN'T WORK.
I CAN'T BLOW AWAY THE ENEMY...
...IF I'M STUCK IN THE HANGAR!
WHOA.
AT EASE, SOLDIER.
NO ONE'S SEEN ANY REAL ACTION IN THE PAST FIFTEEN YEARS.
THE LAST ONES WHO DID ARE ALL DEAD.
ON THE MARTIAN SIDE TOO.
THE POINT IS—ENEMIES, ALLIES, EVERYONE...
...ARE ALL VIRGINS LIKE YOU GUYS.
...NOT EVERYONE.

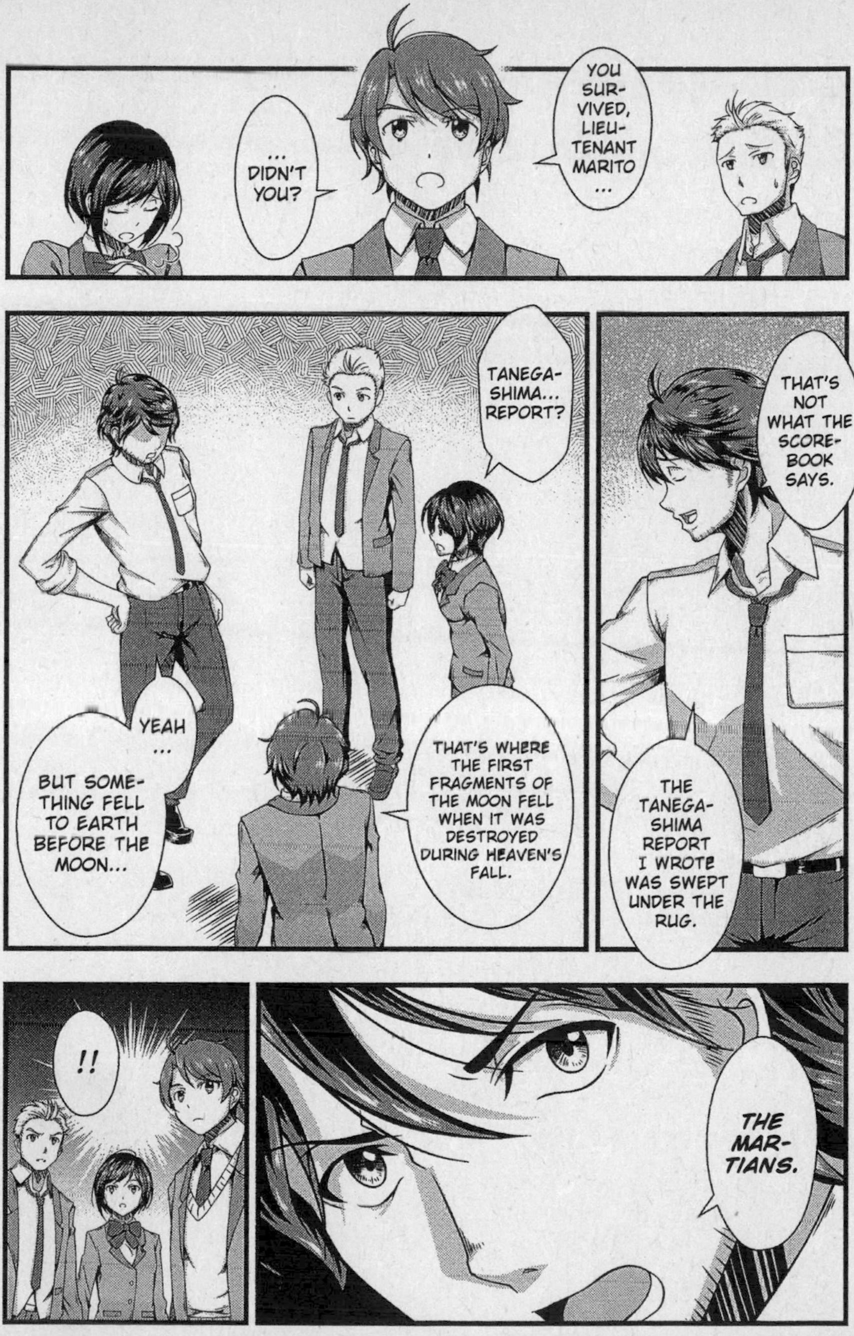
YOU SURVIVED, LIEUTENANT MARITO...
...DIDN'T YOU?
THAT'S NOT WHAT THE SCOREBOOK SAYS.
THE TANEGASHIMA REPORT I WROTE WAS SWEPT UNDER THE RUG.
TANEGASHIMA... REPORT?
THAT'S WHERE THE FIRST FRAGMENTS OF THE MOON FELL WHEN IT WAS DESTROYED DURING HEAVEN'S FALL.
YEAH... BUT SOMETHING FELL TO EARTH BEFORE THE MOON...
THE MARTIANS.
!!

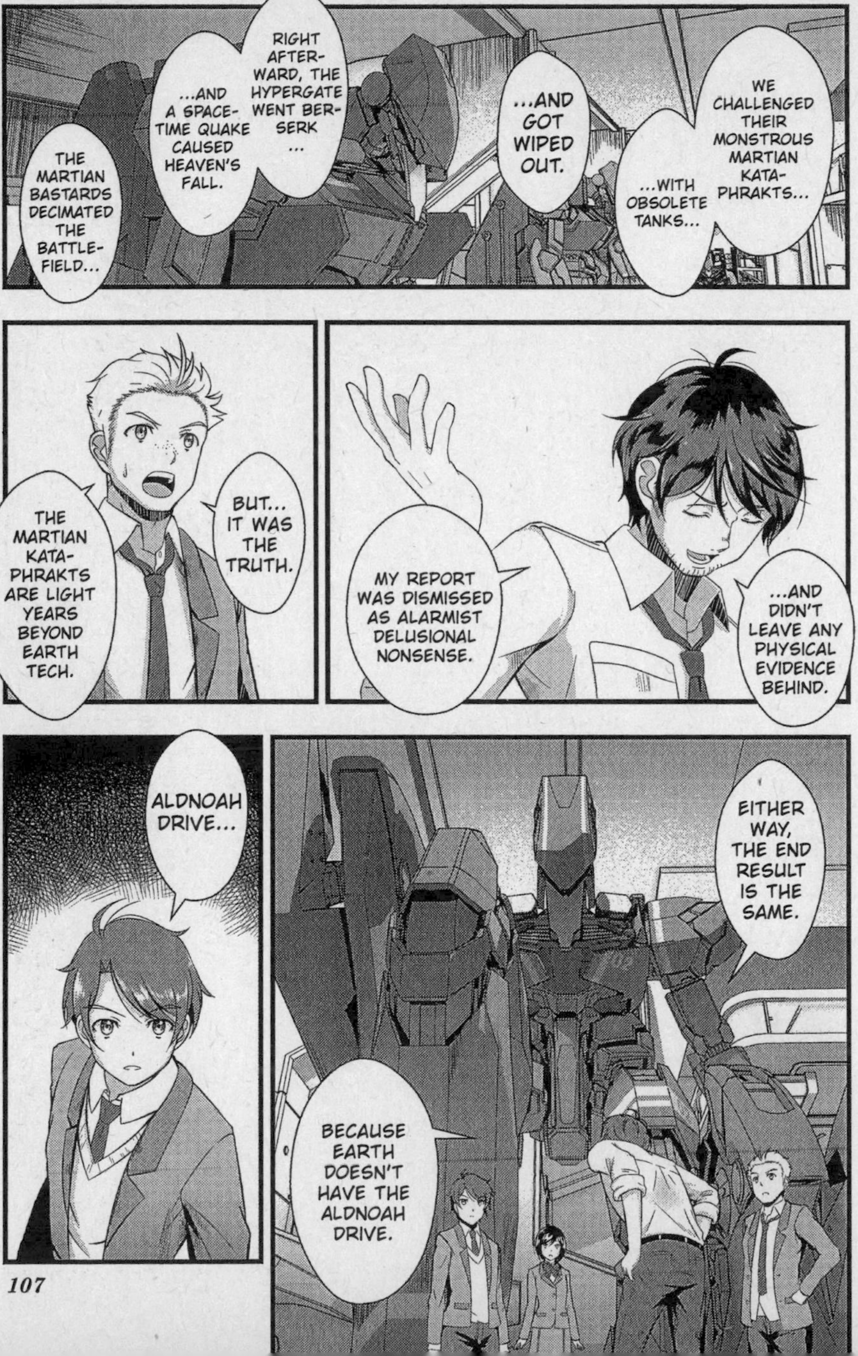

WE CHALLENGED THEIR MONSTROUS MARTIAN KATA-PHRAKTS...
...WITH OBSOLETE TANKS...
...AND GOT WIPED OUT.
RIGHT AFTER-WARD, THE HYPERGATE WENT BER-SERK ...
...AND A SPACE-TIME QUAKE CAUSED HEAVEN'S FALL.
THE MARTIAN BASTARDS DECIMATED THE BATTLE-FIELD...
...AND DIDN'T LEAVE ANY PHYSICAL EVIDENCE BEHIND.
MY REPORT WAS DISMISSED AS ALARMIST DELUSIONAL NONSENSE.
BUT... IT WAS THE TRUTH.
THE MARTIAN KATA-PHRAKTS ARE LIGHT YEARS BEYOND EARTH TECH.
EITHER WAY, THE END RESULT IS THE SAME.
BECAUSE EARTH DOESN'T HAVE THE ALDNOAH DRIVE.
ALDNOAH DRIVE...

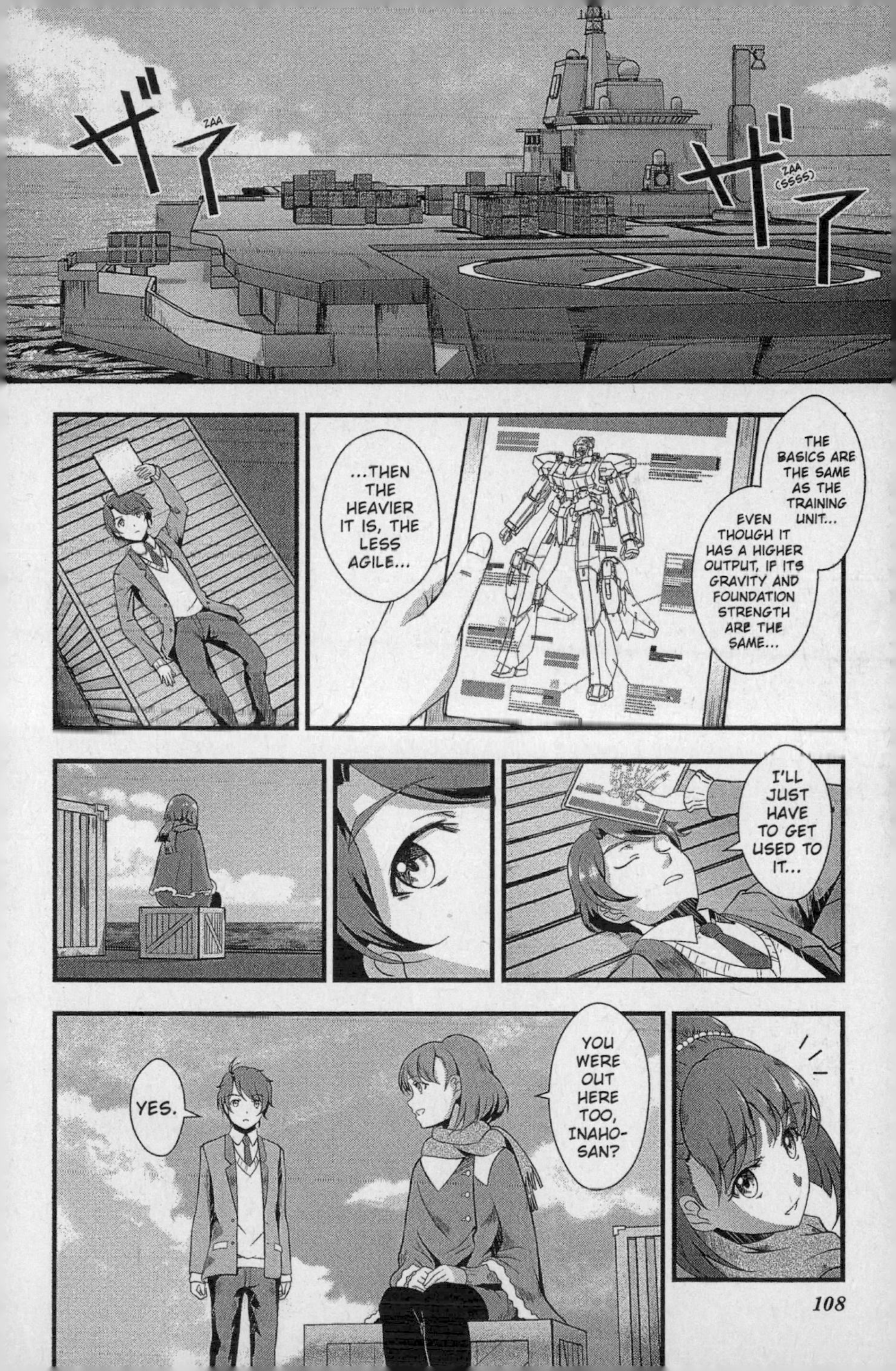
ZAA (SSSS)
ZAA
THE BASICS ARE THE SAME AS THE TRAINING UNIT...
EVEN THOUGH IT HAS A HIGHER OUTPUT, IF ITS GRAVITY AND FOUNDATION STRENGTH ARE THE SAME...
...THEN THE HEAVIER IT IS, THE LESS AGILE...
I'LL JUST HAVE TO GET USED TO IT...
YOU WERE OUT HERE TOO, INAHO-SAN?
YES.

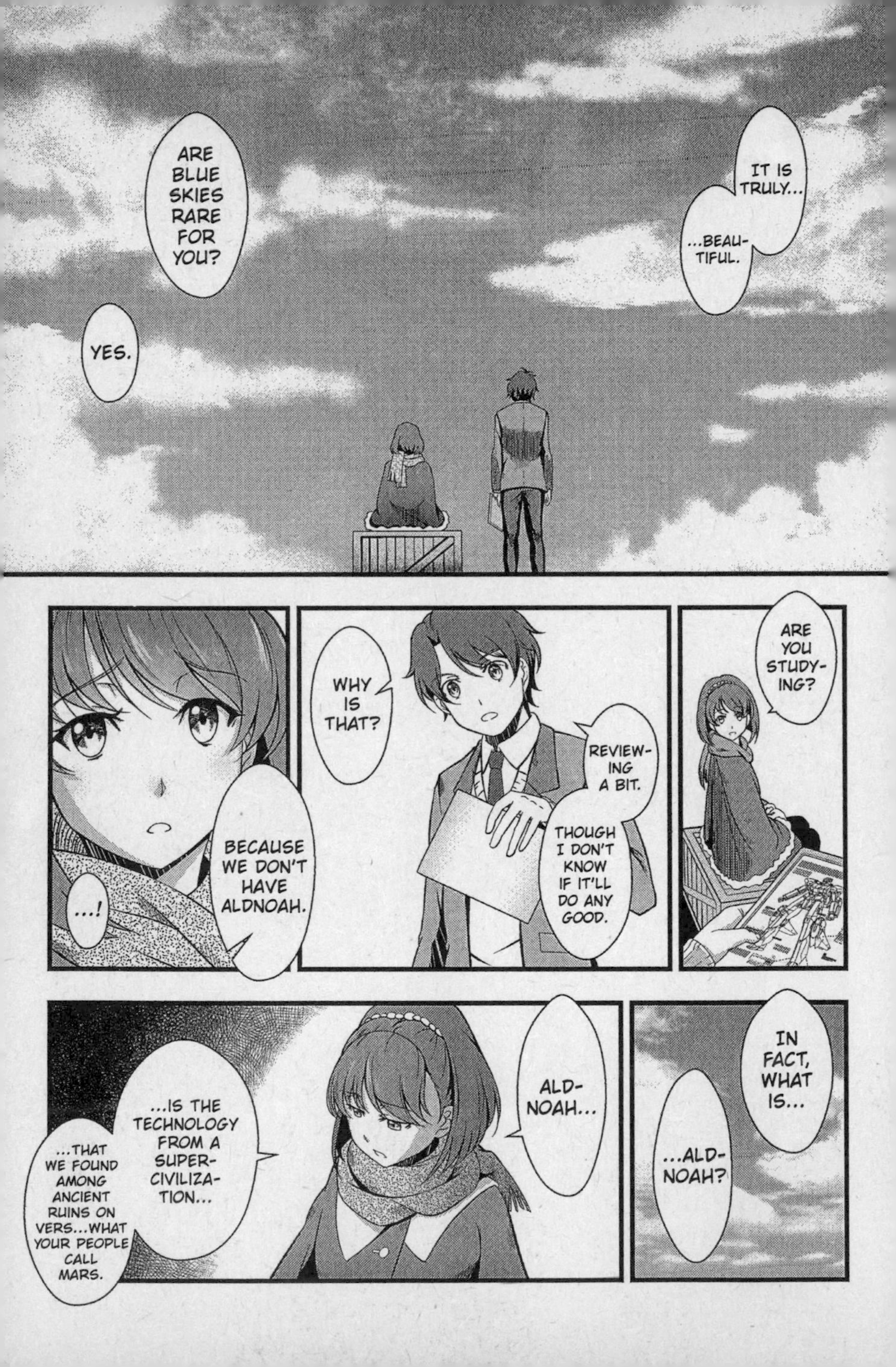
IT IS TRULY...
...BEAUTIFUL.
ARE BLUE SKIES RARE FOR YOU?
YES.
ARE YOU STUDYING?
REVIEWING A BIT.
THOUGH I DON'T KNOW IF IT'LL DO ANY GOOD.
WHY IS THAT?
BECAUSE WE DON'T HAVE ALDNOAH.
...!
IN FACT, WHAT IS...
...ALDNOAH?
ALDNOAH...
...IS THE TECHNOLOGY FROM A SUPER-CIVILIZATION...
...THAT WE FOUND AMONG ANCIENT RUINS ON VERS...WHAT YOUR PEOPLE CALL MARS.

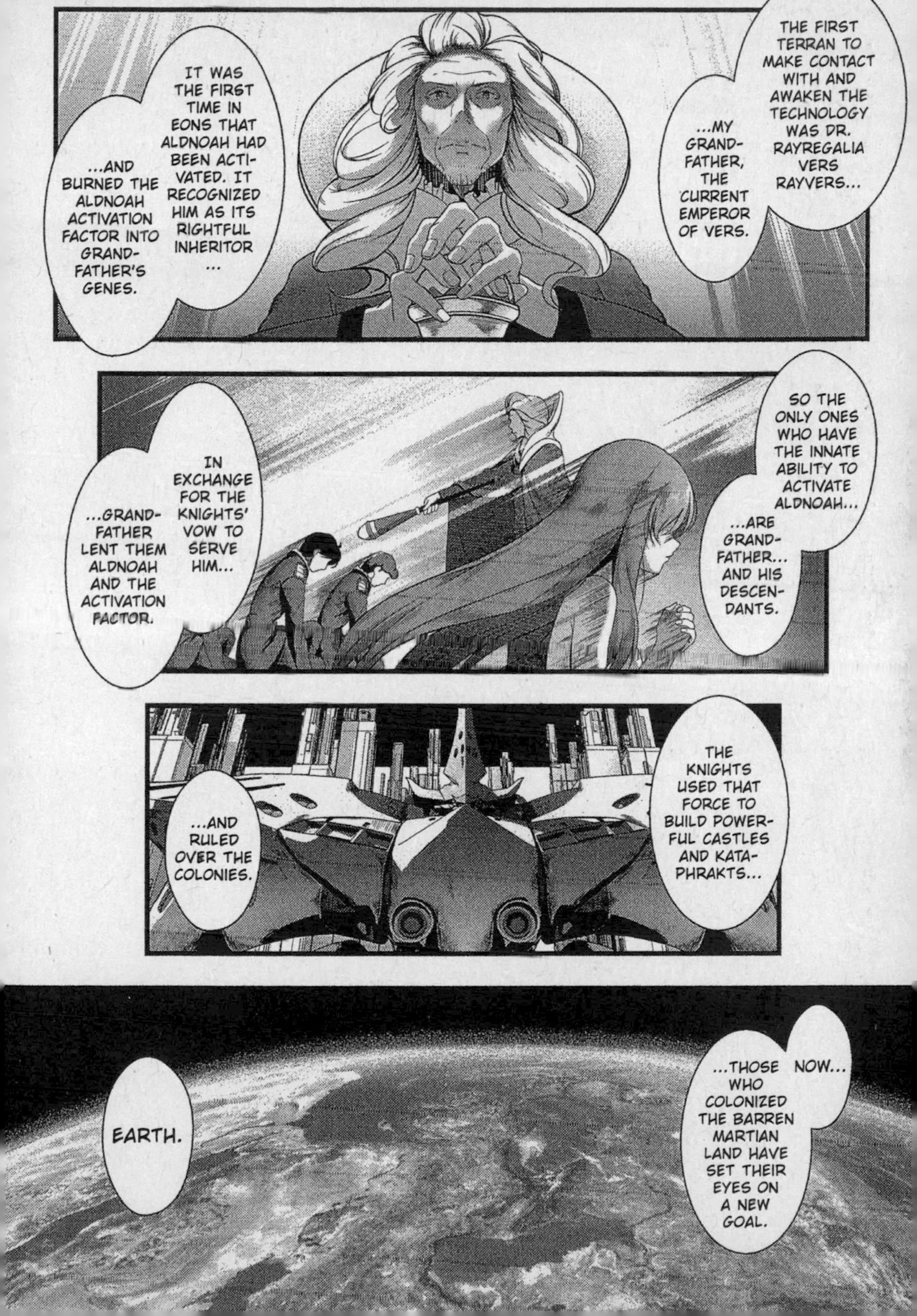
THE FIRST TERRAN TO MAKE CONTACT WITH AND AWAKEN THE TECHNOLOGY WAS DR. RAYREGALIA VERS RAYVERS...
...MY GRAND-FATHER, THE CURRENT EMPEROR OF VERS.
IT WAS THE FIRST TIME IN EONS THAT ALDNOAH HAD BEEN ACTI-VATED. IT RECOGNIZED HIM AS ITS RIGHTFUL INHERITOR...
...AND BURNED THE ALDNOAH ACTIVATION FACTOR INTO GRAND-FATHER'S GENES.
SO THE ONLY ONES WHO HAVE THE INNATE ABILITY TO ACTIVATE ALDNOAH...
...ARE GRAND-FATHER... AND HIS DESCEN-DANTS.
IN EXCHANGE FOR THE KNIGHTS' VOW TO SERVE HIM...
...GRAND-FATHER LENT THEM ALDNOAH AND THE ACTIVATION FACTOR.
THE KNIGHTS USED THAT FORCE TO BUILD POWER-FUL CASTLES AND KATA-PHRAKTS...
...AND RULED OVER THE COLONIES.
NOW...
...THOSE WHO COLONIZED THE BARREN MARTIAN LAND HAVE SET THEIR EYES ON A NEW GOAL.
EARTH.

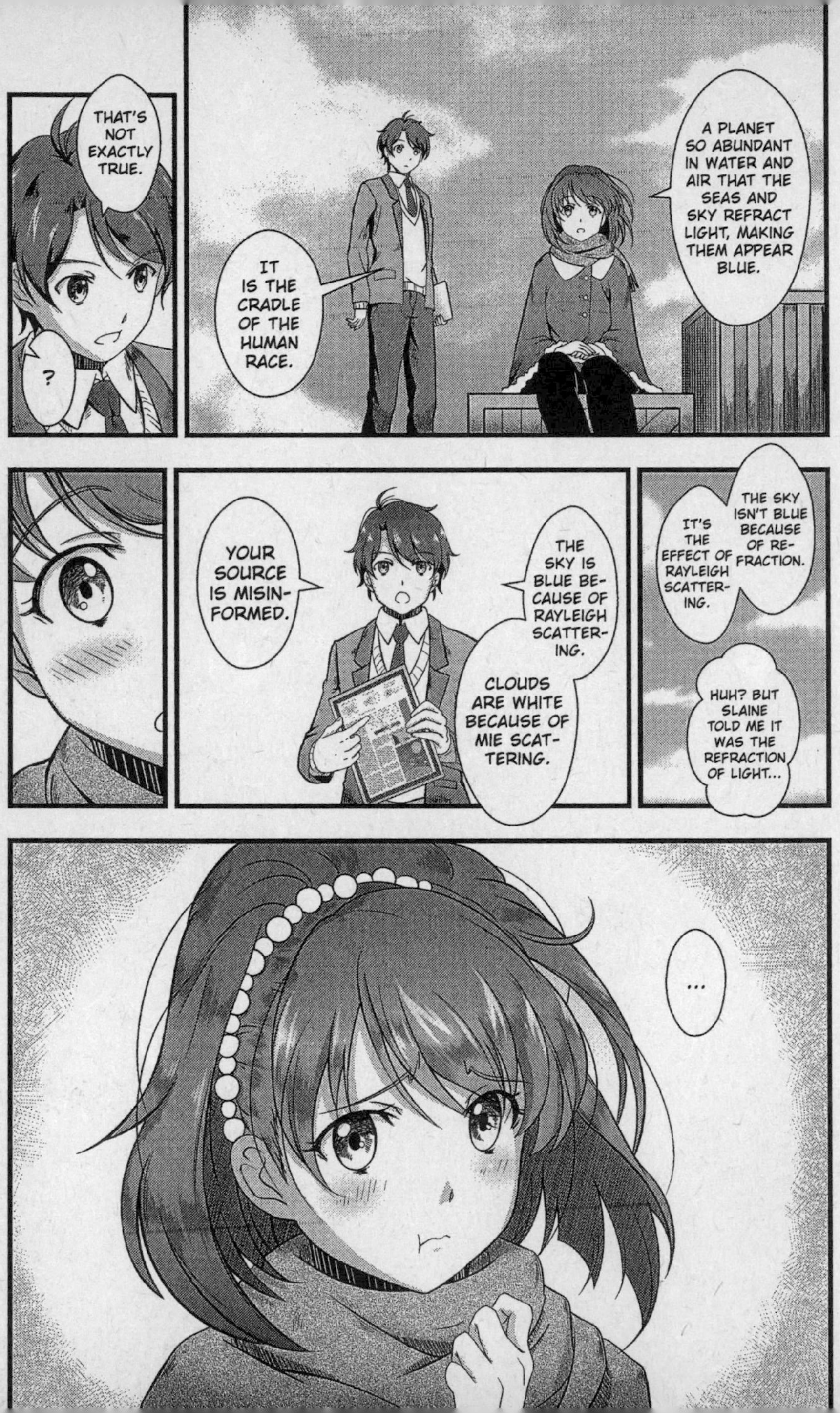
A PLANET SO ABUNDANT IN WATER AND AIR THAT THE SEAS AND SKY REFRACT LIGHT, MAKING THEM APPEAR BLUE.
IT IS THE CRADLE OF THE HUMAN RACE.
THAT'S NOT EXACTLY TRUE.
?
THE SKY ISN'T BLUE BECAUSE OF RE-FRACTION.
IT'S THE EFFECT OF RAYLEIGH SCATTER-ING.
HUH? BUT SLAINE TOLD ME IT WAS THE REFRACTION OF LIGHT...
THE SKY IS BLUE BE-CAUSE OF RAYLEIGH SCATTER-ING.
YOUR SOURCE IS MISIN-FORMED.
CLOUDS ARE WHITE BECAUSE OF MIE SCAT-TERING.
...

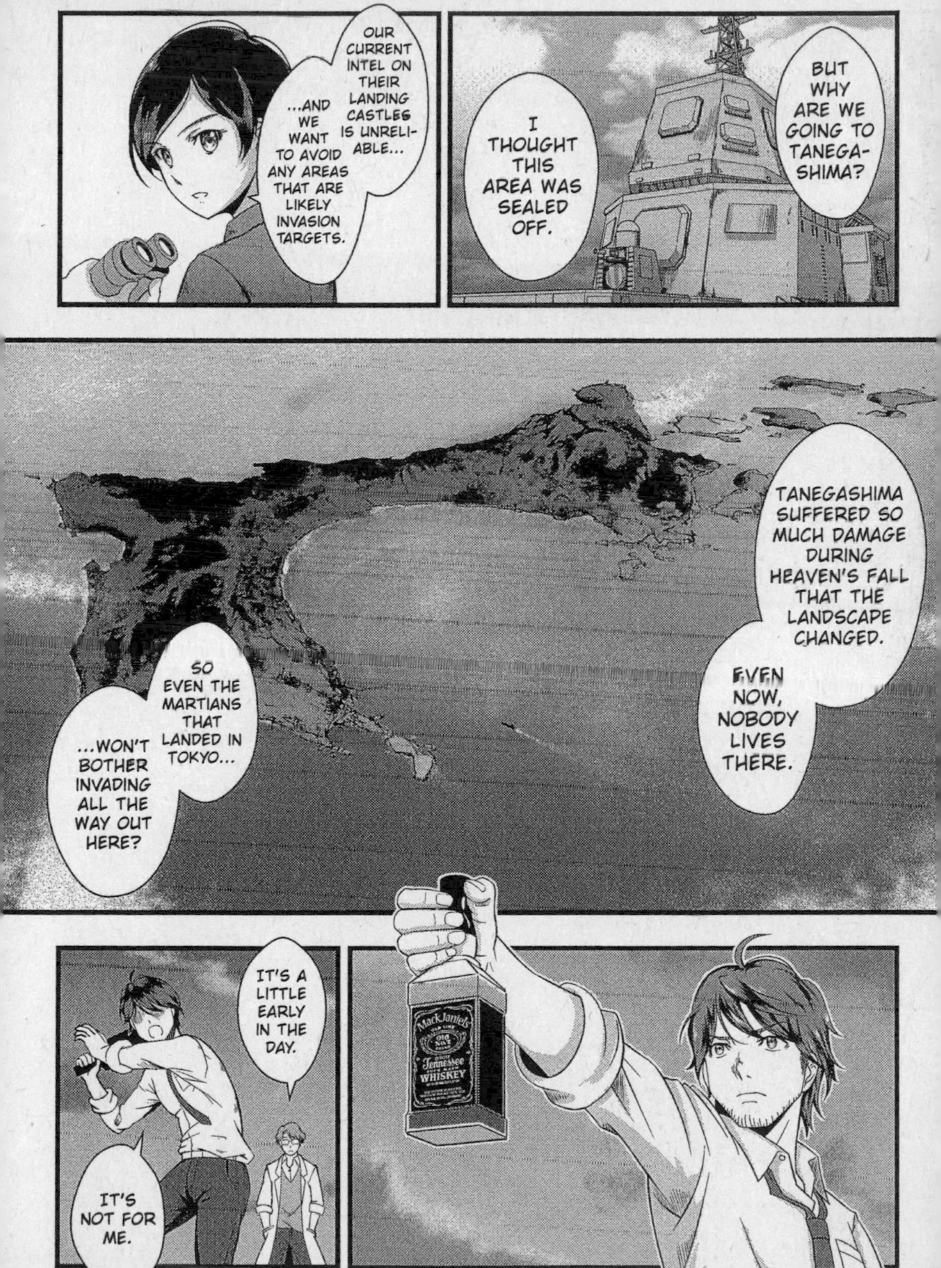
BUT WHY ARE WE GOING TO TANEGA-SHIMA?
I THOUGHT THIS AREA WAS SEALED OFF.
OUR CURRENT INTEL ON THEIR LANDING CASTLES IS UNRELI-ABLE...
...AND WE WANT TO AVOID ANY AREAS THAT ARE LIKELY INVASION TARGETS.
TANEGASHIMA SUFFERED SO MUCH DAMAGE DURING HEAVEN'S FALL THAT THE LANDSCAPE CHANGED.
EVEN NOW, NOBODY LIVES THERE.
SO EVEN THE MARTIANS THAT LANDED IN TOKYO...
...WON'T BOTHER INVADING ALL THE WAY OUT HERE?
Mack Janet's
Tennessee
WHISKEY
IT'S A LITTLE EARLY IN THE DAY.
IT'S NOT FOR ME.

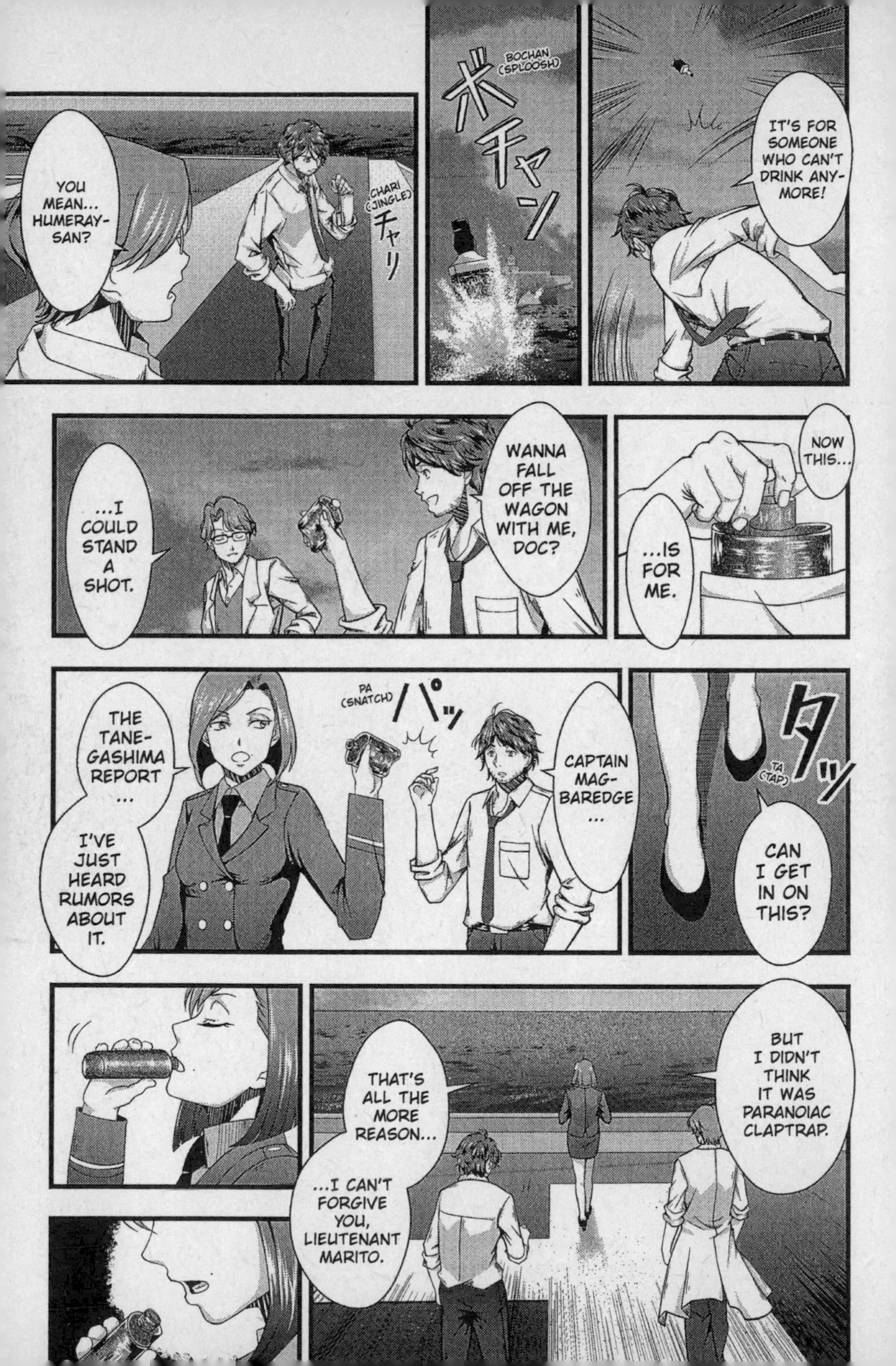
IT'S FOR SOMEONE WHO CAN'T DRINK ANY-MORE!
BOCHAN (SPLOOSH)
ボチャン
CHARI (JINGLE)
チャリ
YOU MEAN... HUMERAY-SAN?
NOW THIS...
...IS FOR ME.
WANNA FALL OFF THE WAGON WITH ME, DOC?
...I COULD STAND A SHOT.
タッ
TA (TAP)
CAN I GET IN ON THIS?
CAPTAIN MAG-BAREDGE...
PA (SNATCH)
パッ
THE TANE-GASHIMA REPORT...
I'VE JUST HEARD RUMORS ABOUT IT.
BUT I DIDN'T THINK IT WAS PARANOIAC CLAPTRAP.
THAT'S ALL THE MORE REASON...
...I CAN'T FORGIVE YOU, LIEUTENANT MARITO.

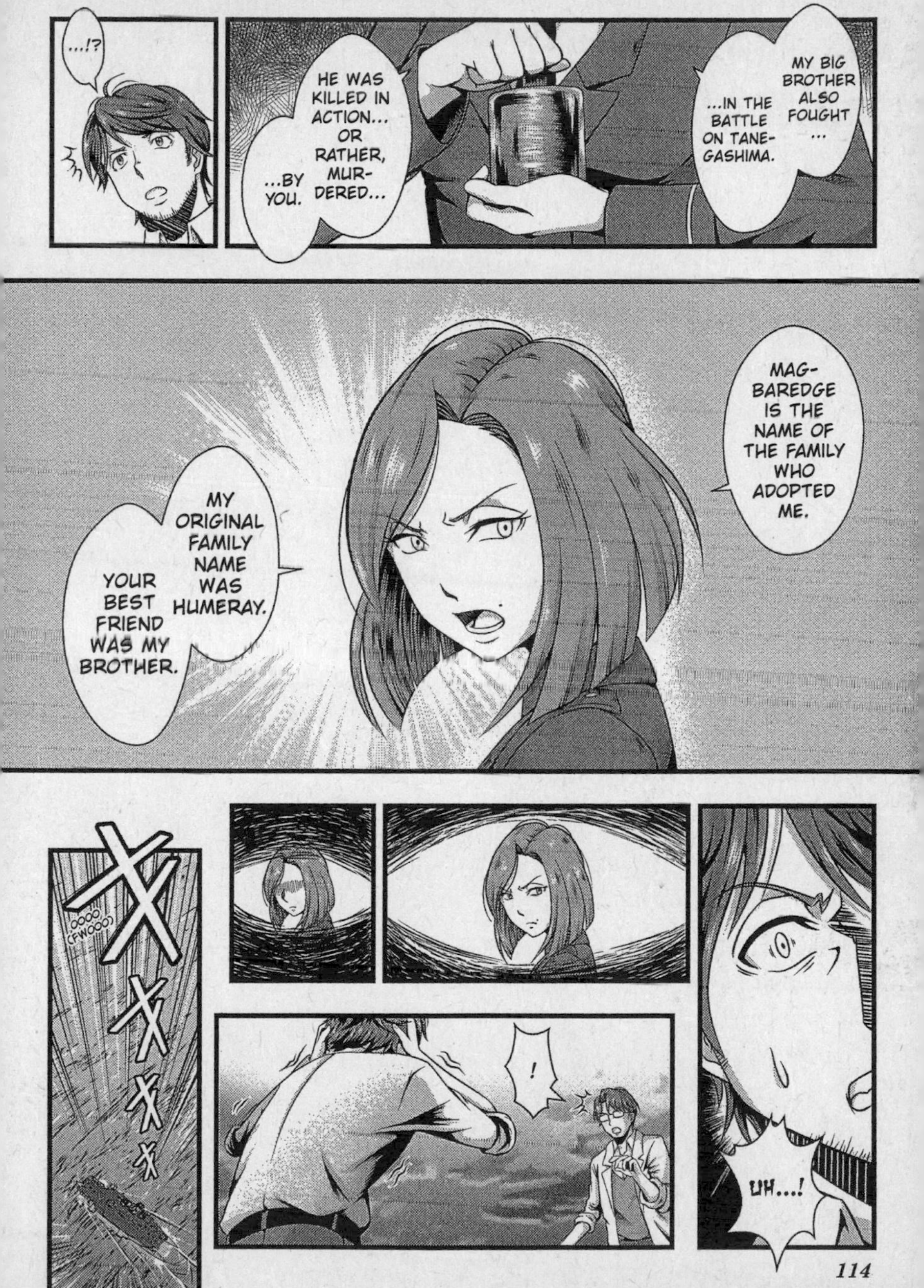
MY BIG BROTHER ALSO FOUGHT ...
...IN THE BATTLE ON TANE-GASHIMA.
HE WAS KILLED IN ACTION... OR RATHER, MUR-DERED...
...BY YOU.
...!?
MAG-BAREDGE IS THE NAME OF THE FAMILY WHO ADOPTED ME.
MY ORIGINAL FAMILY NAME WAS HUMERAY.
YOUR BEST FRIEND WAS MY BROTHER.
UH...!
!
OOOO (FWOOO)

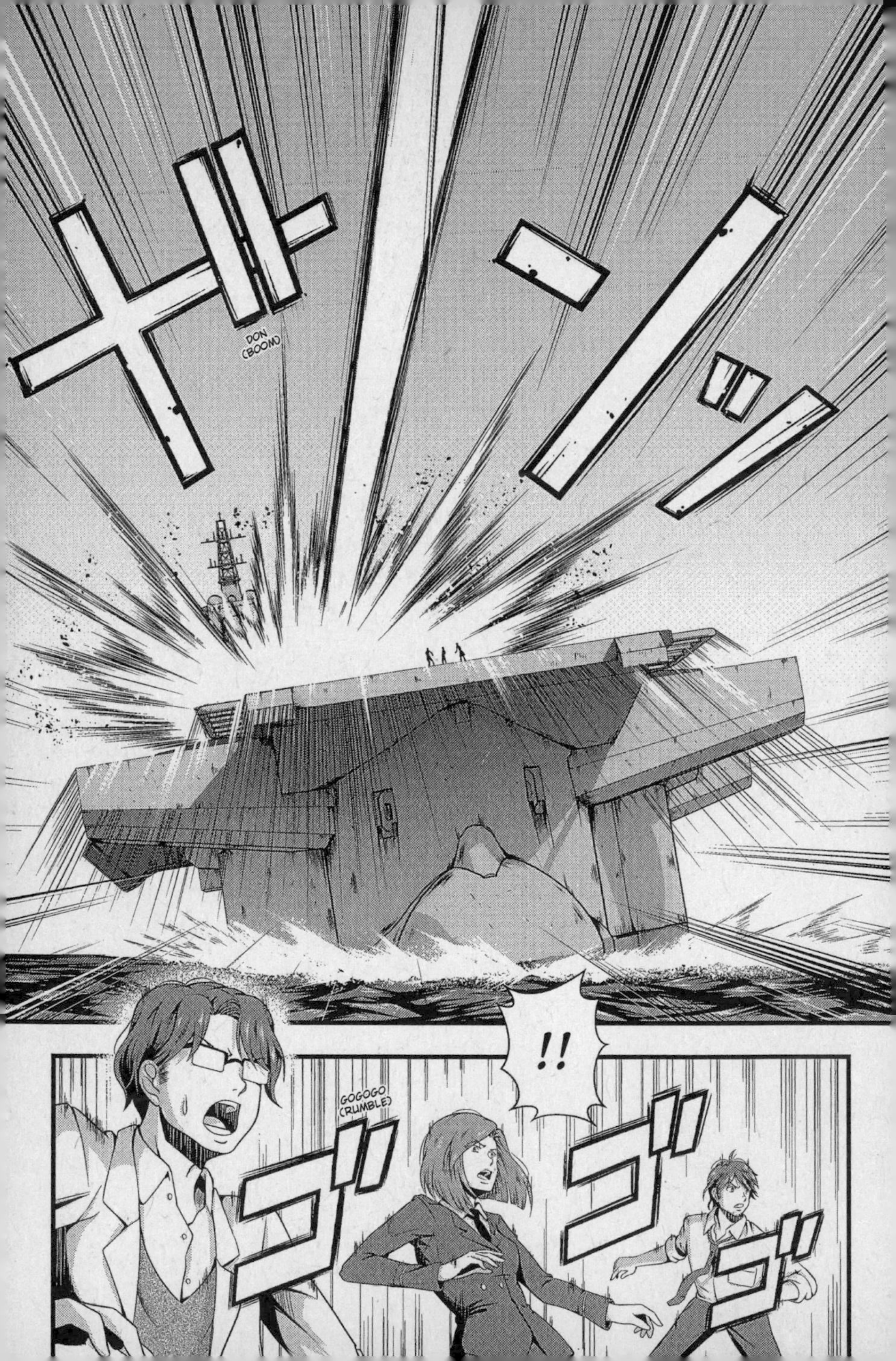
DON (BOOM)
!!
GOGOGO (RUMBLE)

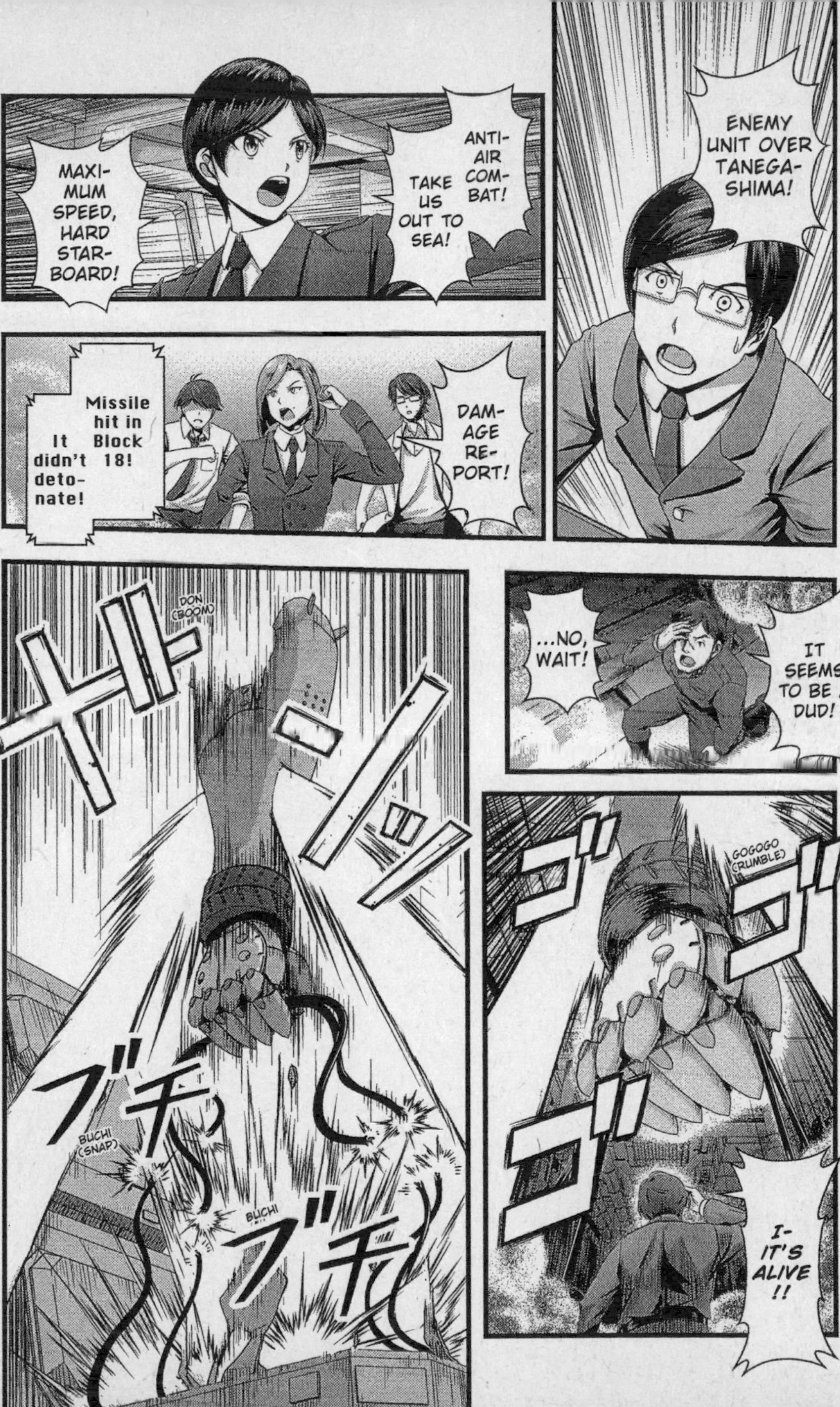
ENEMY UNIT OVER TANEGA-SHIMA!
ANTI-AIR COM-BAT!
TAKE US OUT TO SEA!
MAXI-MUM SPEED, HARD STAR-BOARD!
DAM-AGE RE-PORT!
Missile hit in Block 18!
It didn't deto-nate!
IT SEEMS TO BE A DUD!
...NO, WAIT!
GOGOGO (RUMBLE)
I-IT'S ALIVE!!
DON (BOOM)
BUCHI (SNAP)
BUCHI

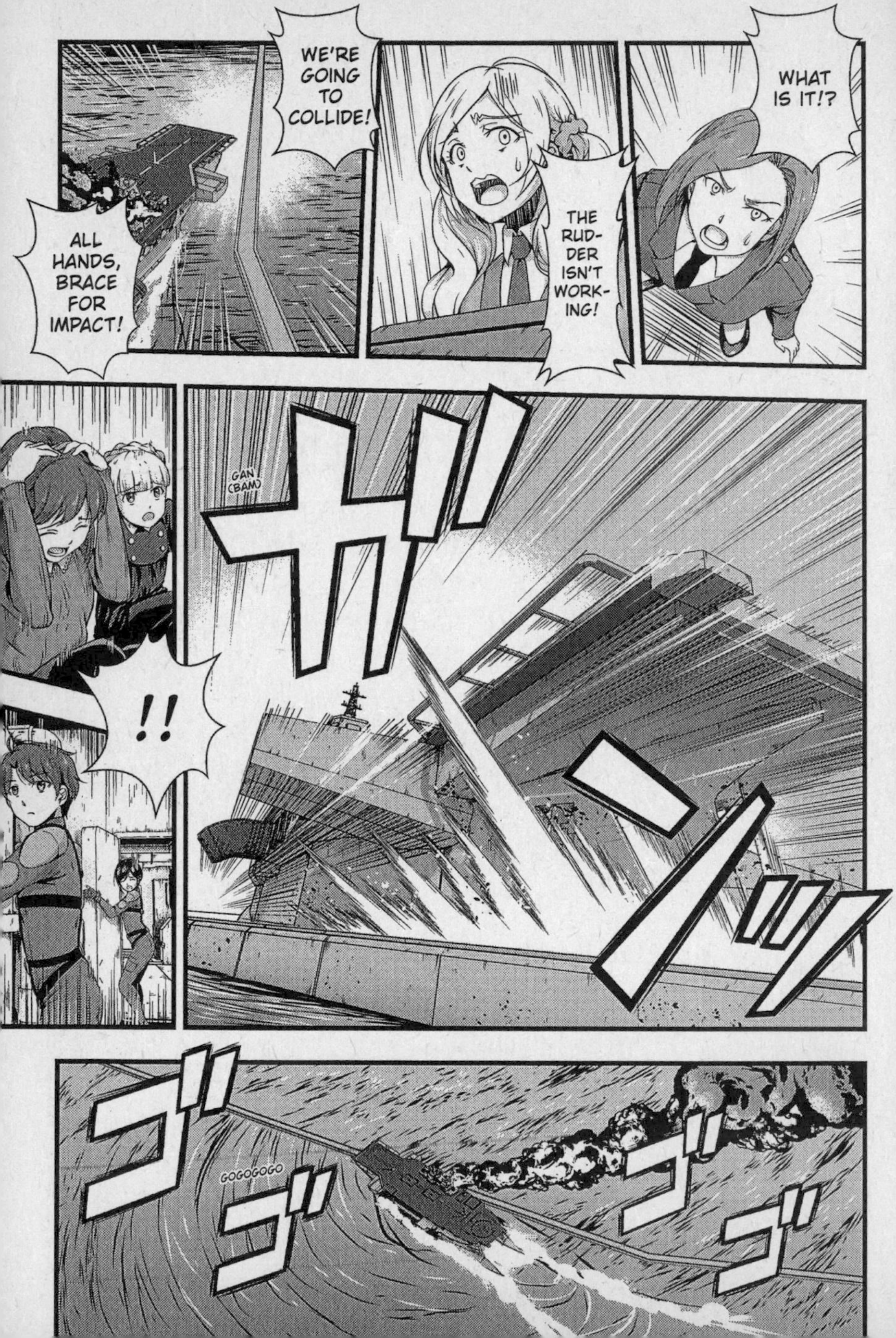

WHAT IS IT!?
WE'RE GOING TO COLLIDE!
THE RUD-DER ISN'T WORK-ING!
ALL HANDS, BRACE FOR IMPACT!
GAN (BAM)
!!
GOGOGOGO

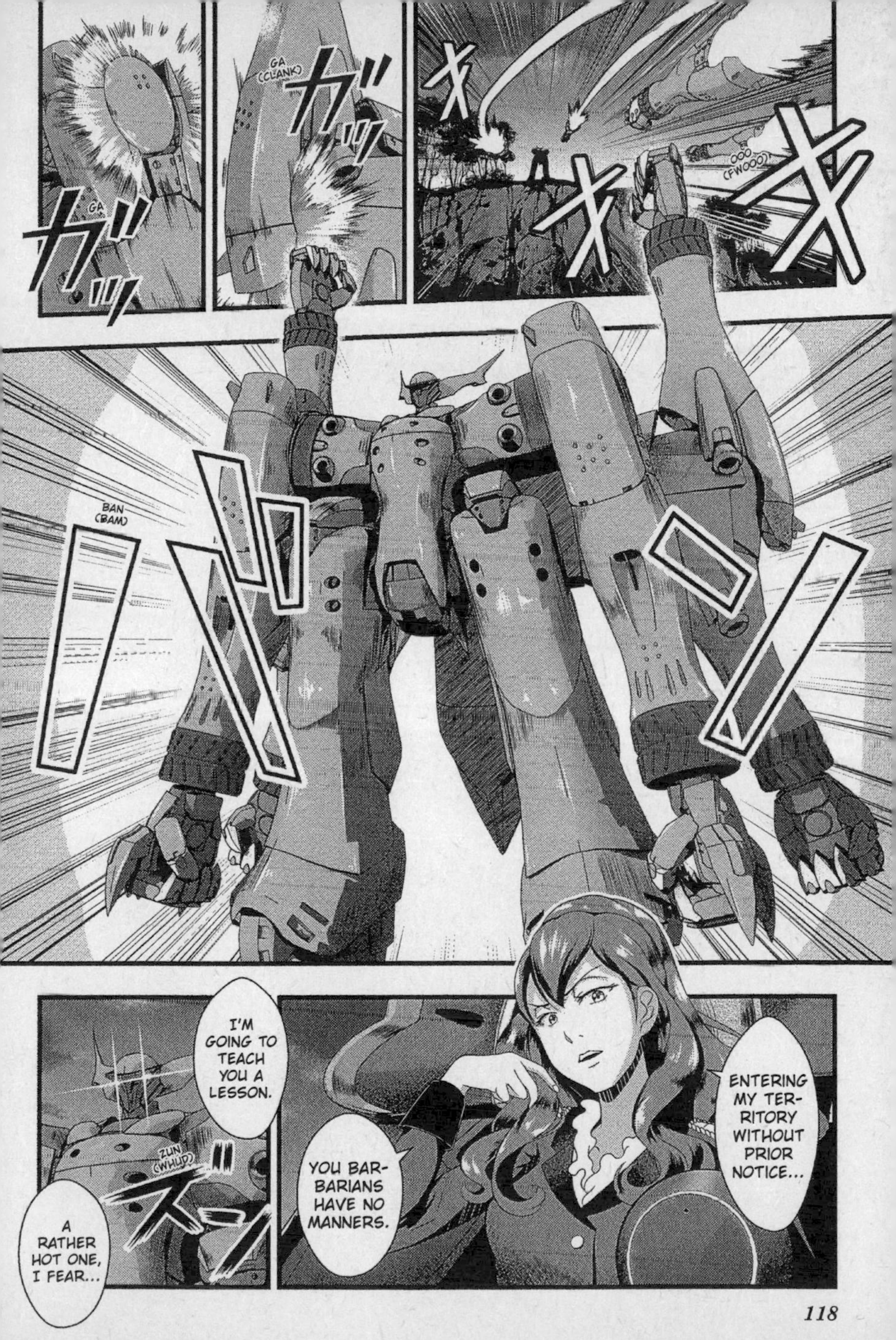
OOO (FWOOO)
GA (CLANK)
GA
BAN (BAM)
ENTERING MY TER-RITORY WITHOUT PRIOR NOTICE...
YOU BAR-BARIANS HAVE NO MANNERS.
I'M GOING TO TEACH YOU A LESSON.
ZUN (WHUD)
A RATHER HOT ONE, I FEAR...

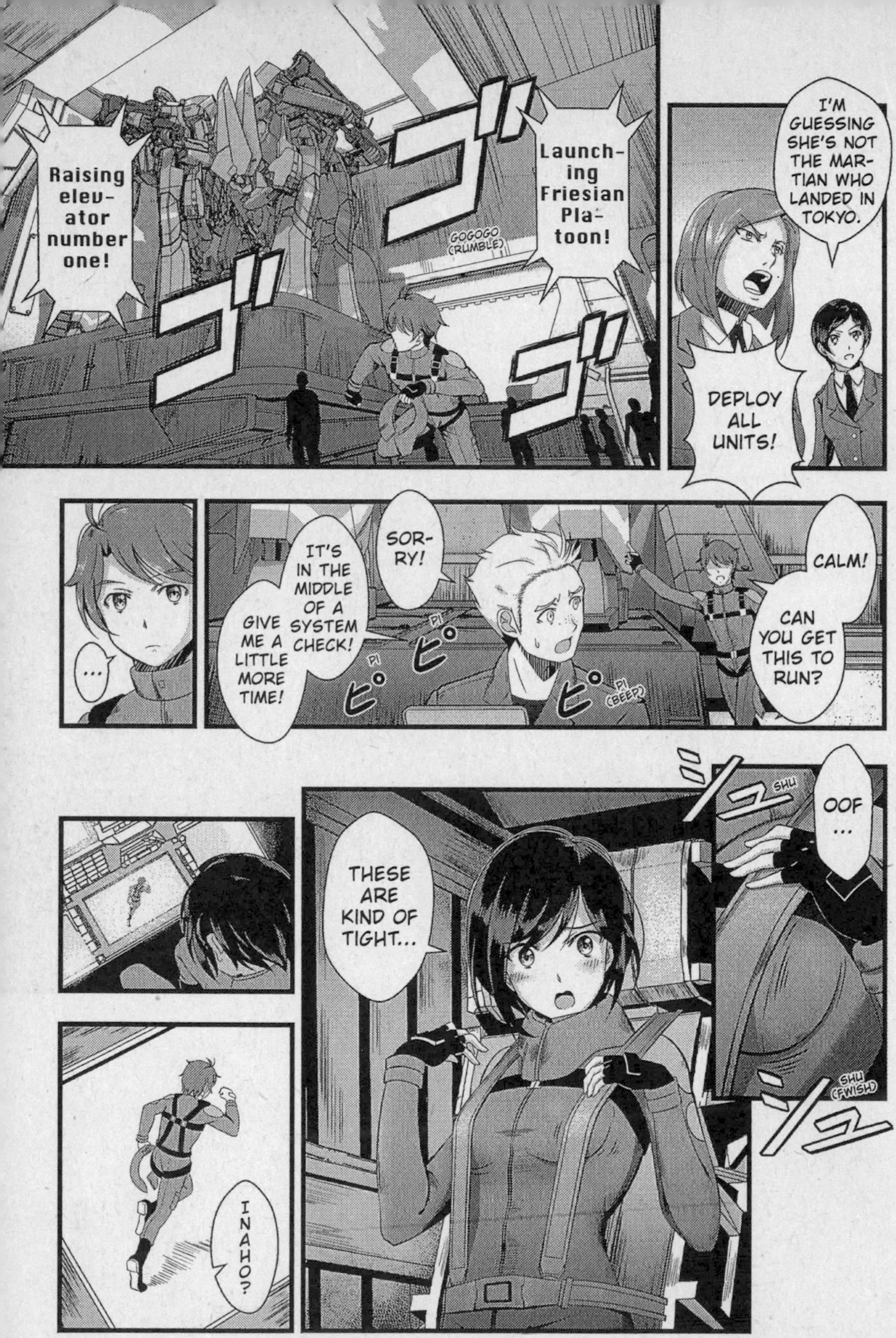
I'M GUESSING SHE'S NOT THE MARTIAN WHO LANDED IN TOKYO.
DEPLOY ALL UNITS!
Launching Friesian Platoon!
GOGOGO (RUMBLE)
Raising elevator number one!
CALM!
CAN YOU GET THIS TO RUN?
SORRY!
IT'S IN THE MIDDLE OF A SYSTEM CHECK!
GIVE ME A LITTLE MORE TIME!
PI
PI
PI (BEEP)
...
SHU
OOF...
THESE ARE KIND OF TIGHT...
SHU (FWISH)
INAHO?

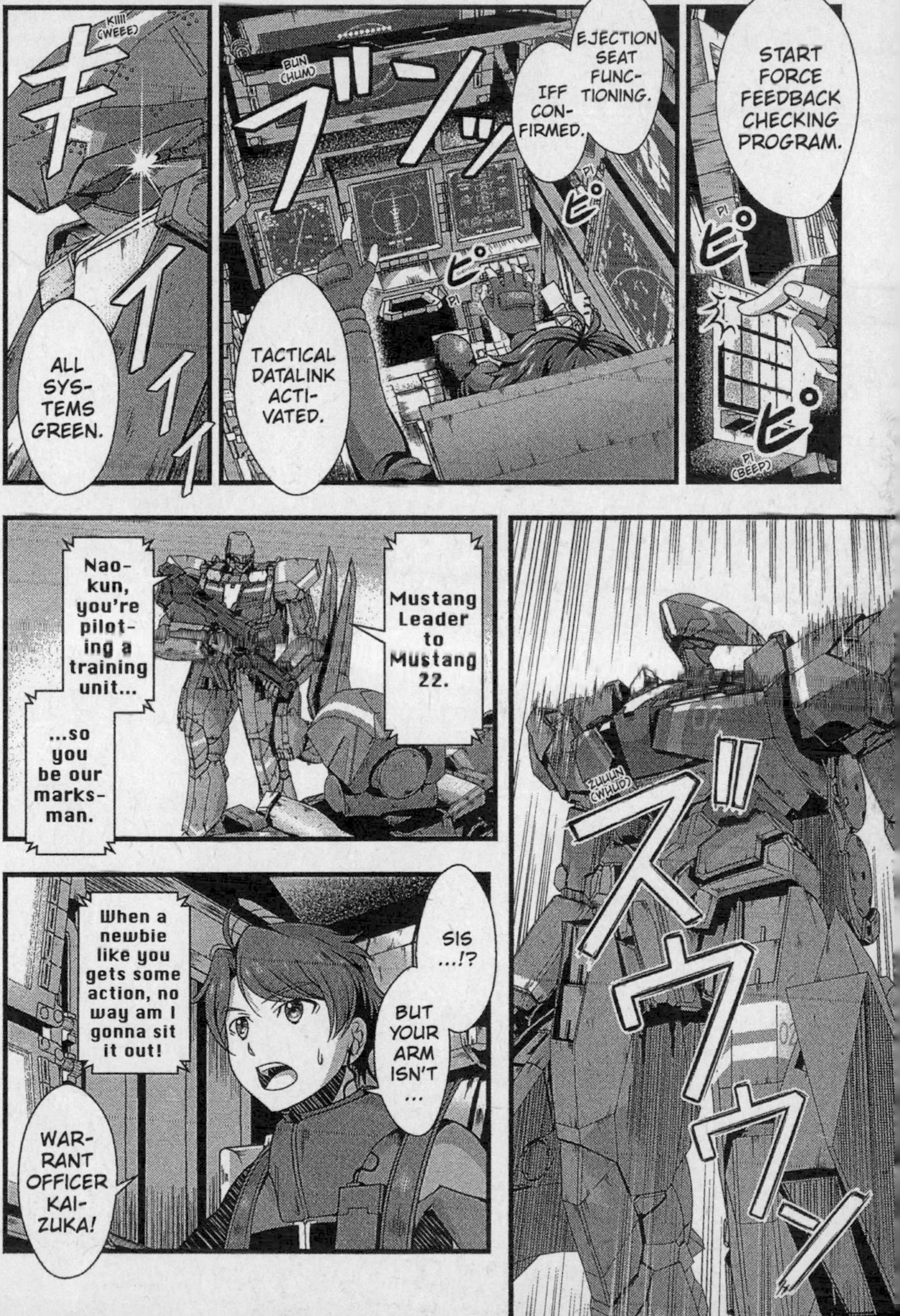
START FORCE FEEDBACK CHECKING PROGRAM.
PI
PI (BEEP)
EJECTION SEAT FUNCTIONING.
IFF CONFIRMED.
PI
BUN (HUM)
PI
TACTICAL DATALINK ACTIVATED.
KIIII (WEEE)
ALL SYSTEMS GREEN.
ZUUUN (WHUD)
Mustang Leader to Mustang 22.
Nao-kun, you're piloting a training unit...
...so you be our marksman.
SIS ...!?
BUT YOUR ARM ISN'T ...
When a newbie like you gets some action, no way am I gonna sit it out!
WARRANT OFFICER KAIZUKA!

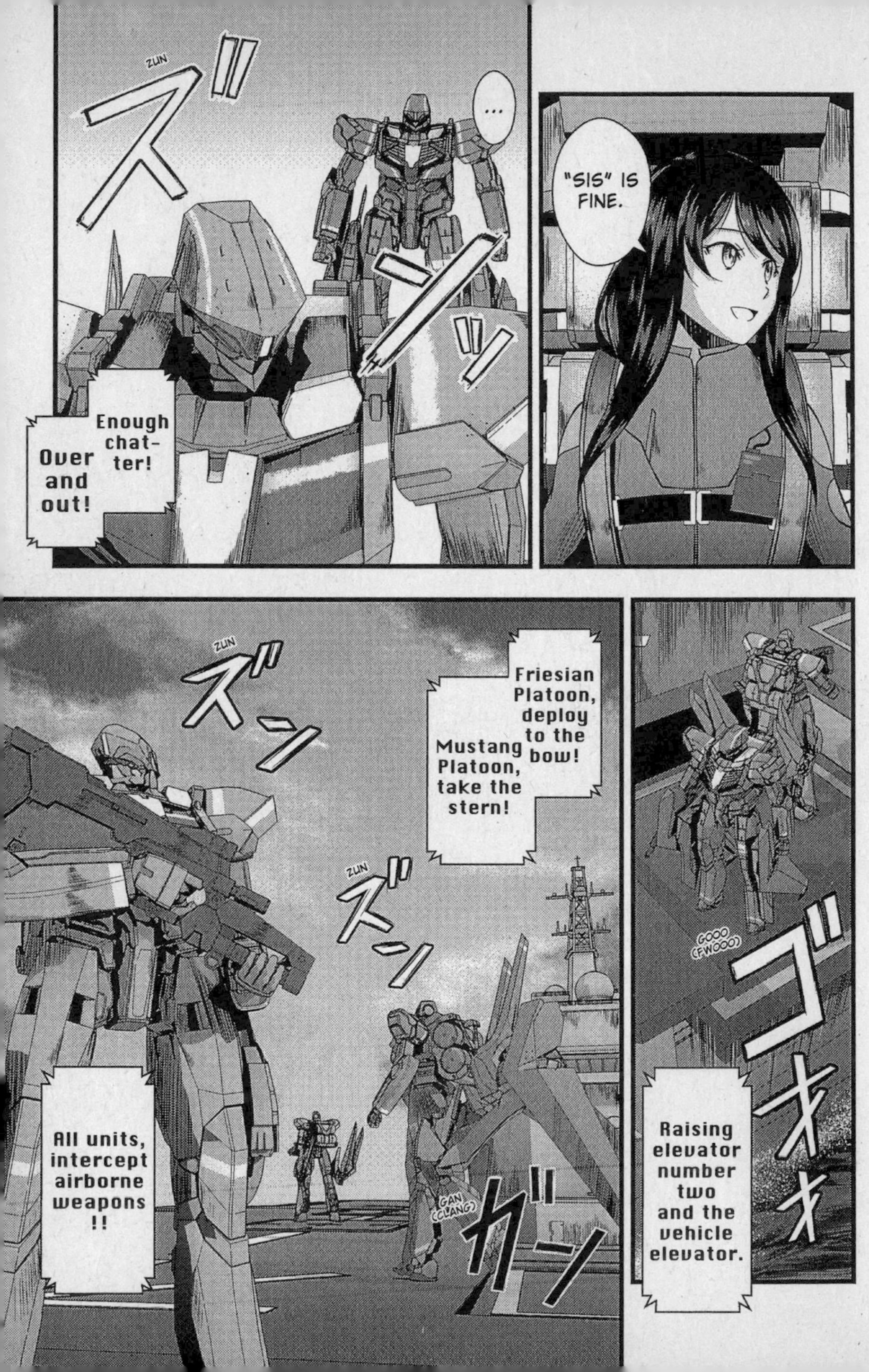

"SIS" IS FINE.
ZUN
...
Enough chatter!
Over and out!
GOOO (FWOOO)
Raising elevator number two and the vehicle elevator.
ZUN
Friesian Platoon, deploy to the bow!
Mustang Platoon, take the stern!
ZUN
GAN (CLANG)
All units, intercept airborne weapons!!

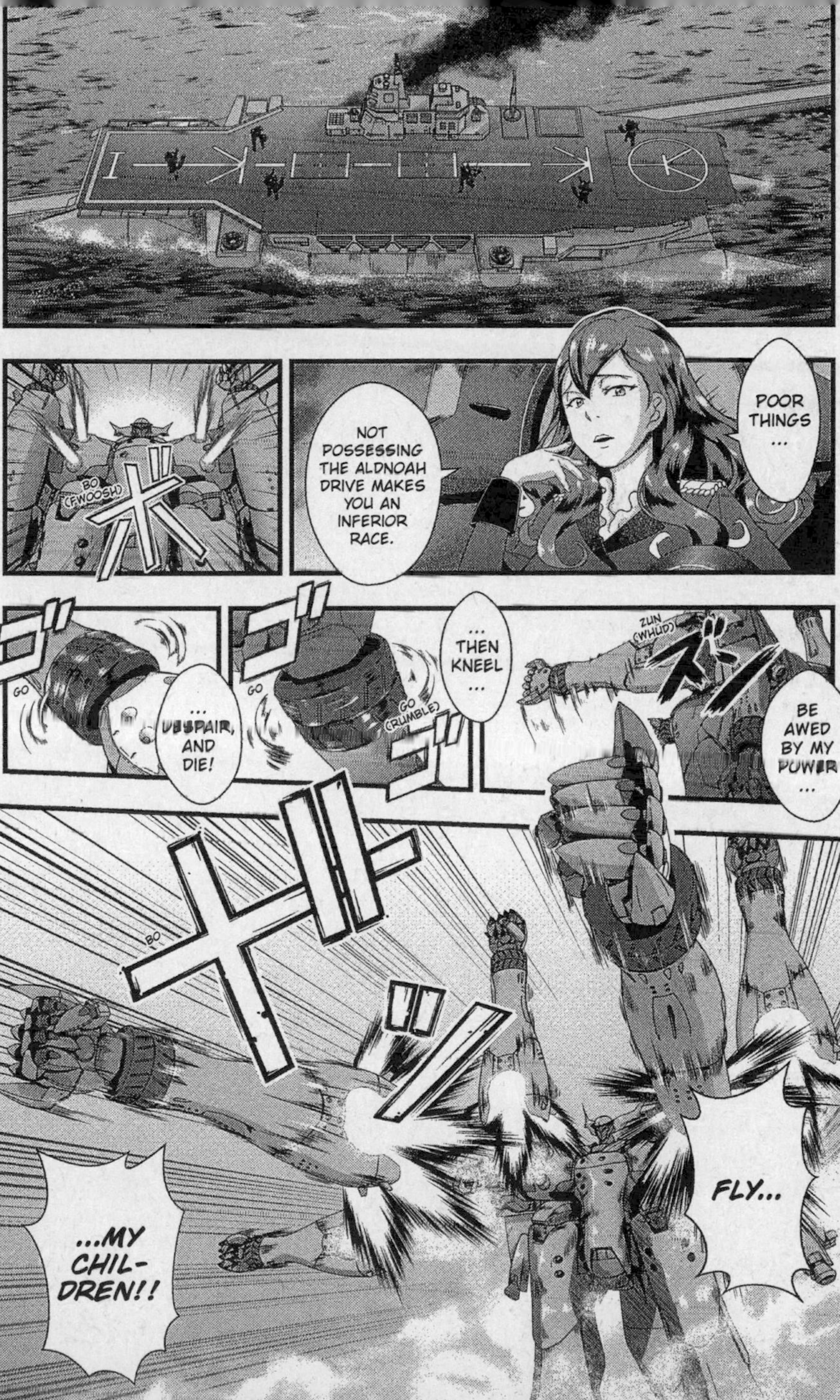
POOR THINGS ...
NOT POSSESSING THE ALDNOAH DRIVE MAKES YOU AN INFERIOR RACE.
BO (FWOOSH)
ZUN (WHUD)
BE AWED BY MY POWER ...
... THEN KNEEL ...
GO
GO (RUMBLE)
GO
... DESPAIR, AND DIE!
FLY...
...MY CHIL-DREN!!
BO

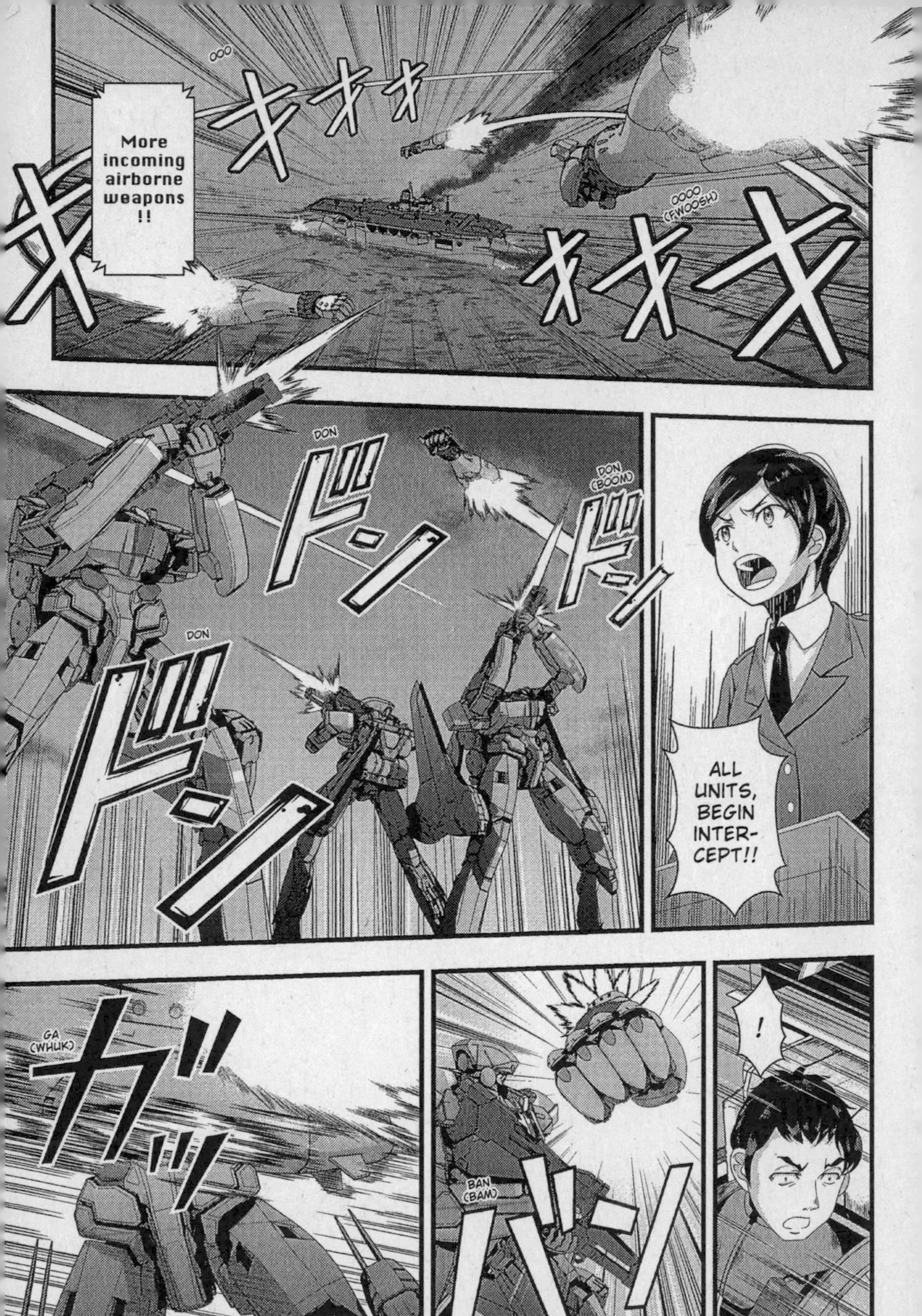
OOO
More incoming airborne weapons !!
OOOO (FWOOSH)
ALL UNITS, BEGIN INTER-CEPT!!
DON (BOOM)
DON
DON
!
BAN (BAM)
GA (WHUK)

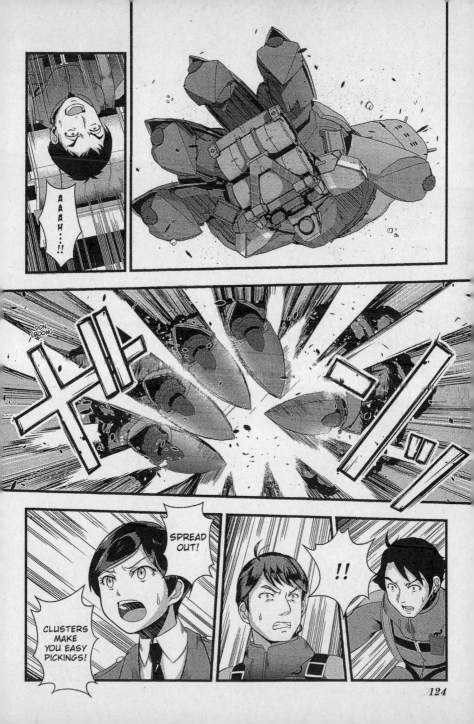

AAAH...!!

DON
(BOOM)

SPREAD OUT!

CLUSTERS MAKE YOU EASY PICKINGS!

!!

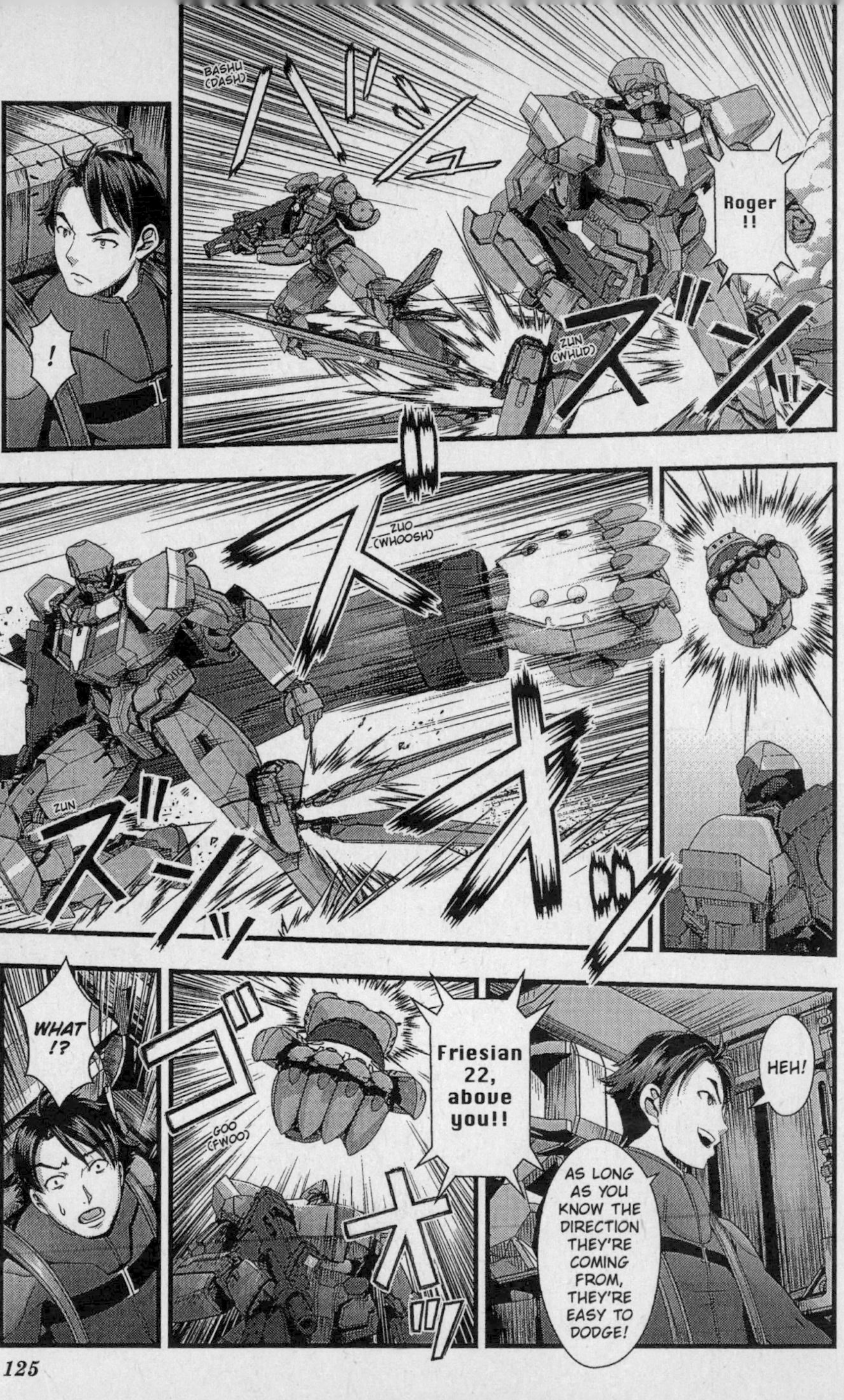
Roger!!
BASHU (DASH)
ZUN (WHUD)
!
ZUO (WHOOSH)
ZUN
HEH!
AS LONG AS YOU KNOW THE DIRECTION THEY'RE COMING FROM, THEY'RE EASY TO DODGE!
Friesian 22, above you!!
GOO (FWOO)
WHAT!?

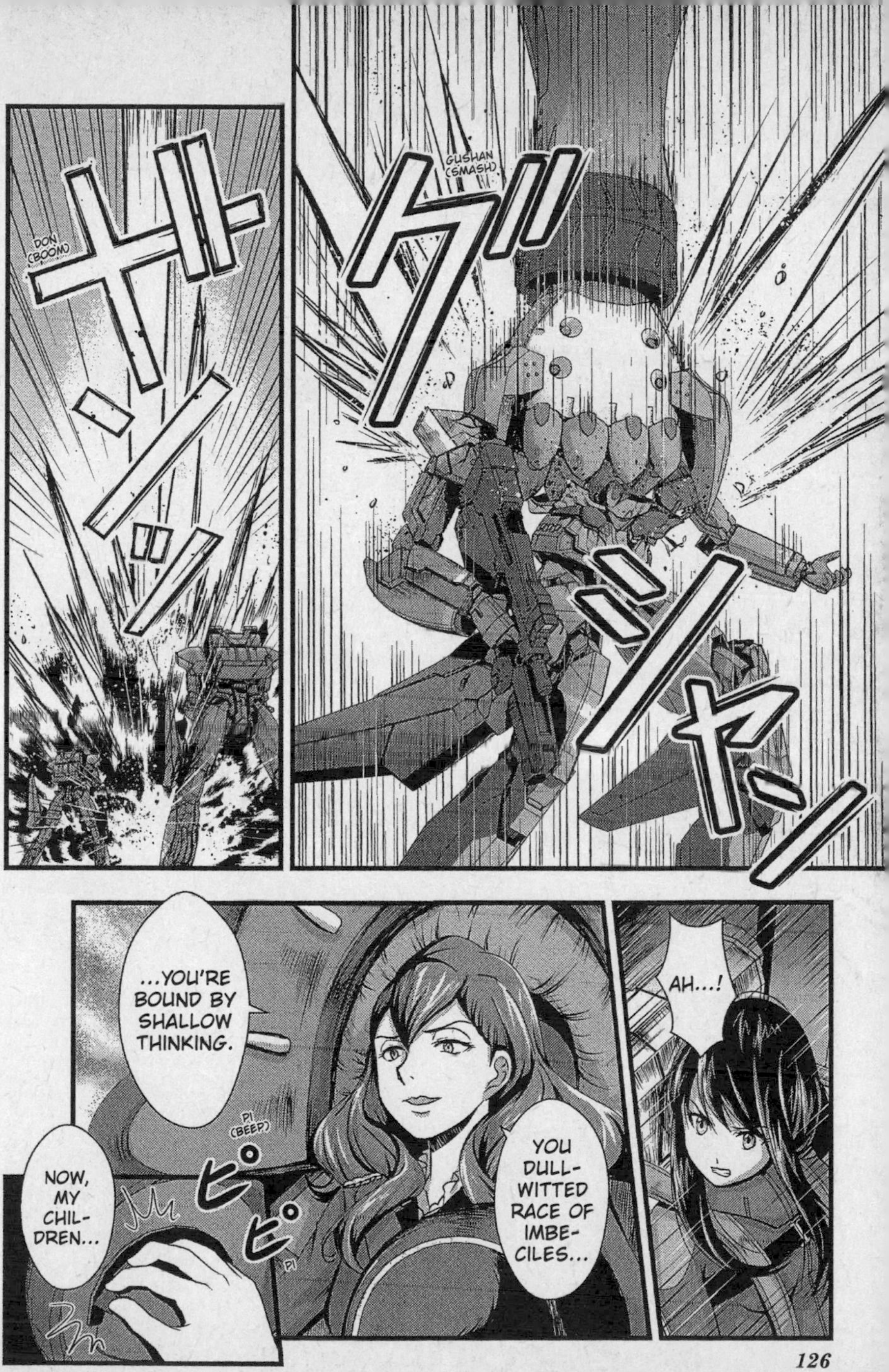
GUSHAN (SMASH)
DON (BOOM)
AH...!
YOU DULL-WITTED RACE OF IMBECILES...
...YOU'RE BOUND BY SHALLOW THINKING.
PI (BEEP)
PI
NOW, MY CHILDREN...

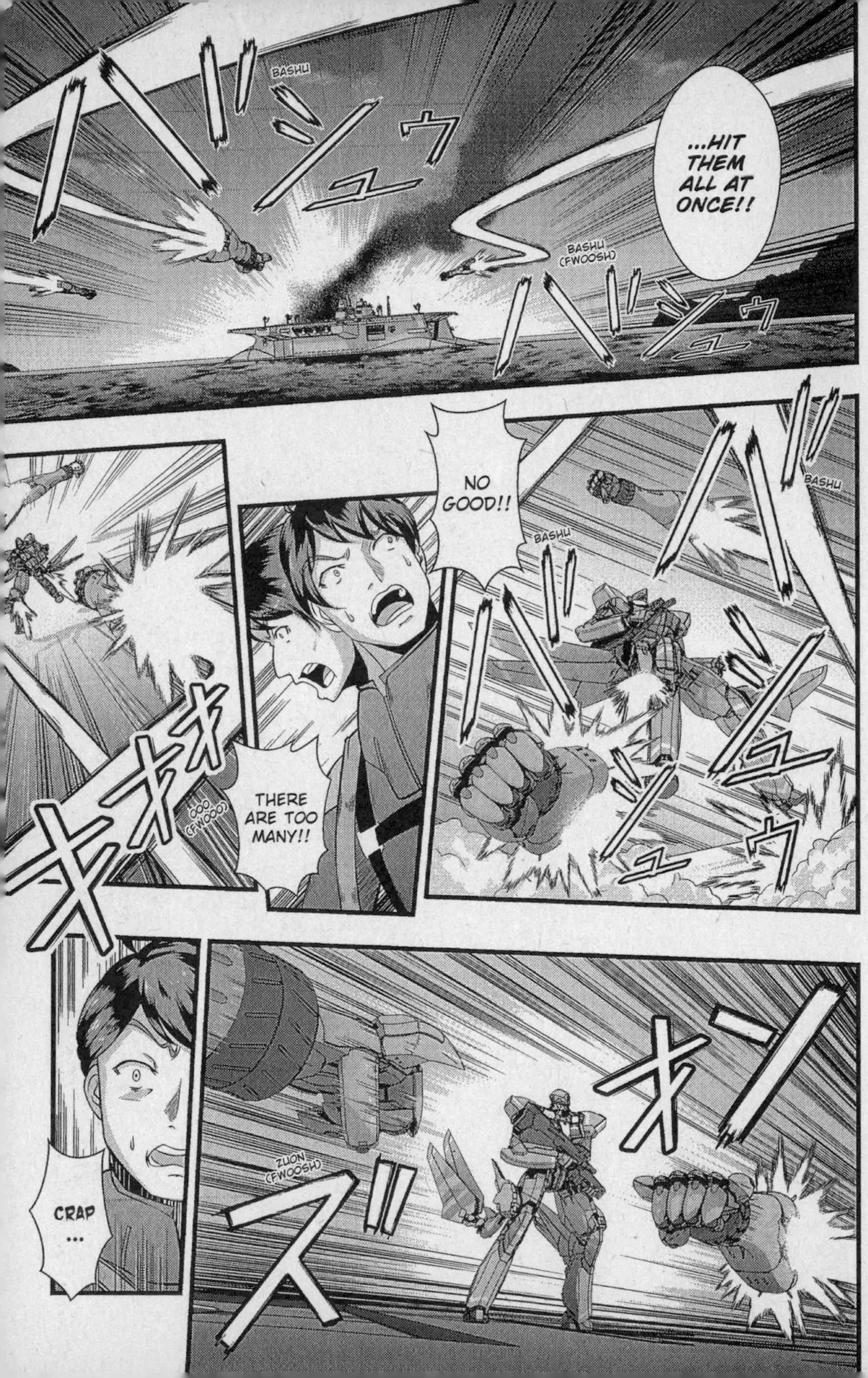
...HIT THEM ALL AT ONCE!!
BASHU
BASHU (FWOOSH)
BASHU
BASHU
NO GOOD!!
THERE ARE TOO MANY!!
OOO (FWOOO)
ZUON (FWOOSH)
CRAP ...

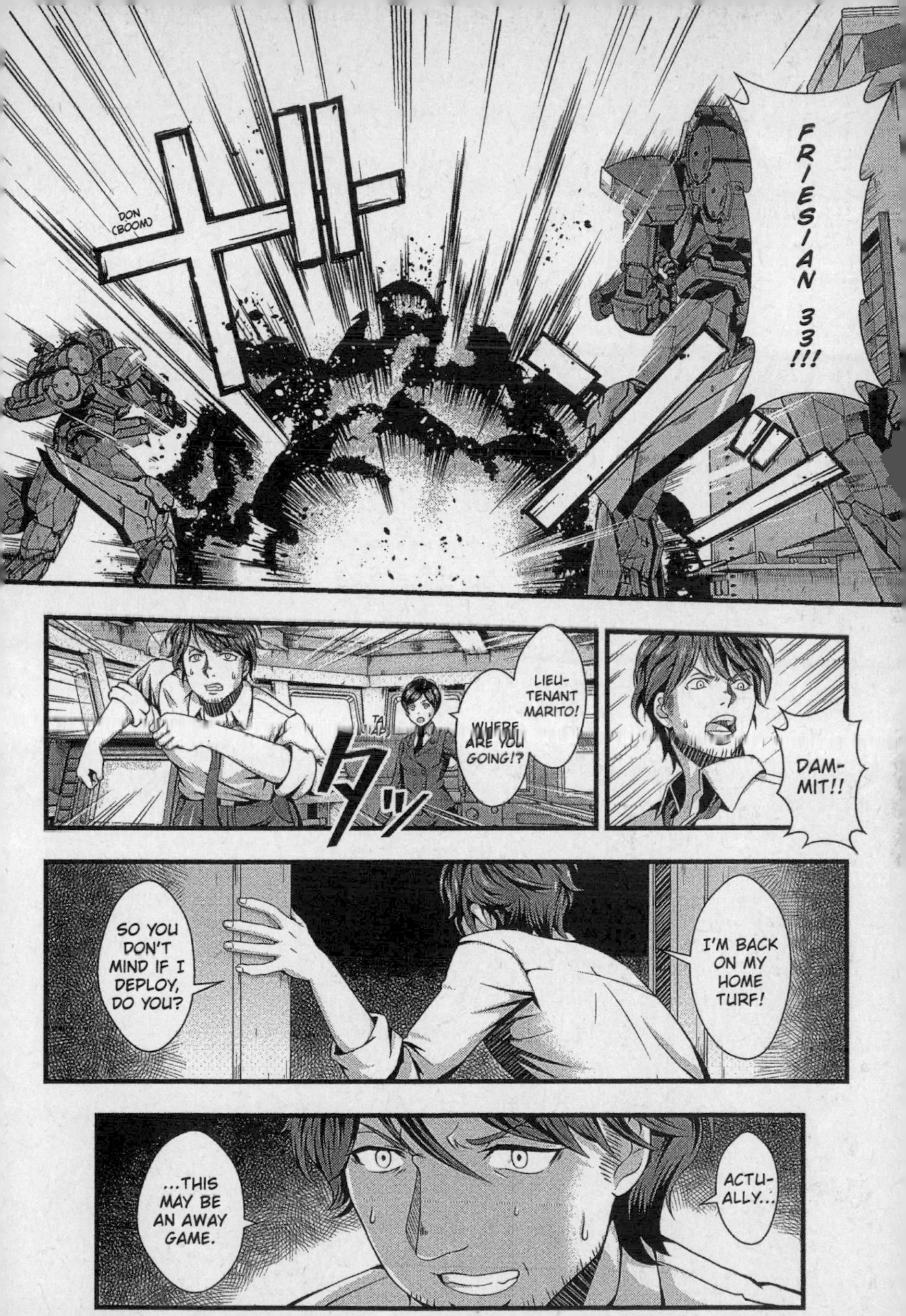
FRIESIAN 33!!!
DON (BOOM)
DAM-MIT!!
LIEU-TENANT MARITO!
WHERE ARE YOU GOING!?
I'M BACK ON MY HOME TURF!
SO YOU DON'T MIND IF I DEPLOY, DO YOU?
ACTU-ALLY...
...THIS MAY BE AN AWAY GAME.

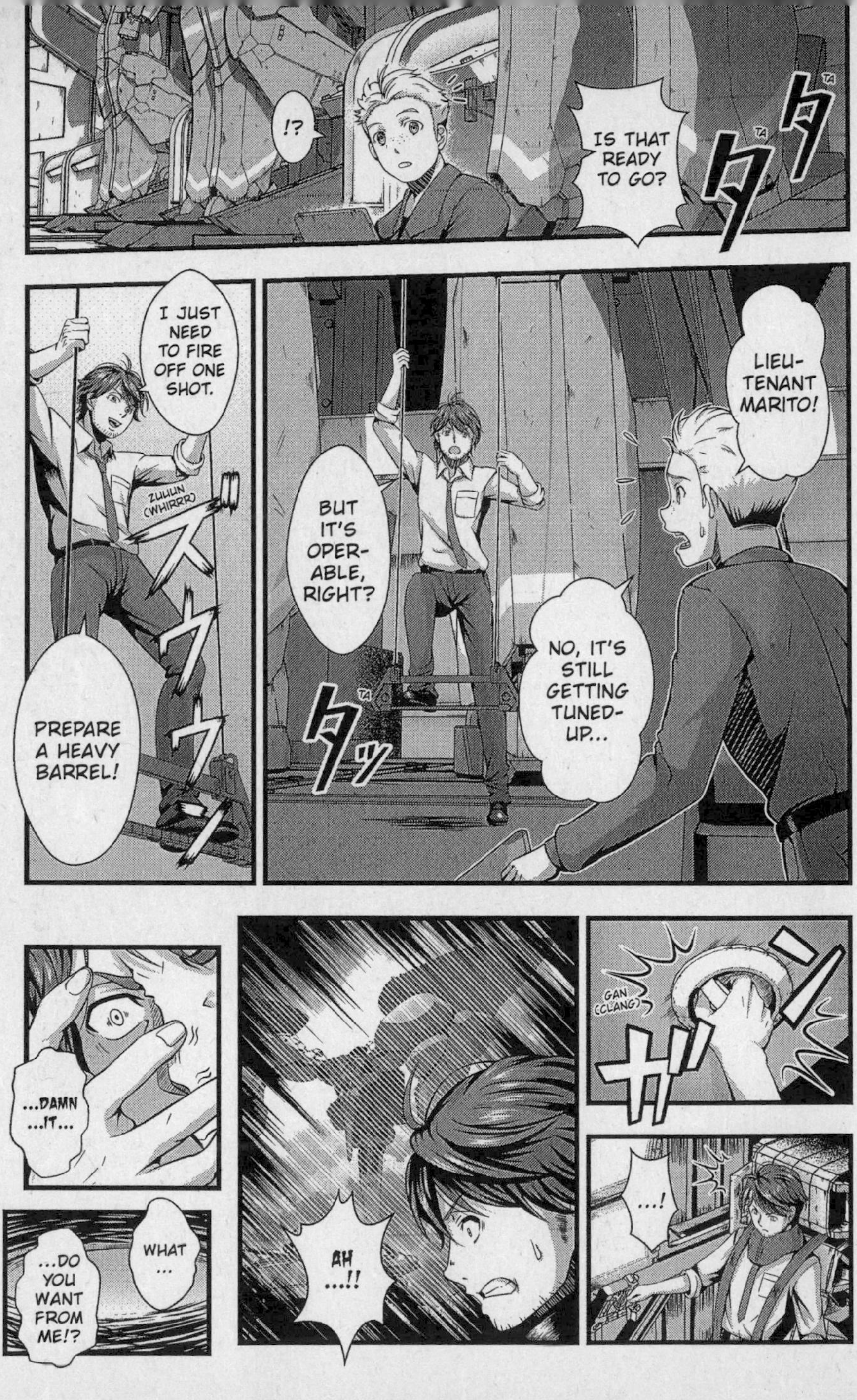
TA
TA
IS THAT READY TO GO?
!?
LIEU-TENANT MARITO!
NO, IT'S STILL GETTING TUNED-UP...
BUT IT'S OPER-ABLE, RIGHT?
TA
I JUST NEED TO FIRE OFF ONE SHOT.
ZUUUN (WHIRRR)
PREPARE A HEAVY BARREL!
GAN (CLANG)
...!
AH ...!!
...DAMN ...IT...
WHAT ...
...DO YOU WANT FROM ME!?

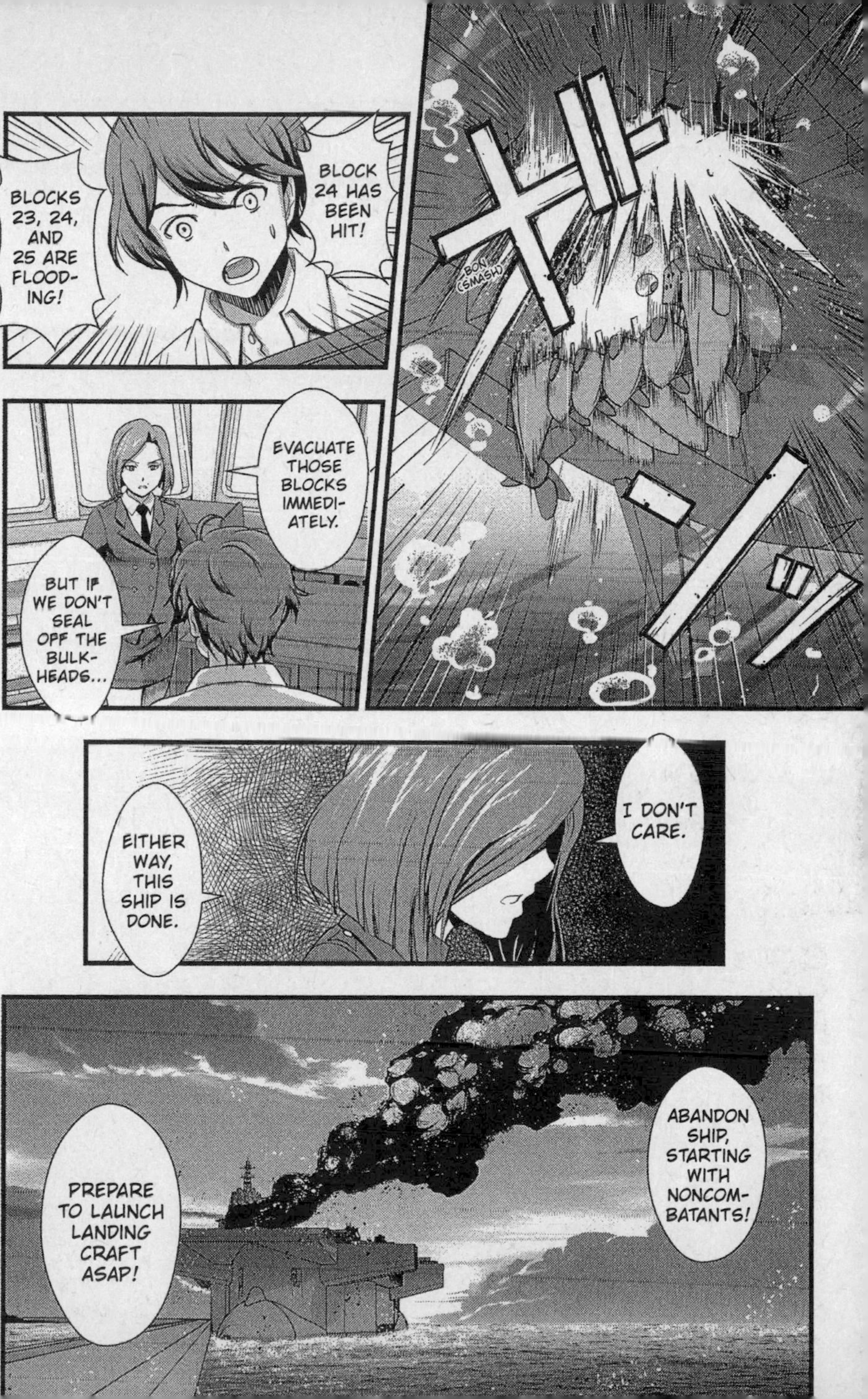
BON (SMASH)
BLOCK 24 HAS BEEN HIT!
BLOCKS 23, 24, AND 25 ARE FLOODING!
EVACUATE THOSE BLOCKS IMMEDIATELY.
BUT IF WE DON'T SEAL OFF THE BULKHEADS...
I DON'T CARE.
EITHER WAY, THIS SHIP IS DONE.
ABANDON SHIP, STARTING WITH NONCOMBATANTS!
PREPARE TO LAUNCH LANDING CRAFT ASAP!

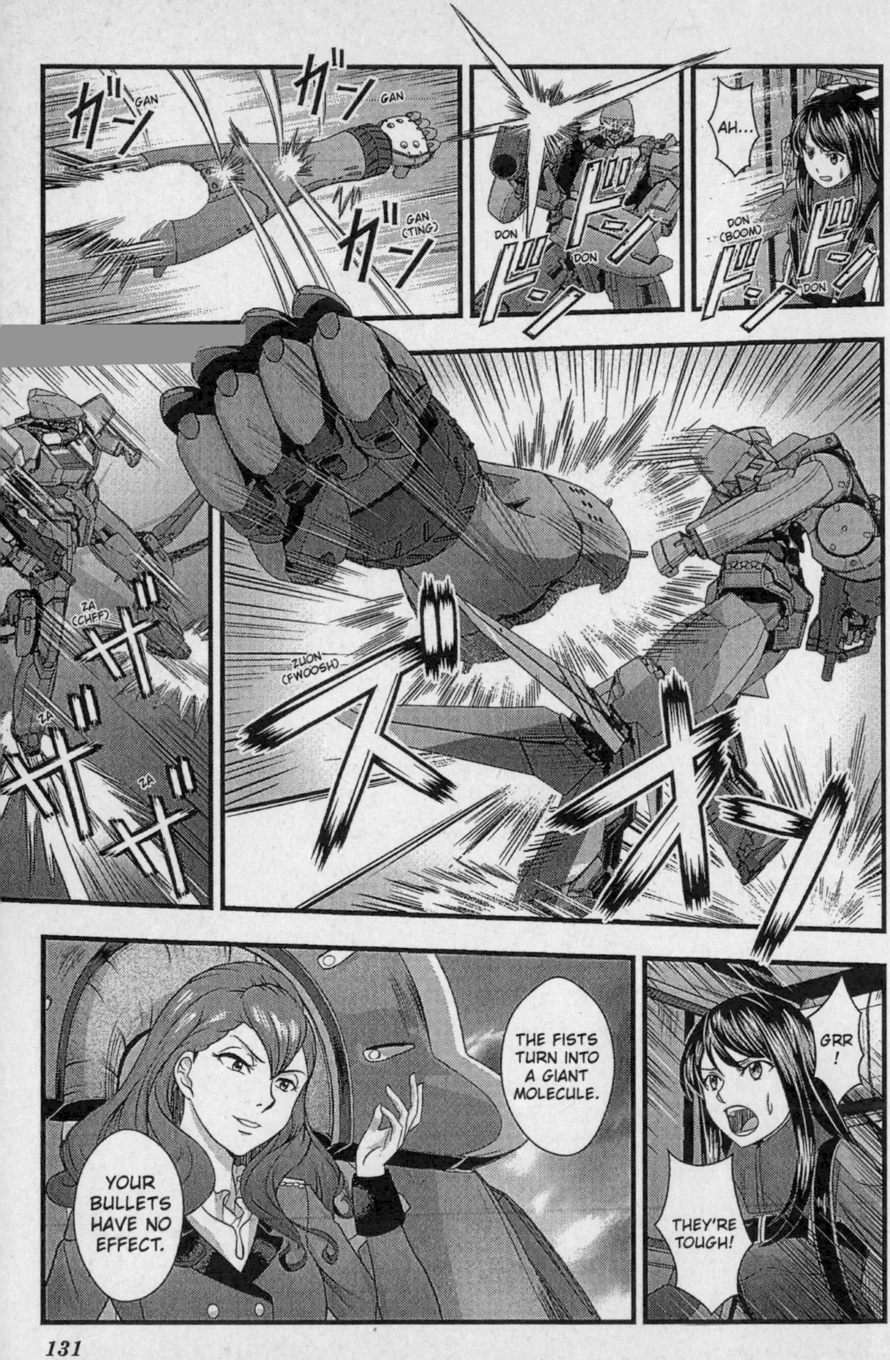

AH...
DON (BOOM)
DON
DON
DON
GAN
GAN
GAN (TING)
ZUON (FWOOSH)
ZA (CHFF)
ZA
ZA
GRR!
THEY'RE TOUGH!
THE FISTS TURN INTO A GIANT MOLECULE.
YOUR BULLETS HAVE NO EFFECT.

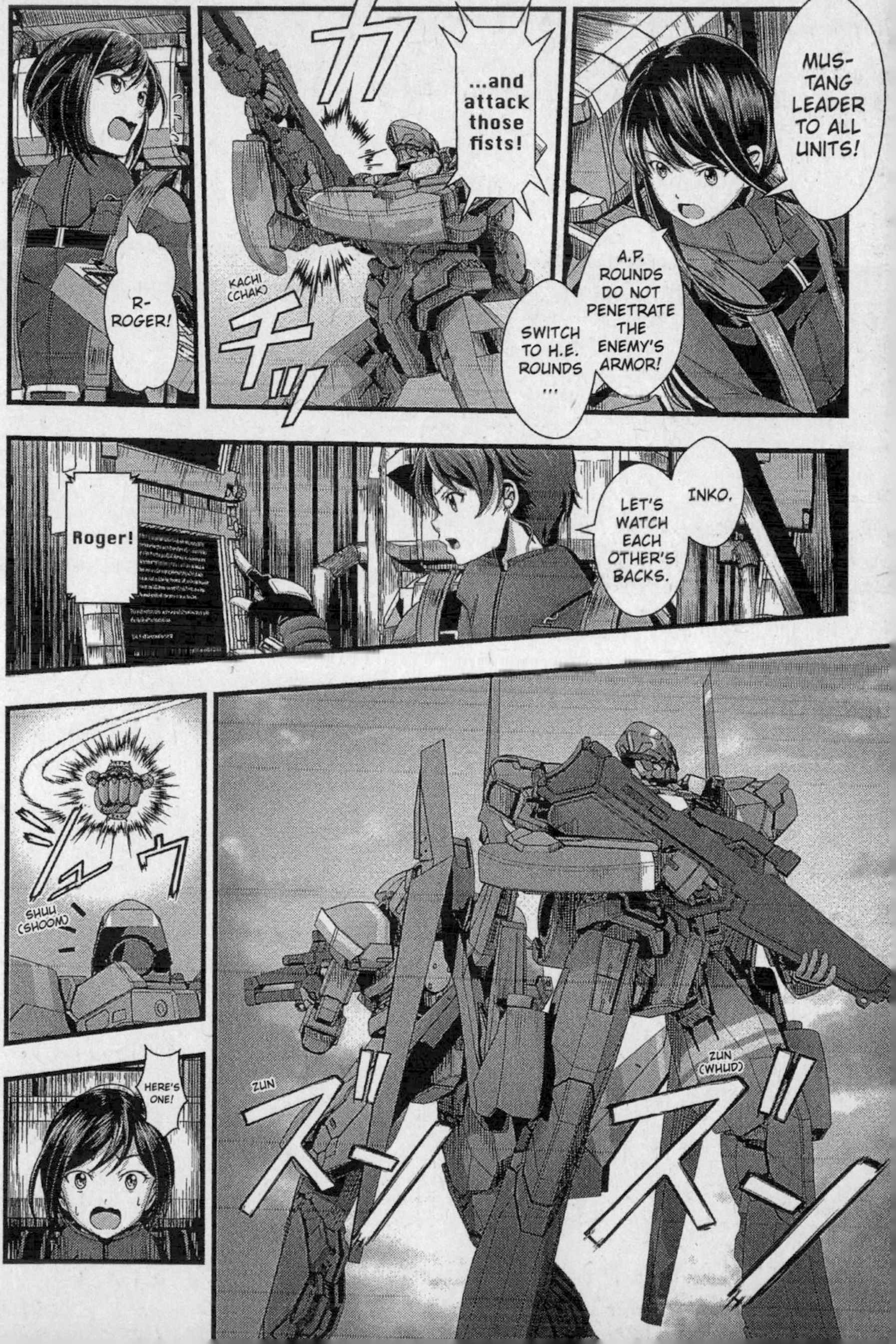
MUS-TANG LEADER TO ALL UNITS!
A.P. ROUNDS DO NOT PENETRATE THE ENEMY'S ARMOR!
SWITCH TO H.E. ROUNDS ...
...and attack those fists!
カチッ
KACHI (CHAK)
R-ROGER!
INKO,
LET'S WATCH EACH OTHER'S BACKS.
Roger!
ZUN (WHUD)
ズーン
ZUN
ズーン
ジュウ
SHUU (SHOOM)
HERE'S ONE!

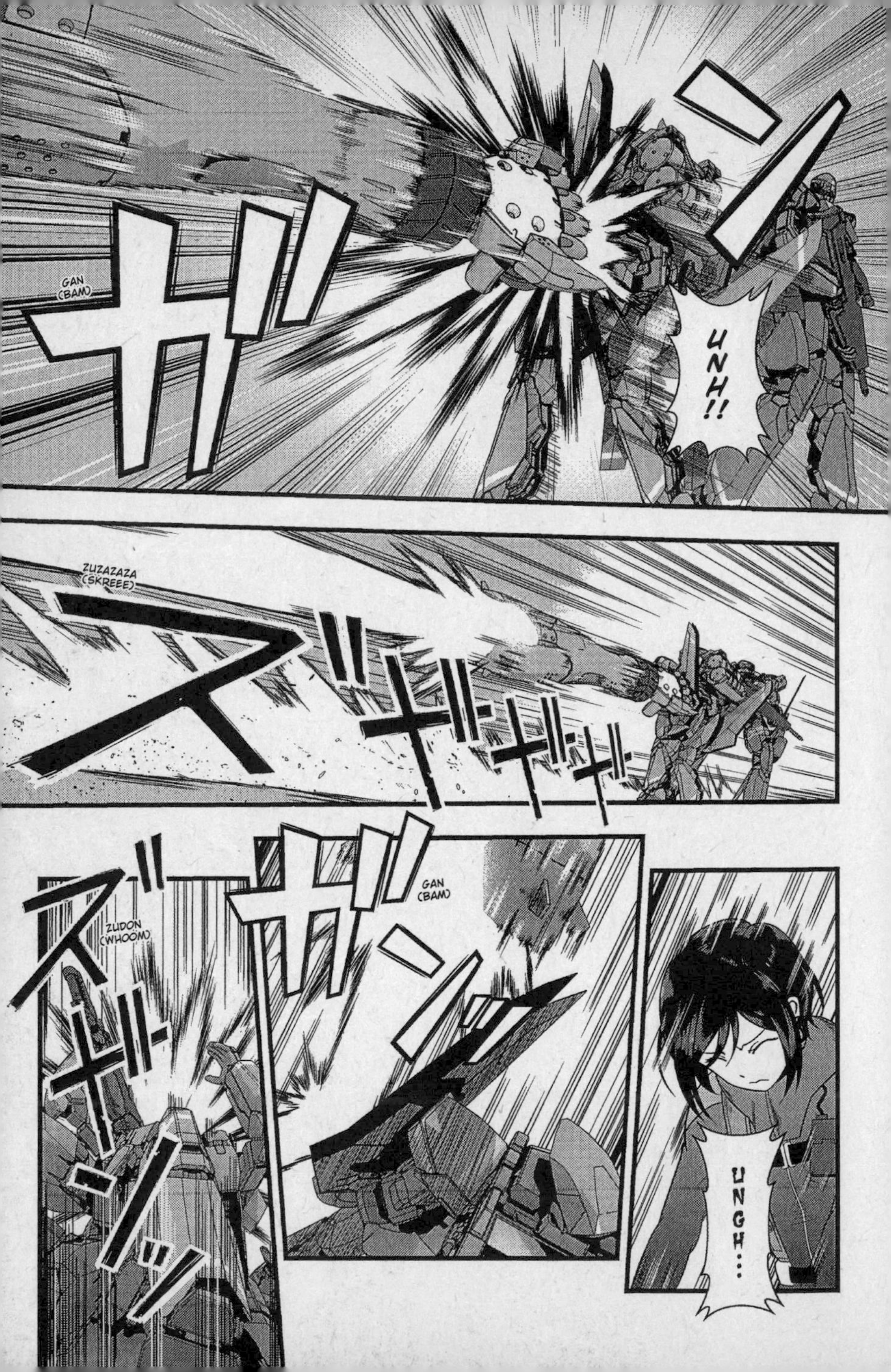
GAN (BAM)
UNH!!
ZUZAZAZA (SKREEE)
UNGH...
GAN (BAM)
ZUDON (WHOOM)

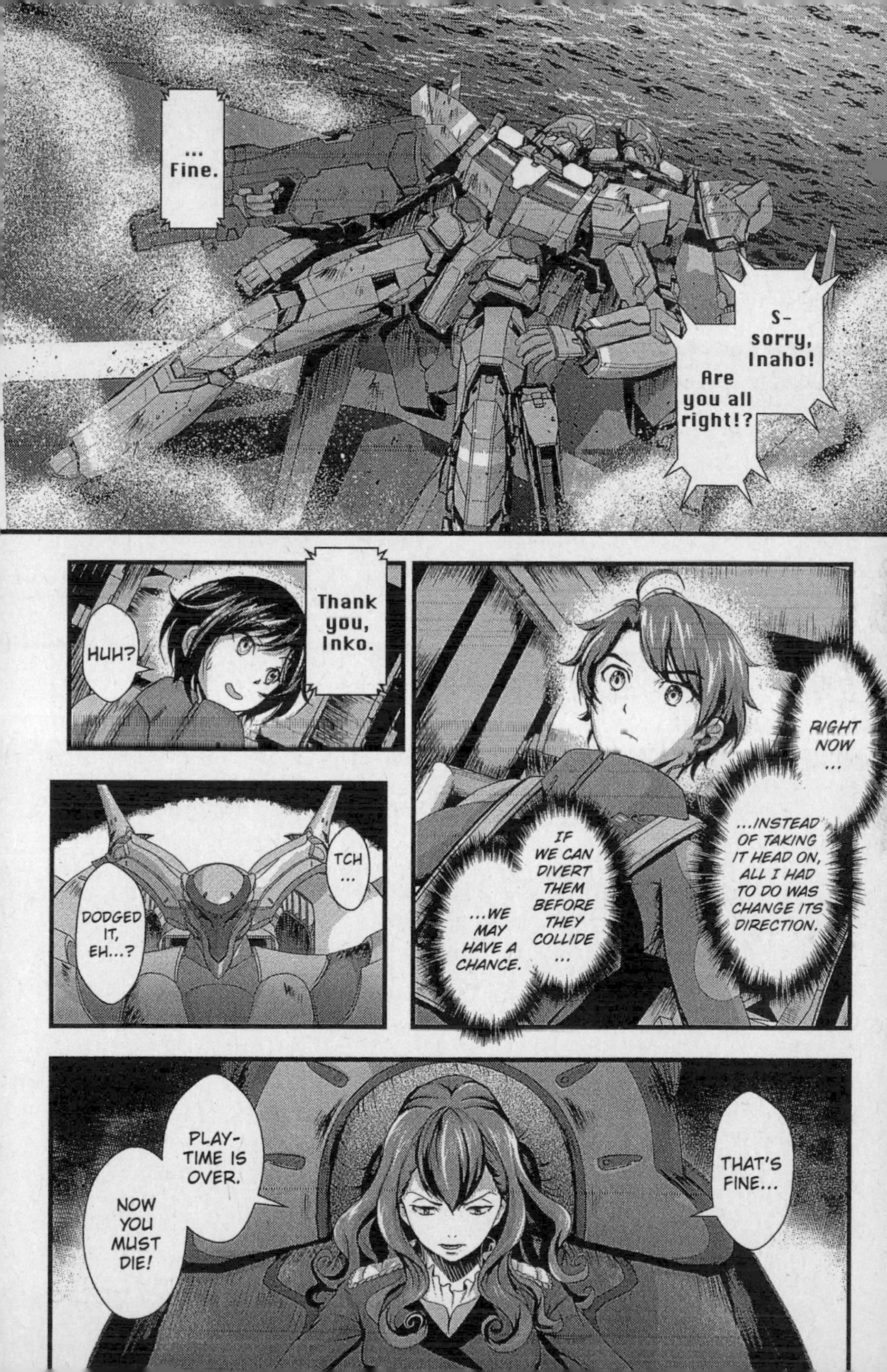
S-sorry, Inaho! Are you all right!?
... Fine.
RIGHT NOW ...
...INSTEAD OF TAKING IT HEAD ON, ALL I HAD TO DO WAS CHANGE ITS DIRECTION.
IF WE CAN DIVERT THEM BEFORE THEY COLLIDE ...
...WE MAY HAVE A CHANCE.
Thank you, Inko.
HUH?
TCH ...
DODGED IT, EH...?
THAT'S FINE...
PLAY-TIME IS OVER.
NOW YOU MUST DIE!

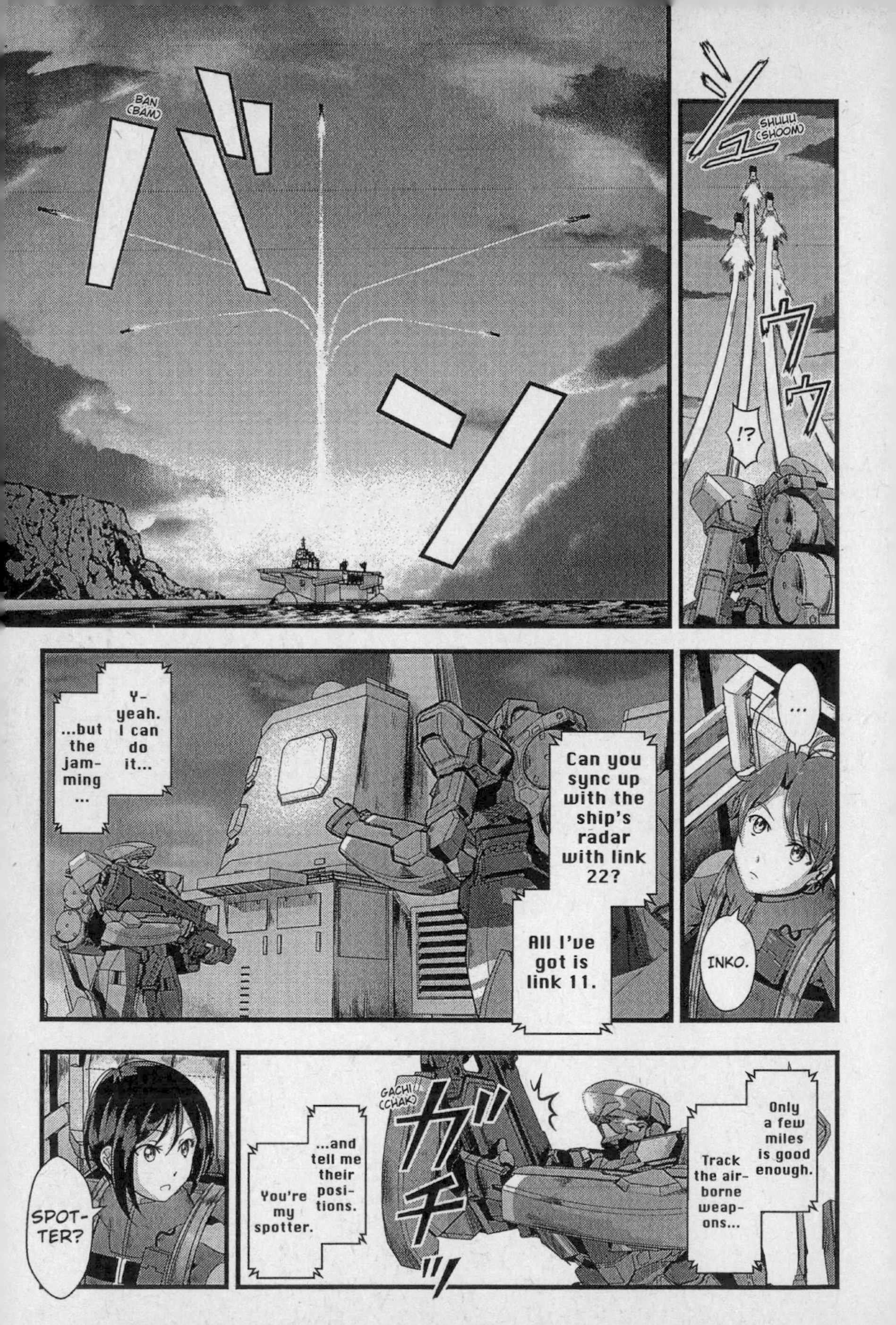

SHUUU (SHOOM)
!?
BAN (BAM)
...
INKO.
Can you sync up with the ship's radar with link 22?
All I've got is link 11.
Y-yeah. I can do it...
...but the jamming...
Only a few miles is good enough.
Track the airborne weapons...
GACHI (CHAK)
...and tell me their positions.
You're my spotter.
SPOTTER?

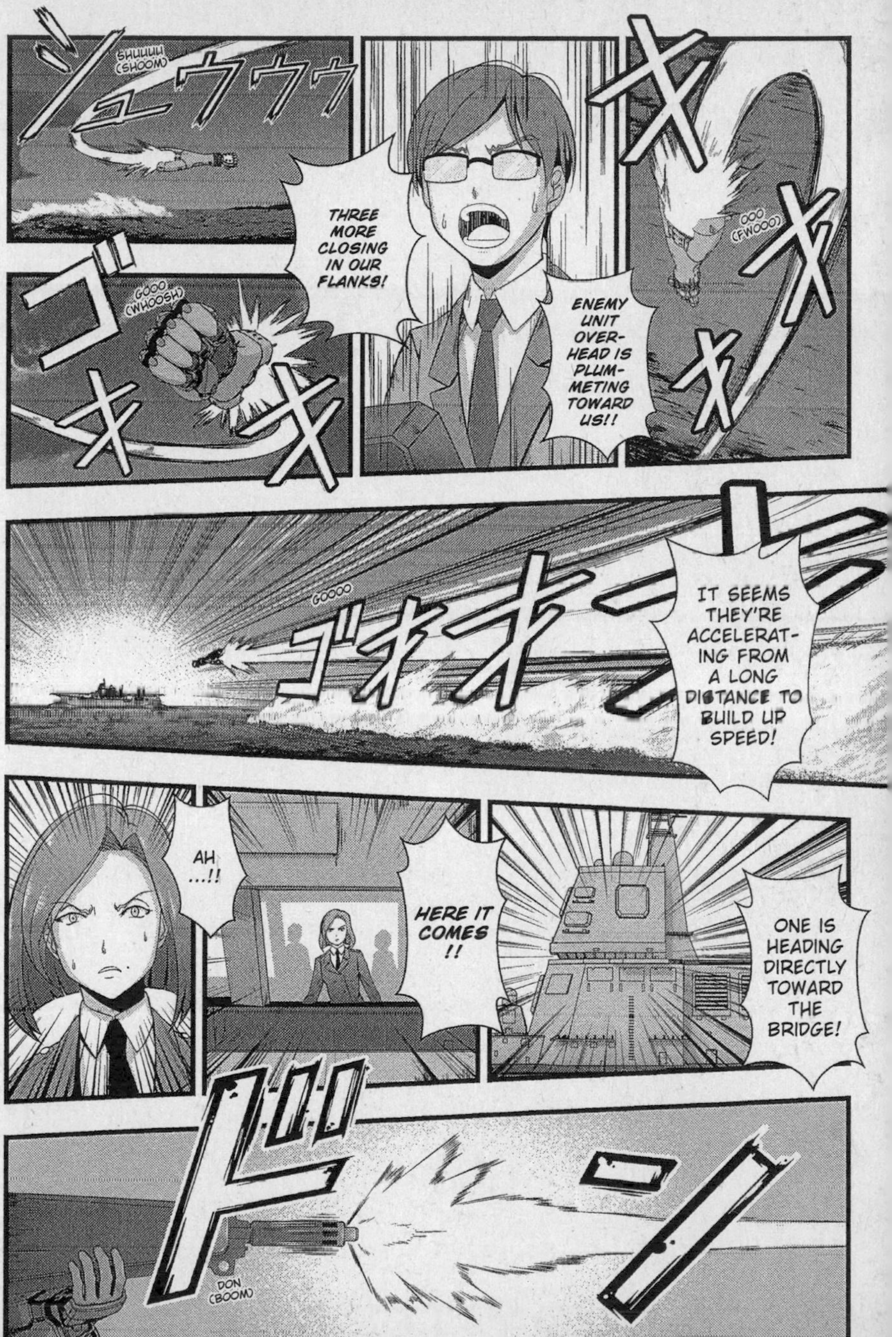
OOO (FWOOO)
ENEMY UNIT OVER-HEAD IS PLUMMETING TOWARD US!!
THREE MORE CLOSING IN OUR FLANKS!
SHUUUU (SHOOM)
GOOO (WHOOSH)
IT SEEMS THEY'RE ACCELERATING FROM A LONG DISTANCE TO BUILD UP SPEED!
GOOOO
ONE IS HEADING DIRECTLY TOWARD THE BRIDGE!
HERE IT COMES !!
AH ...!!
DON (BOOM)

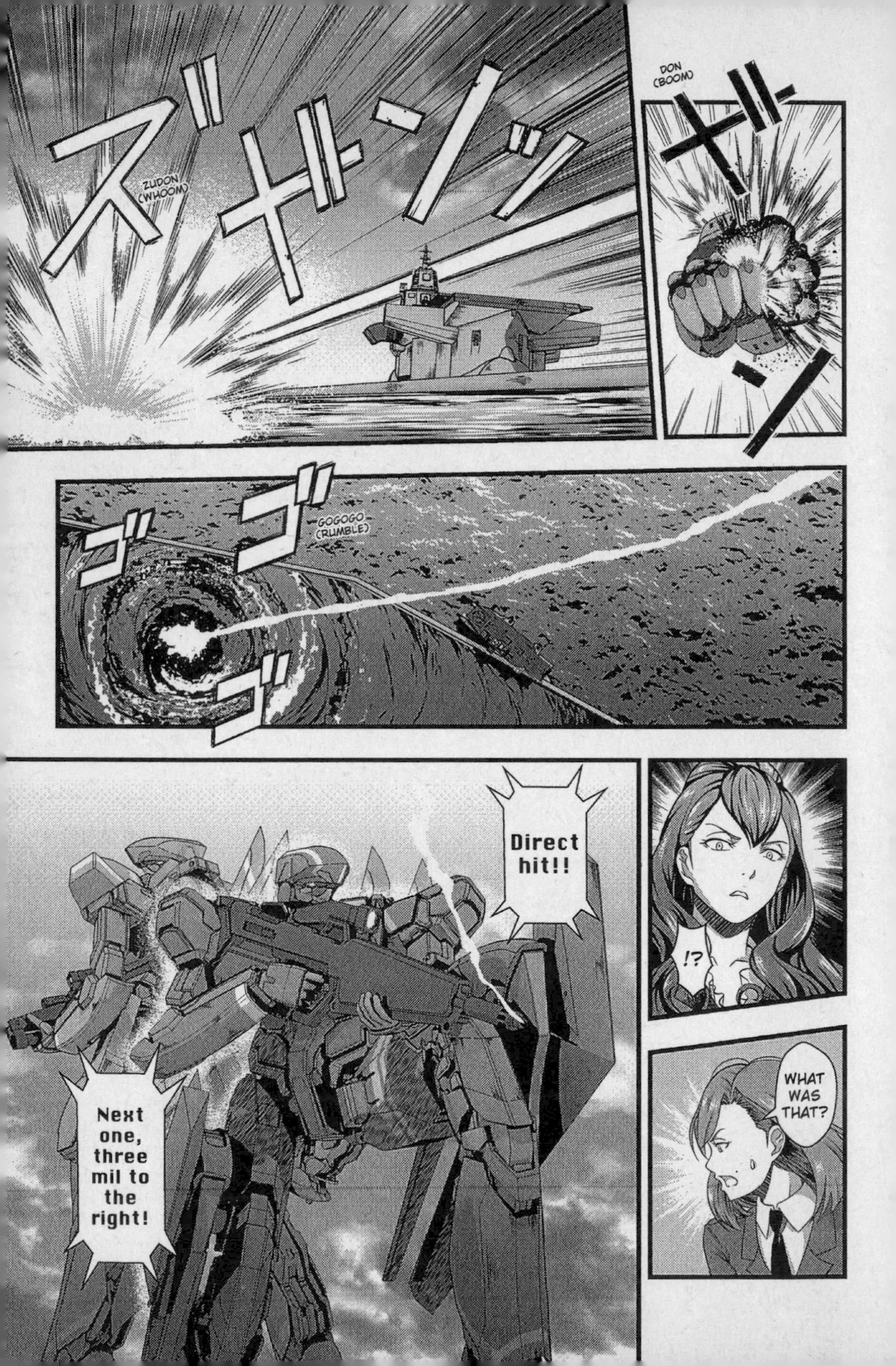

ZUDON (WHOOM)
DON (BOOM)
GOGOGO (RUMBLE)
WHAT WAS THAT?
!?
Direct hit!!
Next one, three mil to the right!

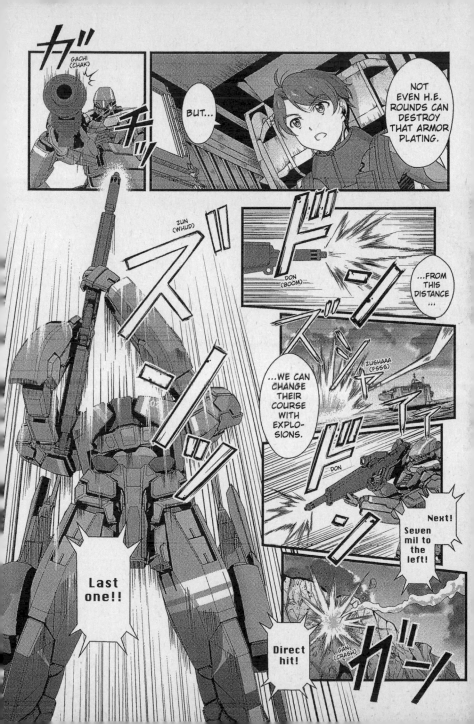

ガチ
GACHI
(CHAK)

チ
チ

BUT...

NOT EVEN H.E. ROUNDS CAN DESTROY THAT ARMOR PLATING.

ズ ー ノ

ズ ー ノ

ズ ー ノ

ズ ー ノ

ズ ー ノ

ZUN
(WHUD)

ドン
DON
(BOOM)

...FROM THIS DISTANCE...

ズシャー
ZUSHAAA
(FSSS)

...WE CAN CHANGE THEIR COURSE WITH EXPLOSIONS.

ドン
DON

Next! Seven mil to the left!

Last one!!

Direct hit!

ガン
GAN
(CRASH)

ガ ー ノ

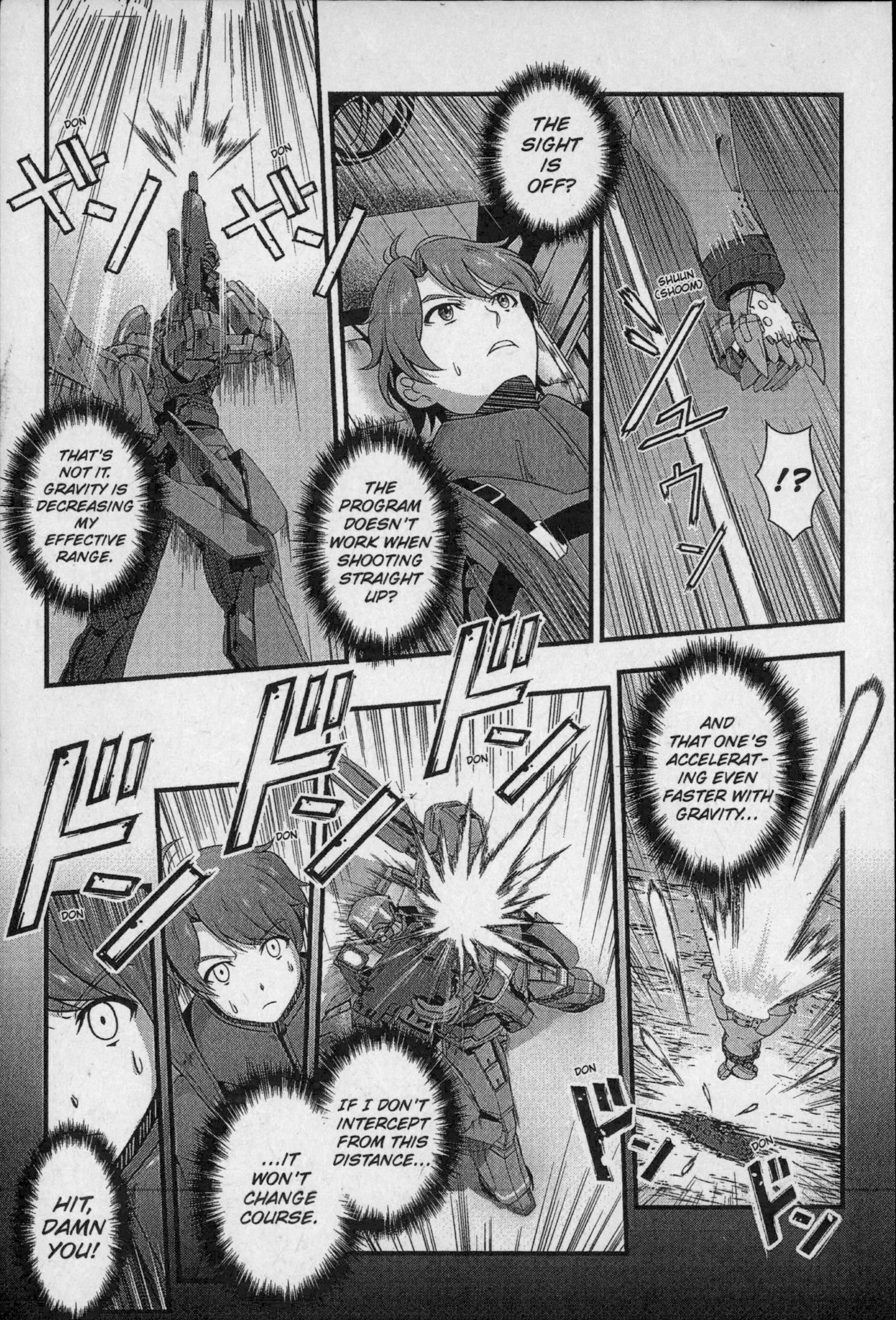

SHUUN (SHOOM)
!?
THE SIGHT IS OFF?
THE PROGRAM DOESN'T WORK WHEN SHOOTING STRAIGHT UP?
DON
DON
THAT'S NOT IT. GRAVITY IS DECREASING MY EFFECTIVE RANGE.
AND THAT ONE'S ACCELERATING EVEN FASTER WITH GRAVITY...
DON
DON
DON
DON
DON
IF I DON'T INTERCEPT FROM THIS DISTANCE...
...IT WON'T CHANGE COURSE.
HIT, DAMN YOU!

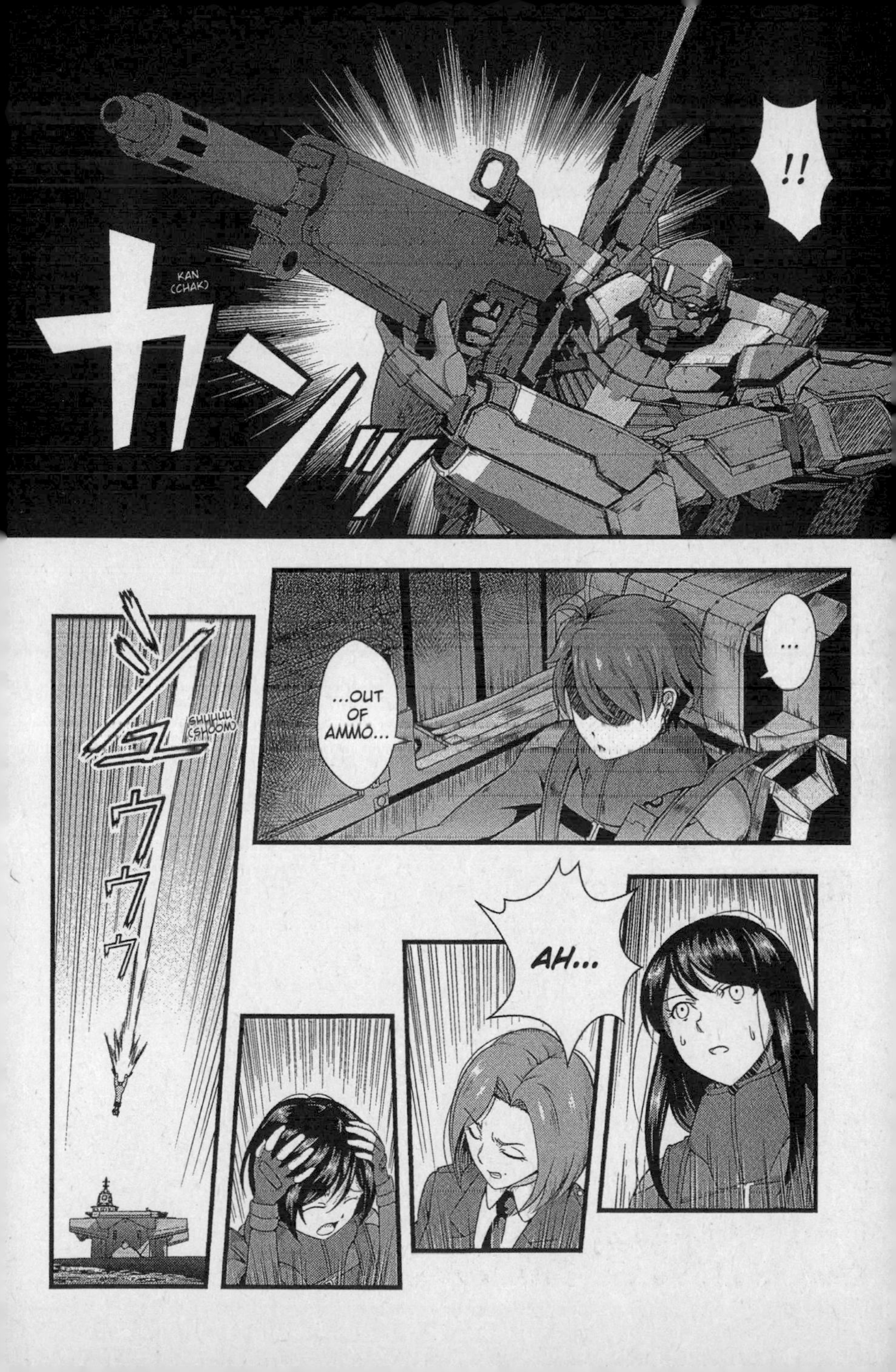
!!
KAN (CHAK)
...
...OUT OF AMMO...
AH...
SHUUUU (SHOOM)

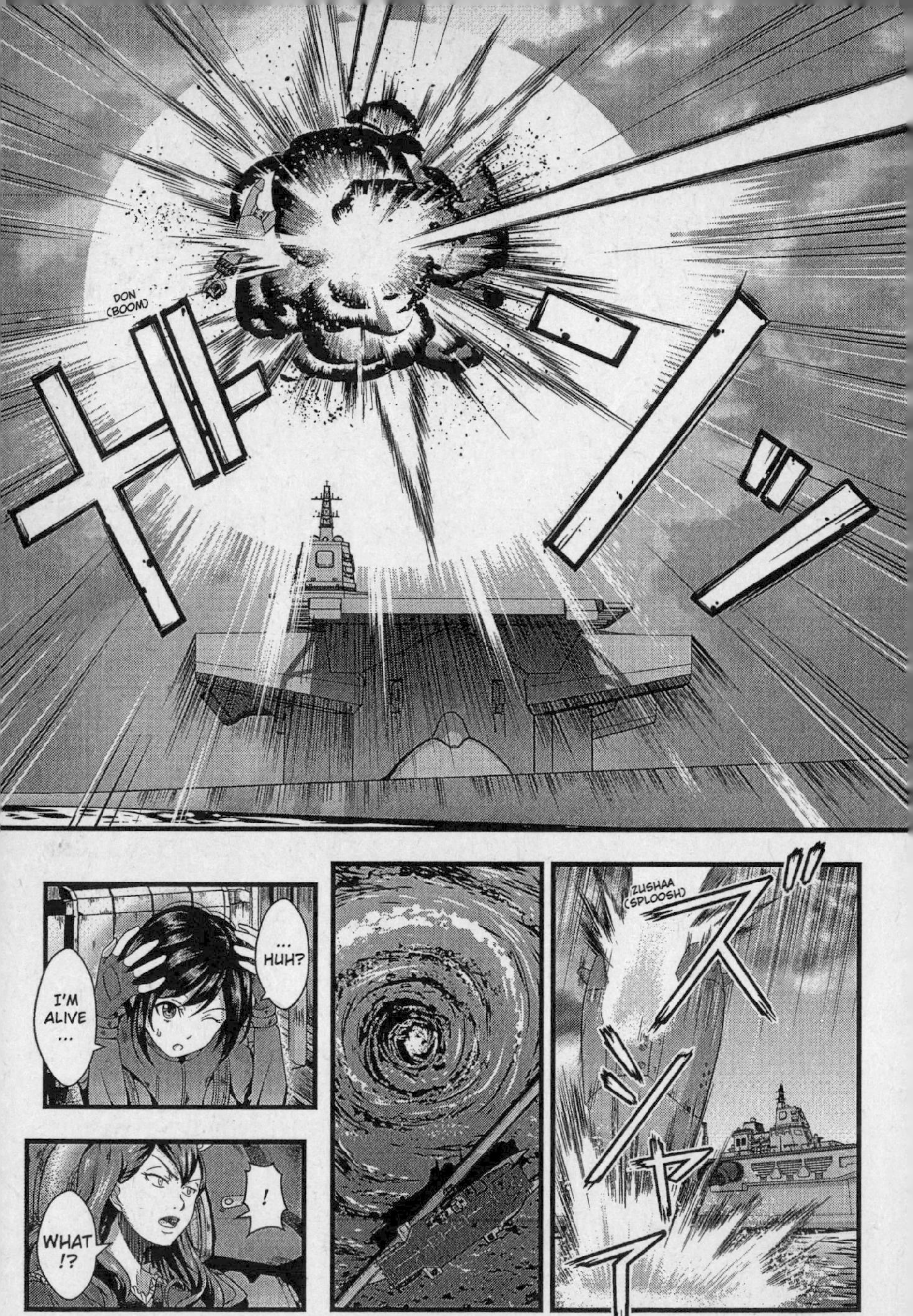
DON (BOOM)
ZUSHAA (SPLOOSH)
... HUH?
I'M ALIVE ...
!
WHAT !?

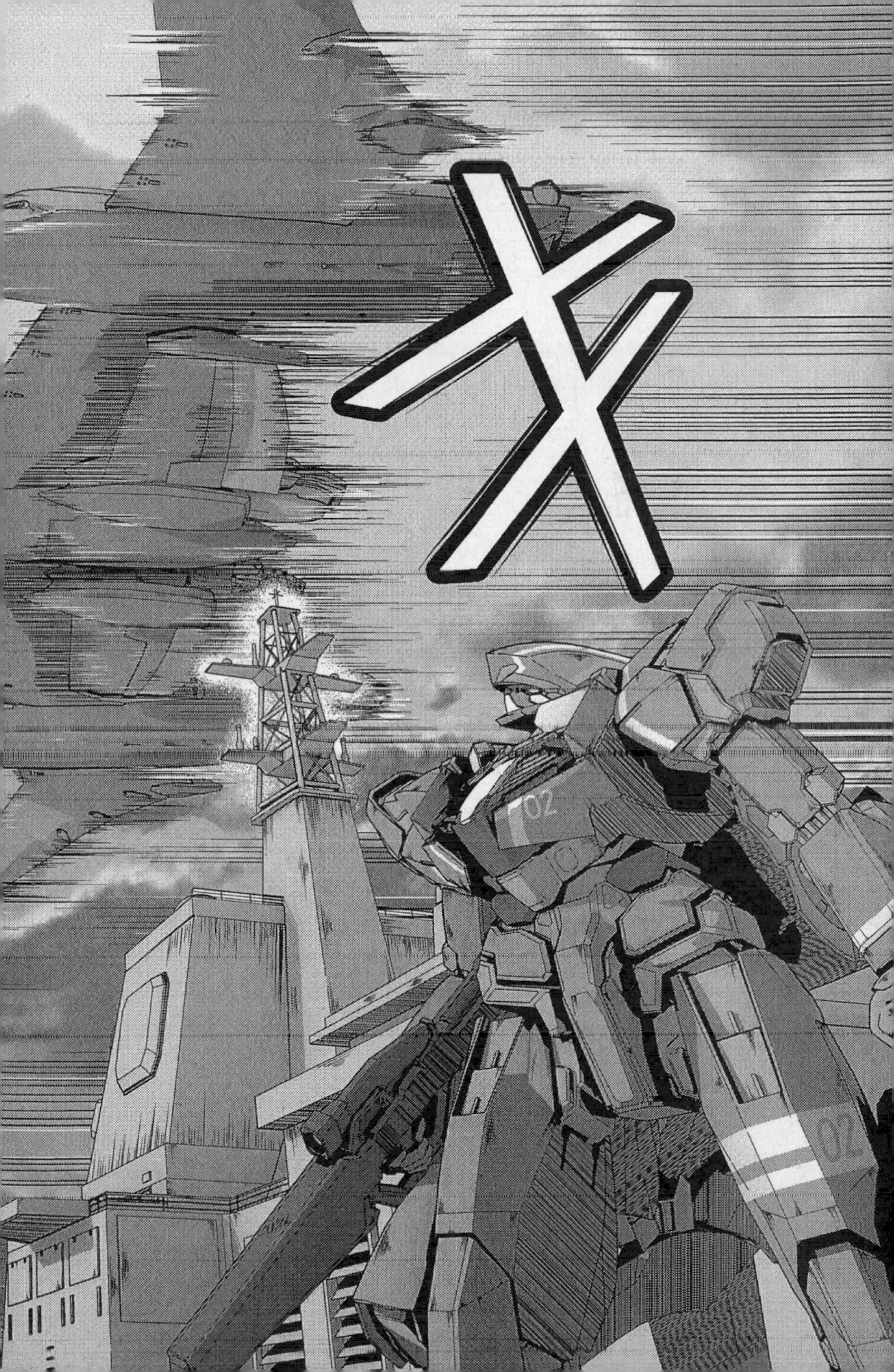

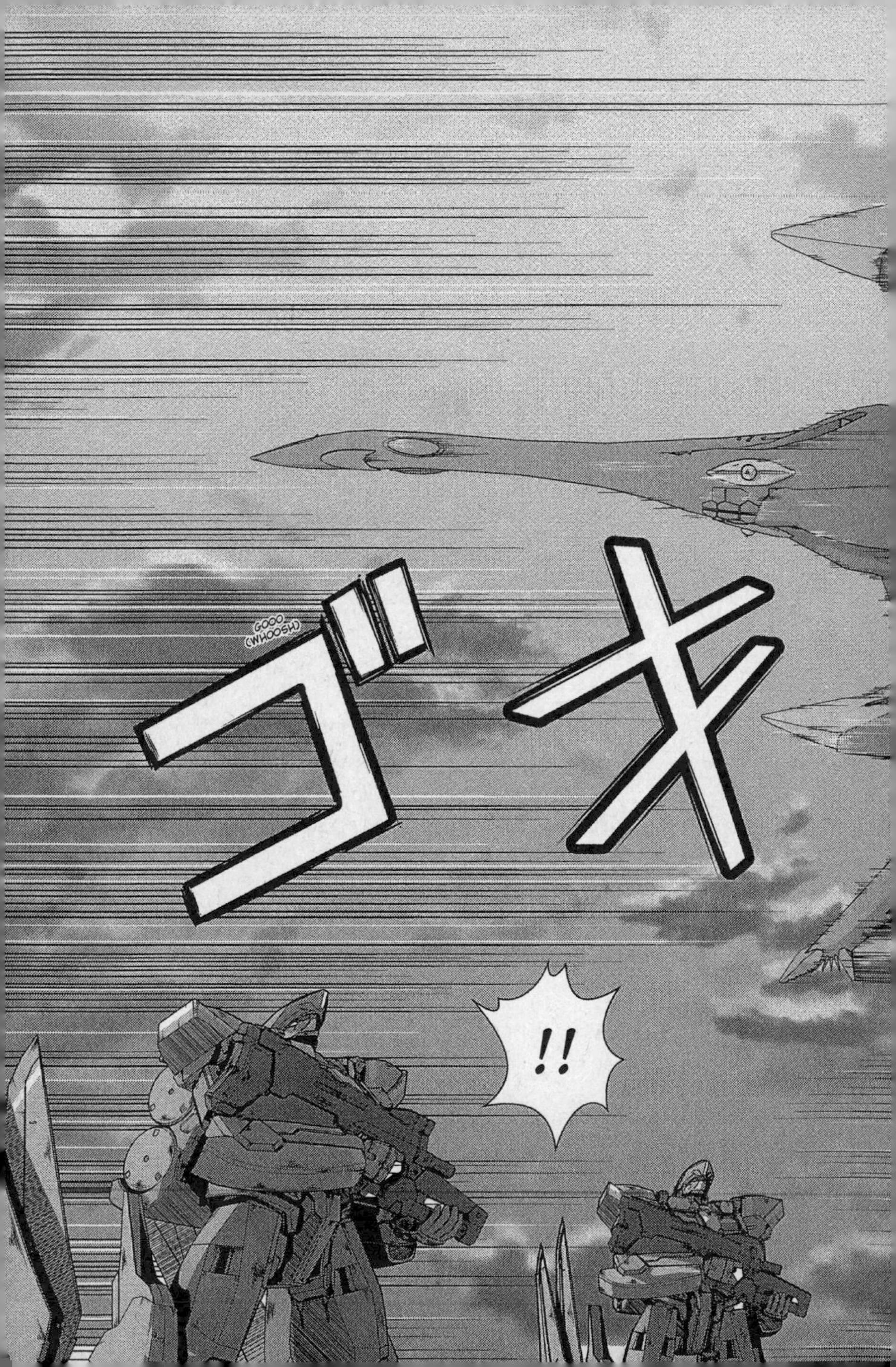
ゴオ
GOOO (WHOOSH)
!!

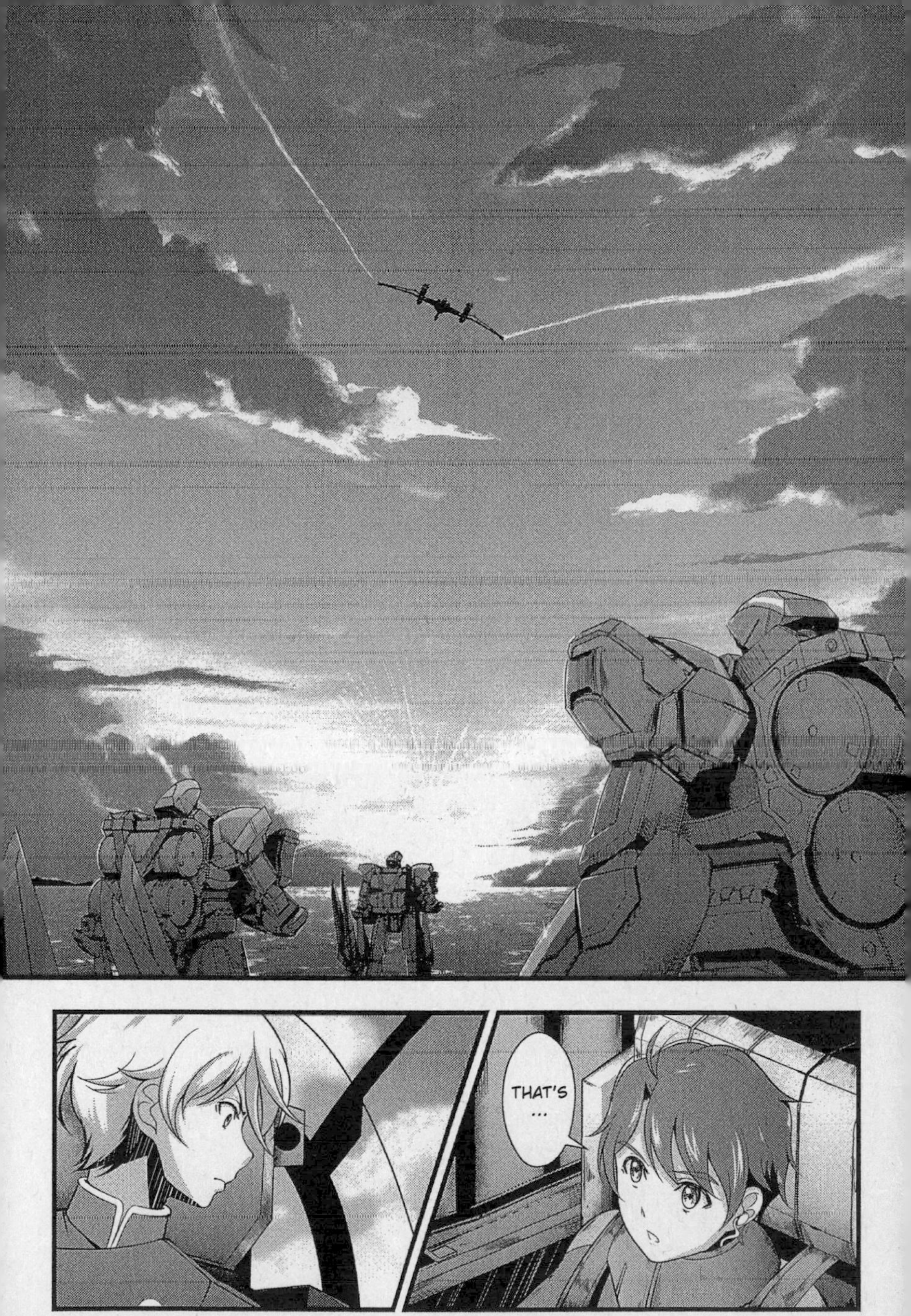
THAT'S
...

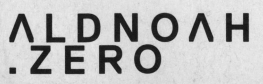

ΛLDNOΛH
.ZERO

To be continued in Volume 3!

ALDNOAH.ZERO
SEASON ONE ❷

OLYMPUS KNIGHTS
PINAKES

Translation: Sheldon Drzka

Lettering: Brndn Blakeslee, Lys Blakeslee

ALDNOAH.ZERO Vol. 2
© Olympus Knights/Aniplex · Project AZ. All rights reserved.
First published in Japan in 2014 by HOUBUNSHA CO., LTD., Tokyo. English translation rights in United States, Canada, and United Kingdom arranged with HOUBUNSHA CO., LTD. through Tuttle-Mori Agency, Inc., Tokyo.

Translation © 2016 by Hachette Book Group, Inc.

Yen Press
Hachette Book Group
1290 Avenue of the Americas
New York, NY 10104

www.hachettebookgroup.com
www.yenpress.com

Yen Press is an imprint of Hachette Book Group, Inc.
The Yen Press name and logo are trademarks of Hachette Book Group, Inc.

The publisher is not responsible for websites (or their content) that are not owned by the publisher.

Library of Congress Control Number: 2015952598

First Yen Press Edition: February 2016

ISBN: 978-0-316-39163-4

10 9 8 7 6 5 4 3 2 1

BVG

Printed in the United States of America